TELEVISION ADVERTISING
AND CHILDREN

TELEVISION ADVERTISING
AND CHILDREN

BRIAN M. YOUNG

CLARENDON PRESS · OXFORD

1990

Oxford University Press, Walton Street, Oxford OX2 6DP
Oxford New York Toronto
Delhi Bombay Calcutta Madras Karachi
Petaling Jaya Singapore Hong Kong Tokyo
Nairobi Dar es Salaam Cape Town
Melbourne Auckland
and associated companies in
Berlin Ibadan

Oxford is a trade mark of Oxford University Press

Published in the United States
by Oxford University Press, New York

British Library Cataloguing in Publication Data
Young, Brian M.
Television advertising and children.
1. Children. Influence of television advertisements
I. Title
302.23083
ISBN 0-19-827280-4

Library of Congress Cataloging in Publication Data
Young, Brian M.
Television advertising and children/Brian M. Young.
Includes bibliographical references and index.
1. Television advertising and children.   2. Television advertising
and children—Great Britain.   I. Title.
HQ784.T4Y68   1990   302.23'45'083—dc20   90-7530
ISBN 0-19-827280-4

Typeset by Graphicraft Typesetters Ltd., Hong Kong
Printed in Great Britain by
Bookcraft (Bath) Ltd,
Midsomer Norton, Avon

To
my parents

CONTENTS

TABLES

I

Introduction

Introductory chapters are best approached as throat-clearing exercises where concepts are prepared, introductions are made, and stalls are set out. I do not intend to deviate from that path. The issue that drives this book is that of television advertising and children. Why is this an issue? Why do people have ready opinions about television advertising, about children, and about how the two go together or, in many cases, don't go together? In order to answer these and other questions it is necessary to explore our images and conceptions of television advertising and children. When the two are put together, they generate passions in people. It will be seen that the emotion stems from the relationship that is presumed to exist between the child and advertising. But before investigating the issue, there are many images and assumptions about the nature of advertising that need to be examined.

FEELINGS AND FEARS ABOUT ADVERTISING

Advertising has always provoked strong feelings. Its presence is difficult to evade and its curious blend of artistry, coercion and sheer banality makes it difficult to place and categorize as a cultural form. Consequently, men and women on Clapham omnibuses are never short of an opinion or two on the subject. They may regard it as an evil, pernicious influence that sells them things they don't want, or they see it as a benign presence that just adds colour to our drab streets or provides a chance to put the kettle on when watching television.

Pollay (1986) has looked at most of the writings from North America on the cultural nature of advertising, excluding the European Marxist tradition on the subject. Because much of what has been written by anthropologists and students of contemporary culture can be viewed as a reflection of the values held by people who are members of that culture, Pollay's review can supply us with a ready inventory of common complaints about advertising— complaints, because the social critic rarely has a good word to say on the subject. Defendants of the role of advertising tend to base their case on its economic functions or claim that it provides us with valuable product information.

One set of criticisms is based on the persuasive and pervasive nature of advertising. Advertising is everywhere, cultivating particular attitudes to problems or creating problems where none existed previously. This way of thinking can be considered as originating from a root metaphor. Root metaphors deeply influence our thinking. They can be specified as principles that guide thought and that can be found in sayings, vivid images, metaphors, and idioms in language. They 'frame' the problems we are dealing with and constrain the ways in which we think about them (see Lakoff and Johnson, 1980).

The root metaphor that guides this thinking about advertising can be described as 'advertising as dry rot'. If society is pictured as an old building, advertising can creep in undetected and affect its very fabric, influencing the basic moral and spiritual values the culture holds dear. Advertising can influence the criteria we use when we make up our minds. For example, buying a car ceases to be a systematic evaluation of the advantages and disadvantages of a particular make and model. Instead, it becomes the selection of a particular life-style that fits with our conception of who we are and what we would like to be. 'Problems' of body odour or of achieving perfect whiteness in washing clothes are created by advertising. Qualities of experience, such as the munching and crunching of foods, are exaggerated at the expense of more meaningful and important characteristics such as their nutritional benefit and relative cost. There is no escape either. If the educated consumer subscribes to *Which?* magazine or invests in a list of E numbers and a pocket calculator for visits to the supermarket, even this attempt at self-defence is appropriated, re-presented, and manipulated by advertisers. No one is immune and no place is safe.

Another set of criticisms centres on the
ture of advertising. Advertising promotes
vices which in turn encourages the adopt
beliefs. These have been characterized in di
example, consumption is glorified within
and much of the life of the characters
situations and scenarios are based on consumpt....
activity is frequently depicted as the solution to most problems, as the means of attaining joy and happiness and, in
general, as the most suitable and available means to that
end. The goal of pleasure or happiness itself is rarely if ever
questioned. The underlying moral philosophy in the world
of advertising is that of secular hedonism, displacing any
references to more spiritual matters.

Placing consumption in such a dominating position with
its inseparable goal of pleasure leads to a vision of a world
where certain political and environmental issues do not
appear to exist. Questions of justice and morality are not
raised and criteria based on questions of ecology are rarely
considered. In certain types of discourse, the question of
consumption would lead naturally to issues concerned with
the morality of encouraging some people to eat more when
many others are being forced to eat less, and the politics of
the European food mountains and wine lakes, or with the
ecology of indestructible plastics and destroyed forests as a
result of the demand for packaging materials. The discourse
of advertising does not permit this competition of ideas.
Given the pervasiveness of advertising one could expect
these other types of discourse to be relegated to special oases
such as conversations with like-minded people, occasional
classes in schoolrooms, and selected courses at colleges and
universities.

Of course, advertising could be seen as symptomatic of a
particular kind of materialistic society which regards consumption as the highest virtue and which has replaced the
local church with a suburban superstore. Much of advertising involves the promotion and, it could be said, the
worship of goods, and this, according to some writers,
leads in turn to a displacement of feeling from people to
objects. Brands are 'loved', 'admired', and 'trusted', using
terms that apply predominantly to human relationships,

...sibly as the result of a process that has ancient origins. The frontier between the world of people and the world of things is not closed and traffic between the two in the form of metaphorical transfer and animistic religious practices is not unknown. We use the world of objects to describe the world of human relations and talk of our feelings for others as if there were a passage between us (see Reddy, 1979). Some cultures attribute human qualities to animals, plants or natural phenomena. Advertising describes the world of commonplace goods and services with the language of human relationships.

Advertising advocates. It presents only one side of a case, rhetorically, using the best techniques available. Why has the advocatory character of advertising been criticized? Presumably, there is an ideal form of information exchange calling for both sides of a case to be presented in a manner of presentation that does justice to the content. In such a balanced presentation the interests of the commentator are regarded as separate from and less important than the recipient's rights to have both sides put forward in an undistorted and fair manner. Whether such presentations exist or not is a separate issue, but it would appear that advertising is not society's only advocatory agency. Pleading, exhorting and generally putting on one's best face are characteristic of much of social life. Society recognizes this in everyday behaviour and in such social roles as 'the politician' or 'the estate agent', and this recognition is acknowledged in parody and other forms of humorous show. The jargon and euphemisms of estate agents or Members of Parliament can be translated into the world of objective reality where 'property requiring some modernization' means an abandoned cottage and a 'vigorous debate' a drunken slanging match.

There are two areas of social life, however, that lay particular claim to a non-advocatory and balanced presentation. They are the schoolroom and, to a lesser extent, the media. It has long been a tradition of Western scholarship that all sides of an issue are explored and the facts of the matter are presented transparently, not made opaque with rhetoric. Schools, colleges, and universities have a responsibility to cultivate this style of inquiry and teachers have a duty to see that all sides of the matter are presented. The media cannot remain completely immune from advocacy in all its forms, but they do attempt to compartmentalize and corral communication which is advocatory in intent or persuasive in its effect. Comment is traditionally regarded as separate from news in newspapers and advertising in magazines is framed with such conventions as 'advertiser's announcement', or enclosed in separate boxes, or relegated to the back pages of a magazine.

The tradition of public broadcasting in Britain meant that the BBC cultivated an image of factual, informative reporting and balanced, argued comment. This image was satisfying both to broadcaster and public because it provided a suitable face for Britain to show the outside world, lent moral authority to government activities at home, and conveyed an impression of credibility and authority. How can broadcasting policy based on presenting the facts be married with advertising that trades in half-truths? When advertising was first introduced into non-BBC broadcasting in Britain in 1955, it was made clear that it would be in the form of 'spot' advertising rather than sponsorship so that the station and not the advertiser would be responsible for the programmes. The only exceptions were to be documentary films and shoppers' guides prepared by advertisers, a format that was short-lived (Henry, 1986, p. 29). The introduction of commercial broadcasting was violently opposed by many establishment figures, and advertising was kept at a distance from the unbiased and informed comment that constituted much of the tradition of British broadcasting.

In North American culture there is a particular paradox inherent in the use of advocatory techniques in the selling of goods and services. The presence of advertising is seen as a threat to reason simply because of its advocatory nature. The market place is held to be an area of social life where reason should dominate.

The market place occupies a special position in the pantheon of North American cultural values as both a metaphor and a metonym. It is a metaphor in that a vivid concrete image transposes an abstraction from economic theory into a comprehensible vision of a place where people buy and sell. It is a metonym because this simple symbol stands for a host of complex processes. The market place is an arena reserved for rational decision-making where transactions between informed consumers and honest but tough sellers take place. But it is also a territory where individuals can exercise their rights. One of these is the right to advertise, extol or promote one's wares. The metaphor can be extended by populating the market place with hucksters jostling for position and shouting loudly. The one who gets the best position and makes the best pitch will sell more and make more money. This scenario is one of the linchpins of a capitalist economy and any threat to its sanctity has to be taken extremely seriously. This is not to say that irrational decision-making is not permitted, provided it takes place in other contexts. People fall in love at first sight and, in popular culture, they make life-long commitments on this irrational basis—behaviour that is often presented approvingly in such cultural forms as romantic novels and magazines.

The paradox inherent in the cultural vision of the market place can be solved and reason can be made to co-exist with unreason by appealing to 'fairness' and 'truth'. Advertising is allowed and welcomed as long as certain rules of reason are obeyed. The 'truth' about a brand or product is presumed to exist and any rhetoric employed must use fair means of presenting certain aspects of that truth. Advocates who present 'the other side' should be allowed a fair hearing and not be jostled out. The fact that 'the other side', which includes health education or consumer advocacy, doesn't have as much money as the advertisers and promoters does not enter into the argument. It is presumed that differences in power based on wealth have been attained by fair means and that there is nothing preventing anybody making money if they work hard enough.

Advertising, according to Pollay (1986), has been criticized because, by appealing to the individual, it encourages greed and selfishness and leads to people being less community-orientated, less cooperative, less compassionate, and less charitable. It is difficult to lay the blame for this state of affairs at the door of advertising since the act of consumption represented is itself an individual act of acquiring and using something that someone wants. The desires to own, hoard or consume are common in any capitalist society and can be found in many socialist and communist societies too. Indeed, this human propensity could be a cross-cultural universal.

The argument that advertising enhances and emphasizes this underlying acquisitive and selfish tendency is tempting; after all, the pervasive and persuasive character of advertising should reinforce these acquisitive motives and drive people to self-centred activities. Advertising, however, is more complex than that. Certainly, the ultimate purpose of television commercials and other media ads is to get the viewer and reader to purchase and use the advertised brand, and they are designed to achieve these ends. Many commercials will also emphasize a certain life-style that characterizes users of that brand. This is often portrayed as sharing with fellow-users of brand X. Advocacy of this nature can certainly be said to encourage social activity among certain groups in the population although that communal behaviour is driven less by altruistic feelings of sharing and helping and more by a desire to be one of a crowd that wears that brand of jeans, or eats at this fast-food restaurant, or drinks that soft drink. The self-centred ethos that characterizes much of British culture towards the end of the twentieth century has come about as a result of a combination of historical, political, social, and cultural forces that cannot be properly unravelled until the next century.

One area of self-centred activity has less to do with advertising than with the changing nature of services and advances in technology. The rise in popularity of video rentals, the easy availability of ready-to-eat packaged foods, the increase in off-licence sales, all work towards loosening leisure from specific places and times. The occasions when we used to meet people in the pub, or go to the cinema, and the friendly relationships formed in the corner shop and at the butcher's are less regularly maintained than previously. Instead of making appointments with leisure we turn it on like a tap when it is needed. Leisure becomes a way of satisfying our needs rather than a process of relaxing with others. The home becomes the focus of leisure, and leisure becomes a solitary activity or, at best, one shared only with a few members of the family or close friends and neighbours. Advertising emerges as a home companion, because almost every home has a television set with at least one channel that carries regular advertising. In 1986, 97 per cent of the British population had access to a television set and well over half the population lived in households with more than one set (Independent Television Companies' Association, 1987).

Certain characteristics of the content of advertising have been assumed to have unintended effects on audiences. One is the use of generalities, either because of the mass nature of the audience or because of the nature of advertising discourse or both. The reality that is portrayed in the world within the ad is a highly stereotyped place where the rules that underlie social conduct are very simple, or where the problems that are posed are soluble in an unrealistic way, often with the help of the product displayed. For example, Berger (1974) argues that there is a relationship between drug abuse and advertising. The argument is as follows. Drug commercials (for example, for aspirin) supply models of how the world works and provide the solution to its problems. The basic model can be characterized as the 'pain–pill–pleasure' syndrome. Advertisements create the 'problems'. Pills are purchasable commodities which solve this problem and, in the process, give pleasure. This model is then generalizable to solving problems in real life. Berger does admit that these strategies could be a product of North American culture. He argues that one of the reasons Americans find it difficult to think of drug abuse as a social problem is because they are 'prisoners of psychology'. Americans, according to Berger, account for the successes and failures of people with a limited range of explanations based on individual initiative, will-power, and motivation.

There seems to be a good case that the social categories presented in advertising and the roles and rules that can be inferred from the activities of people-in-ads are at the same time simple and distorted versions of everyday life. Although one would not expect the represented reality of television to correspond exactly to real life, which can be routine, repetitive, complex, and often extremely uninteresting, the social world of the ad is not the same as that of other comparable genres, like drama, cinema, or poetry. And yet television advertising is developing into other creative fields such as pop videos (Kaplan, 1987) and there is a demand for these forms to be taken seriously as an artistically and aesthetically respectable medium of communication. It is not possible to categorize advertising as separate from and inferior to the high cultural varieties, just as it is not really possible to see advocacy as completely separate and altogether different from 'telling the truth'. The very pervasiveness of advertising would suggest that it is not a self-contained phenomenon that can be isolated from other social arrangements.

The presence of stereotypes is another aspect of the use of generalities in advertising and this, according to Pollay (1986), encourages and aggravates existing '-isms' such as sexism, racism, and ageism. It can be argued that stereotyping is bad because these simple social categories do not do justice to complex human individuals. Consequently, stereotyping should be fought against wherever it is found. This argument is, I feel, basically unsound and aims at the wrong target.

Stereotyping is a basic fact of human cognitive activity. Making categories and drawing relationships of similarity and difference is an inescapable part of the process of constructing mental worlds that guides our thinking and predicts our actions. The world of people is no different from the world of things in this process and social categories have a vital part to play in any person's thinking about people. What is important is where these categories are used and to what purpose they are put.

The casual eavesdropper in a public bar may be excused if he imagined this world to consist of little beyond 'poofters' and 'Pakis'. Similarly, the world of McGill postcards consists of ludicrously obese middle-aged women and their hen-pecked husbands. One can feel morally outraged and criticize all these stereotypes wherever they are found as dehumanizing caricatures of humanity and argue that the more they are reproduced the more they are reinforced, independently of the context of and purpose behind their expression. However, the use of the term 'poofter' for homosexual in the context of a bar conversation for the purpose of a cheap laugh is different and, I would contend, less derogatory and dangerous than using it in the context of, for instance, a popular newspaper to describe a group in society to a mass readership. Stereotypes are dangerous when they provide a false and misleading picture of what people actually are like.

The danger of stereotyping in advertising will arise when the conventional purpose and accustomed context of such stereotyping become blurred. Take the typical ad stereotype of the housewife who lives in an ideal home with perfect children. May (1981) has argued that advertising can be categorized as a type of communication where certain ground rules apply, such as expecting the source behind the communication to put on 'a best face' and presenting only favourable information. (This argument is developed further in Chapter 5 where theories of advertising are discussed.) If the reader of the ad is equipped with these assumptions, then the presence of an ideal representation comes as no surprise. It would be surprising if the kitchen floor was a mess and the child always cried. We would then presume that this apparent breach of the 'best face' ground rule for advertising was there for some purpose and try to work out why. This stereotype is relatively benign. In other words, if the world of people-in-ads is stereotyped but the ad itself or the advertising discourse is distinguishable from other media representation and the reasons for stereotyping can be attributable to the intent behind ads to place things in their best light, then stereotyping is comprehensible. This does presume an understanding of the purpose behind advertising and an ability to recognize where the ad begins and ends. These constitute the basics of advertising literacy, and are important when the special audience of children is discussed in Chapters 7 and 8. The beast is elusive, complex and reflexive and the literacy required to recognize stereotypes for what they are involves a sophisticated set of skills.

Another characteristic of advertising lies in its use of symbols and poetic language which, it has been argued, devalues hallowed institutions such as Christmas and dilutes the more important experiences in life. This argument should be particularly important when considering the development of children whose education includes exposure to and understanding of poetry and art. Advertising, it is claimed, appropriates the forms and content of art in the service of a lesser god which is mammon. This criticism is part of a more general view which polarizes and labels culture 'high' and 'low', or 'aesthetic' versus 'vulgar', or possibly 'sacred' as opposed to 'profane'. Advertising transcends these boundaries and appropriates forms and content of the 'high' in service of the 'low'.

Advertising idealizes 'the good life'. Many advertisements promote life-styles which the average reader of that magazine or viewer of this television commercial can only dream about and which can never be lived. They create aspirations which are perpetually dissatisfying; they breed a sense of powerlessness which leads to frustration and sometimes criminality. This sort of argument is used to explain why unemployed youths steal. The glossy world of advertising with its affluent and successful life-style is contrasted with the reality of poverty and material loss. The disparity between the two can act as an inducement to make good the difference by criminal activities, like stealing or making false benefit claims.

Pollay (1986) summarizes what writers have said about the way advertising uses different forms to appeal to the public's needs and wants, and about the consequences for society. For example, advertising rhetoric appeals to status which in turn promotes social competitiveness and induces envy and false pride. Advertising plays on people's fears and constructs irrational ones which may be based on artificially created worries about shirts not being gleaming white or the smells of carpets, armpits or vaginas. These fears in their turn produce anxiety and insecurity, especially in the target groups the ads are aimed at. The continual emphasis on novelty in advertising, which is understandable in view of the demands for goods and services, results in a lack of respect for experience and a distrust of history and tradition. The focus on youth and the youth culture of fads and fashions reduces the authority of the family and devalues old age. Advertising uses sexuality as part of the sell and in this way encourages sexual preoccupation and the rise in pornography. Since advertising deals with mass markets, it encourages the growth of conformity by depicting all people as tending to use the same things and behave in the same way.

All of these criticisms about television advertising have been voiced at some time. Although there may be some truth in them, they may not all be relevant to Britain, and are best taken as symptomatic of the anxieties that have been felt and may still be felt about the beast. For example, as will be seen in Chapter 6, much British advertising uses nostalgia and a rather false image of the recent past. This may produce an obsession with history instead of disrespect for it. But historical experience remains distorted, thus fuelling the criticism that advertising represents reality in an unreal and false way. Not only are certain groups, including women, ethnic minorities, and old people, seriously misrepresented in the world-in-the-ad but historical situations are inadequately portrayed.

The recognition by advertising of pluralism in society and the subsequent rise in importance of the concepts of market segmentation and life-style marketing have meant that there is, paradoxically, more conformity but a wider range of alternatives within which that conformity is enjoyed. For example, a young single consumer can choose from a wide range of different life-styles. If the buyer identifies with and selects, for example, a brand of clothing from a Next shop, then marketing strategy pressurizes him or her to adopt and purchase a whole range of consumer goods and services that conform to the life-style of a Next customer. The conformity lies within the total consumer package that is purchased and is different from that found in some communist countries where the choice of brands is limited or non-existent.

It should be apparent from the above that advertising is a subject on which a host of opinions can be expressed, frequently charged with emotion and feeling, although not without reason. Advertising has been seen as pervasive, persuasive, materialistic, advocatory, simple, and rhetorical. The best way of summing up these attributes is in relation to the audience under consideration. Consequently, the root metaphor does not describe advertising but rather the relationship between advertising and children. But we need first to define children, and look at their territory and the period of life that some of us remember with nostalgic pleasure and others as a place of fearful memories: childhood.

IMAGES OF CHILDHOOD

Childhood is not a concept that is constant, immutable and unchanging across the years or from culture to culture. It is a social construction and, as such, will redefine itself, and occasionally disappear, depending on how other socially constructed aspects of society drift and change. The boundaries of childhood and the categories used to define the different ages of man fluctuate from century to century. The classic work in this field was done by Aries (1973) although the conclusions he drew are not without critics (Pollock, 1983). Certainly the field known as 'the history of childhood' has developed since the writings of Aries and is well stocked with erudite claims and counter-claims on whether child-rearing practices really did change in eighteenth-century Europe (Pollock, 1983; bibliography). The principles laid down by Aries still remain valid, however, and are relevant to the study of the range and variety within different images of childhood in society.

Aries argued that the child in French medieval society did not exist beyond the basic distinction between an infant person who was essentially dependent on caretaker(s) for protection or help, and a member of adult society. In other words, there was no evidence of childhood as a period of special treatment, where children were subject to different institutional arrangements from adults, where there were different degrees or grades of youth and where the emotional and intellectual treatment of children was identifiable as different from adults. Whether this really was so at that time in history is not central to the argument. What is important is that, in certain respects, it is possible for a culture at a particular time and in a particular place to represent childhood socially in a different way from the age-span with which we are familiar and perhaps even to do away with the concept altogether.

At some stage in the sixteenth and seventeenth centuries, a conception of childhood appeared 'in which the child, on account of his sweetness, simplicity and drollery, became a source of amusement and relaxation for the adult' (Aries, 1973, p. 126). That is, adults related to children in a way that was different from their interaction with other adults. Adults expected children to behave differently from adults. Children, if they were treated this way and gained attention and reward for behaving in the expected fashion, would then be more likely to behave in a sweet, simple, and droll manner. Both parties become locked into stereotypical ways of behaviour as a consequence of occupying these stereotypical roles, and an image of childhood will have been created. It will not be the only image of the period, and the evidence for its emergence at that time and place may be too flimsy to be acceptable to all scholars. Nevertheless, such an image can be regarded as an available cultural resource that might be taken off the shelf, dusted down, and fitted to the child. A social identity does not provide a complete account of the person, however. It could be said that the available images of childhood are like suits in a wardrobe. Which suit fits will depend on the occasion and the mood of all concerned. But the wardrobe is not limitless, although certain fortunate groups may have a greater freedom and range of display because the available repertoire is more generous. For example, it could be argued that the available range of images for a woman is less than for a man and that this restricts the expression of gender identity.

So far, we have established one such image of childhood. Aries argues that the invention of the child as an amusing and sweet creature was not welcomed by all sectors of society. Other images were created, perhaps in reaction. Interest by moralists and pedagogues of the seventeenth century in what would now be seen as the psychological development of children led to schooling for boys with its concern with discipline in order to instil correct conduct and the application of reason to problems. The child at about 5 to 7 years of age was entering a different phase of childhood. He was no longer seen as an amusing, inadequate creature, but as a suitable case for educational treatment.

Each period in history has its privileged age, according to Aries. Youth was the privileged age of the seventeenth century, childhood of the nineteenth and adolescence of the twentieth. It is this last invention that some older members of the society of today might remember as not being present and certainly not being emphasized and that all of us can see changing and being reconstructed from decade to decade. As age bands shift and change, so will the stock of available images of childhood and images of different ages in childhood alter and be replenished. It is to some of the images of childhood in present-day society that we now turn.

There are a variety of different images of childhood available in contemporary Britain. For example, some British television programmes for children, such as *Play School*, appear to address them as simpler versions of adults. They are communicated to by means of a code that is stripped of much of the natural intonation and non-verbal characteristics of normal adult-to-adult conversations. Presentation is simple with considered pauses between chunks of information. Indeed, the code used to 'communicate with children' in these programmes is distinctive enough to merit parody. The content is earnest and worthwhile and the concern, although dominated by the need to 'entertain', is often educational in the sense that the child will learn and benefit from listening and watching. There are several images here: the child as in need of education, the child as different, the child as less than adult in some way. On the other hand, alternative images of childhood are found in the British media, such as the ITV Saturday morning programme of the late 1970s called *Tiswas*, which treated the child as a 'kid', a blend of potential anarchist and hyperactive maniac. In this context, children are communicated with in a code that is fast, idiomatic, and heavily loaded with non-verbal and prosodic features. Kids are streetwise and should be

treated as fun. This is the world of the *Bash Street Kids* and
Dennis the Menace, without the violence. Children may not
respond in an adult way with adult wit and wisdom but a
child's puzzled reply is good for a laugh from the grown-
ups watching, including the men behind the cameras. The
image adopted is not so far removed from Aries's description of the child as a source of amusement even though it
is a more raucous version of sweetness, simplicity, and
drollery.

Each of these 'images' of children contains an element
of truth, but is also a distortion and a caricature of the
individual child. When we consider social issues and how
they concern and influence children, we tend to borrow,
from the cultural shelf, one or more of the available
stereotypes of children. There are more than the few described. For example, the symbol of the child as innocent
and pure is a very relevant creation to employ when sexual
abuse takes place, and the popular press will reflect the sense
of public outrage that results. The youth of the child involved is frequently emphasized as if to establish without
doubt that the victim was firmly within the category of
'child', and to avoid other culturally available stereotypes,
such as 'the child as mini-adult', that would complicate the
simple drama. The offender is cast in the role of sub-
human, as 'beast'. Stock phrases used, such as 'beast preying
on young children', evoke ancient images and representations that can be found in Red Riding Hood.

CHILDREN AND ADVERTISING PUT TOGETHER

When advertising is aimed at this special audience called
children the relationship between child and advertiser becomes a psychological minefield. One image that can be
appropriate is that of the child in need of protection. The
emotional and irrational drives of young children can be
exploited as, unlike adults, they are not as capable of protecting themselves and defending themselves against such an
onslaught. In addition, there is the added image of childhood as an age of innocence.

This image can be found in one of the most famous, or notorious, books on advertising, *The Hidden Persuaders* by Vance Packard, published in 1957. This volume caught the public imagination with its lurid vision of people manipulated by advertisers with sophisticated techniques into behaving irrationally and purchasing products they didn't really want. Much of Packard's rhetoric falls flat today and occasionally lurches into self-parody—for example, in the following vision of the perils of advertising: 'Seemingly, in the probing and manipulating nothing is immune or sacred. The same Chicago ad agency has used psychiatric probing techniques on little girls' (p. 5). Some of his claims sound plain silly. In a discussion of soup and why people buy it Packard quotes a psychoanalyst as saying that the symbolism of soup may lie 'in the prenatal sensation of being surrounded by the amniotic fluid in our mother's womb' (p. 102). Packard's own knowledge of different kinds of work done by psychiatrists, psychologists, and psychoanalysts seems rather flimsy as he frequently uses the terms interchangeably. The relationship of advertiser as seducer and child as innocent is readily detectable in Packard's book.

It is this relationship that is found in much of the thinking and talking about how advertising influences children, and may be detected between the lines of some of the research examined in Chapters 3 and 4. The obverse of this relationship, which can certainly be detected between the lines of some of the research done by those within the advertising industry, is of the advertiser as friend and equal to the child who, in this scenario, is a streetwise, robust kid with abilities that academics have underestimated.

In conclusion, this chapter has described some of the fears and views writers have expressed about the nature of advertising. This social issue would appear to evoke deeply felt emotions. The cultural images of childhood were also explored. When the two concepts are brought together they are cast in a fundamental relationship of seducer and innocent and it is this that influences and moulds much of the thinking on the problems of advertising to children, and their solution.

2

Seducers and Innocents: A Political Affair

INTRODUCTION

In this chapter, the issue of television advertising and children will be examined in its social, political, and historical context. It has been argued in Chapter 1 that the images, myths and fears created in the public's mind by the idea of 'advertising' results in a vision of innocence versus seduction when combined with the prevailing conception of childhood that is provided as a cultural package. The advertiser is seen as the seducer and the child is cast in the role of the innocent.

Researchers and those who fund research are not immune to the consequences of such images and it would be naïve to assume the scientist and researcher is a completely dispassionate and objective assessor of the human condition. Consequently, the published research on the relationship between children and television advertising cannot be considered and evaluated independently of the social context in which it was conducted. 'Social context' is a very general term and it is difficult to imagine a research programme in any discipline that is independent of the rest of society's functioning and interests. The most obvious relationship between social context and a flurry of research aimed at solving a particular problem is concerned with funding priorities. Scientists are aware of the 'rich' areas of research that attract considerable financial support whether for solving important medical problems such as cancer or achieving technical and political goals such as President Kennedy's determination to send an American to the moon by the end of the 1960s.

Another aspect of the relationship, however, seems to affect the social sciences in particular. This concerns the questions asked rather than the answers provided. Not only is the problem defined and delivered by non-scientists to researchers and 'back-room boys' but, implicit in this delivery, is a set of questions or procedures that partially determine how the problem is to be answered. Alternatives may not be obvious at the time and it is with the benefit of hindsight only that we can look back on a particular period of research and see how the range of questions asked was restricted and how ways of thinking about the problems imposed limitations on the questions that could have been asked.

This is more of an issue in the social sciences than, for instance, in the physical sciences, for two main reasons. Firstly, the physical sciences tend to have a more predictable and trusted body of theory on which to rely and this means that the hypotheses to be tested can emerge from existing theory. Secondly, the physical sciences frequently argue their case in highly specialised or artificial languages such as mathematics or the language of computer programs. These codes are private, and consequently insulated from the influence of non-experts in non-scientific circles. As a result, the physical sciences are relatively independent of other forms of social discussion.

Theories in the social sciences are much less predictable, however, and not at all private, and their subject matter is often common knowledge. This would explain why most people will have some idea of what television advertising does to children and some of the intelligent ideas or opinions of lay people will be present in the theories of social scientists on the relationship between television advertising and children. It is unlikely that they will have such set ideas and opinions on, for example, the principles of genetic engineering, although they may be aware of the social consequences and effects of this new technology.

There are good reasons, then, to look at the social context of children and television advertising research. The place to look is North America, and in particular the United States, where broadcasting and selling have always been intimately related. The story that unfolds can be found in various sources (Adler, 1980; Choate, 1981; Dorr, 1978; Griffin, 1980; Hughes, 1983; Horowitz, 1979; Melody,

1973; Melody and Ehrlich, 1974; Shaw, 1983) and the material for the remainder of this chapter is taken from these commentaries.

THE DEVELOPMENT OF CHILDREN'S TELEVISION IN THE UNITED STATES

The origins of television advertising directed at children in the United States coincided with the growth of television programming for children in that country. The reasons for this are not hard to find given the primarily commercial function of broadcasting in the USA. Melody (1973, p. 13) demonstrates that the commercial broadcasting system operates on a very simple principle. The product is the audience, the buyer is the advertiser and the programme acts as bait to attract viewers. In other words the commercial broadcaster is in the business of selling audiences to advertisers. This concept of the three-way relationship between advertiser, audience, and broadcaster may disturb British minds. That country is more accustomed to broadcasting in the service of the audience and a vision of the broadcaster as part of a national institution reflecting important cultural values and standards. Advertisers, in the British picture, are a necessary evil and are allowed in so that broadcasting may survive financially. In commercial broadcasting in the United States, however, it is the advertiser who occupies the centre stage and programmes are there to provide a market of audiences.

In the United States in 1950, television programming for children was designed to attract a young viewing audience seen as an important influence in the purchase of television sets. Consequently, a great deal of specialized children's programming of high quality was produced and much of this was presented without advertising sponsorship. For example, in 1949, 42 per cent of children's programming was of this kind (Melody, 1973, p. 36). In the 1950s, however, the number of television sets in use in the United States rose dramatically. Melody (1973, p. 37) cites an increase from 190,000 in 1949 to over 16 million in 1952. As a result, programmes were produced that would appeal to sponsors rather than to potential purchasers of television sets. Advertisers at that time general did not consider the child as an effective marketing device and, as adults made the purchases, they believed it was better to attract them as viewers, with the bait of attractive programmes.

By the mid-1950s this situation was changing. ABC-TV broadcast a series of programmes in 1954 and 1955 called *Disneyland* aimed at children both in terms of content and associated advertising for Walt Disney products such as his amusement park and his films. *Disneyland* was a success, attracting large audiences and winning an Emmy award for best adventure series in 1955. Here was effective bait that lured a large child audience, and had quality as well. But most of this material, with associated advertising, was shown during morning and afternoon periods. Prime-time programming was geared to a mass audience which by the late 1950s was a family audience including a percentage of interested child viewers. Gradually, the quality children's productions which had been relegated to non-prime-time periods were dropped and by 1956 many had disappeared. The 4 p.m. to 7 p.m. slot, for example, often contained locally-based children's shows consisting of a battery of cartoons loosely linked by a local 'personality' introducing the cartoons and selling the advertiser's products.

The year 1960 marks an important shift in the balance of control between advertiser, broadcasters and audience in the United States. In the 1950s the trend was for the advertiser to sponsor a programme, thereby controlling the programming schedule as well as the associated advertising. The rise of prime-time programming with the concept of the mass family audience and the decline and relegation of children's programmes to unprofitable morning and afternoon slots were largely a result of sponsors' decisions. From 1960, sponsors became more hesitant to take the financial risks associated with programme sponsorship and the networks (NBC, CBS, and ABC) began to finance programme production. As the control over programming swung from advertisers to broadcasters, a more integrated strategy of network management developed. The whole schedule of programmes, advertisements, and potential audiences could now be considered in comparison with those of competing networks. Management had to plan a strategy to line up programmes and attract advertisers in the face of competition from the other networks.

Another consequence of the growth of the television industry was the development of non-prime-time periods for specialist audiences. These attracted a smaller audience and brought in less income from advertisers but programme production costs were lower. It was discovered that weekday viewing, which had an audience largely composed of housewives, was a profitable period. In addition, the early 1960s heralded the discovery and development of the so-called 'youth market' to take advantage of an increase in wealth and consumption by young people.

Saturday morning was the chosen time for advertisers to sell to a large and cheap audience of children using the inexpensive bait of animated film. The animated film developed by Disney, for example, was an expensive and time-consuming medium to work in. Two animators from the old MGM animation unit, William Hanna and Joseph Barbera, developed a limited animation technique which was faster and cheaper and ideally suited to the needs of television production. Saturday morning children's television acquired a certain notoriety in the United States as the 'kidvid ghetto' (Melody and Ehrlich, 1974).

Now that a group of children who could be attracted by advertisements using cheap programmes had been discovered, the broadcasters proceeded to refine the market. The Saturday morning 'kidvid ghetto' was ripe for exploitation. One of the principles of selling in this type of specialized market is to seek a relatively high response rate from a smaller, selected audience. The concept of 'demographic purity' is often mentioned in this connection. This means that only a certain type of audience should watch a particular programme and advertisements as the impact of the sales pitch would be wasted on non-target groups. Demographic purity was the aim of Saturday morning programming, where different age groups of children were attracted selectively at different times in the morning. The aim was to build a continuous audience flow through the morning, moving from programmes for younger children early in the morning to those appealing to older children later. This flow was to be designed to minimize network switching.

In summary, the early promise of quality television programmes for children was a false one, based primarily on the interests of the industry in persuading its potential audience to purchase television sets. Once this was achieved, the basic economics of United States commercial television broadcasting dominated the development of children's television. To use a fishing analogy, the programmes are only bait or differently meshed nets to catch audiences for advertisers. Prime-time television may have been the dynamite in the pool but Saturday morning soon became the place to catch children. Once hooked, they could be sold to. How American people reacted to this concentrated onslaught by advertisers on their children will be discussed in the following section.

CHILDREN IN FRONT OF THE SMALL SCREEN: THE AMERICAN PUBLIC'S GROWING CONCERN

The history of concern with television advertising to children in the United States can be dated back to January 1968. A group of mothers met in Boston that month to found an organization called Action for Children's Television (ACT). One of their first jobs was to monitor the content of children's programmes. They had to watch for many hours to compile statistics on what was being shown and how often, in order to have an influence on programming policy. It soon became apparent that one main issue concerned the separation of programme from commercial. For example, early in 1969 ACT discovered that in a programme broadcast in the Boston area called *Romper Room*, products, including a line of Romper Room toys, were sold directly to the audience by the programme's host. An attempt to discuss this issue with the major networks proved fruitless as both ABC and NBC refused to meet the group. In February 1970, ACT petitioned the Federal Communications Commission (FCC). This body had acquired broad discretionary powers in terms of the Communications Act of 1934 that gave it the authority to regulate broadcasting 'consistent with the public interest, convenience and necessity'. Its authority includes monitoring industrial activities and performing quasi-legislative functions such as holding hearings and making rules. Its power derives from its authority to grant, review or deny licences to television stations and to levy fines for certain violations (Adler *et al.*, 1980, p. 4). The FCC was petitioned on three points:

1. There shall be no sponsorship and no commercials on children's programmes.

2. No performer shall be allowed to use or mention products, services or stores by brand name during children's programmes, nor shall such names be included in any way during children's programmes.

3. Each station shall provide daily programming for children and in no case shall this be less than 14 hours a week. This obligation will be part of each station's public service requirement.

The FCC published these proposals and asked for comments. As might be expected, this produced a strong negative response from advertisers and broadcasters. The controversy served to fuel public discussion of the issue and by the end of that year ACT had received much media attention and had held a symposium on children and advertising. The proceedings were also published (Sarson, 1971).

ACT developed from the concern of a group of articulate East Coast mothers of children about the content of television programmes and advertising watched by their children. The Council on Children, Media and Merchandising (CCMM) was created as a result of a rather different set of anxieties felt by nutritionists who were unhappy about the marketing practices of the food industry in the United States. Robert B. Choate figures prominently in this controversy (Choate, 1972; 1981). His testimony to various United States Federal government committees and his articles in the popular and trade press aroused public concern. Middle-class Americans started to look at just what the food industry was feeding their children. 'Empty calories' became a popular term. CCMM was created out of this concern and recruited personnel who were experienced in the complexities of the US Federal administration in Washington and skilled in the art of lobbying members of Congress. It was suggested that research into the area of television advertising and children should be undertaken.

This upsurge of concern with television advertising in relation to a child audience was reflected in academic circles by the emergence of a few funded studies in the area. Before 1970, virtually all the research into children's advertising had been conducted by advertising agencies or private research firms working under contract to sponsors. Much of this private work was, and still is, shrouded in expensive mystery. For example, in 1973 the Gene Reilly Group started publishing what was to be a multi-volume research report entitled *The Child*. Between 1973 and 1978 the contents of the report were not available to public organizations, to CCMM, ACT, or even the United States government. It was sold to clients who were large corporations such as Burger King Corporation, Kellogg Company and General Mills Incorporated, and who could afford the astounding price of $15,000 per edition. For this investment, clients were privy to such gems of information as: 'Mothers either "usually" or "sometimes" bought the child's favorite roughly nine times out of ten with one exception: frozen television dinners' (quoted by Choate, 1981).

The first studies by independent academics were content analyses of commercials directed to children (Barcus, 1971*b*; Winick *et al.*, 1973). Barcus's study was sponsored by ACT and Winick's work was partly supported by the National Association of Broadcasters (NAB). The FCC sponsored a study by Pearce which examined the financial contribution of children's advertising to overall network revenues (Pearce, 1972). ACT also supported an important investigation into the economics of children's television.

The US broadcasters themselves were not unresponsive to public pressure as applied by the ACT and CCMM groups. The National Association of Broadcasters revised its own Television Code from 1 January 1973 to reduce the amount of 'non-program material in weekend children's

programs' from 16 to 12 minutes in an hour and the number
of interruptions in those programmes from eight to four.
Children's programme hosts or primary cartoon characters
were forbidden to deliver commercial messages during, or
adjacent to, their own programmes. Although not all television stations were members of the NAB, the three national
networks were, so this was a small step forward in the
direction of industry self-regulation.

As well as approaching the FCC, the ACT and CCMM
pressure groups lobbied the Federal Trade Commission
(FTC). Relations between the FTC, consumer interest
groups, broadcasters and commercial interests provide a
complex but fascinating story that occupies most of the
recent industry of television advertising and children in the
United States from the mid-1970s to 1981.

The Federal Trade Commission was established in 1914
and is the agency with principal responsibility for regulating
interstate commerce in the United States. Since 1938, the
FTC's brief has included the protection of consumer interests
and private competition. This is done by prohibiting 'false
advertisements' and preventing 'unfair or deceptive acts and
practices'. The Commission has the power to act on commercials on a case-by-case basis, and to restrict or require
certain advertising practices. In practice, the procedures of
rule-making are extremely laborious and time-consuming
involving staff investigations and reports, proposals, public
hearings, consideration of evidence and the (eventual) publication of trade regulation rules which may then be challenged by opponents in the Federal courts.

The effectiveness, or 'clout', of the FTC has been called
into question. Shaw (1983, p. 169) states that it was generally agreed that for more than fifty years the FTC went about
its job with the vigour of a sleepwalker trudging through
molasses and was dubbed 'the little old lady of Pennsylvania
Avenue'. Choate (1981, p. 332) argues that the effectiveness
of the FTC depended very much on the drive and sym-
pathies of the leaders of the Commission, and on their
resistance to the pressure of business interests. Certainly,
during the five-month period from December 1971 to April

1972, ACT petitioned the FTC on several matters, including the prohibition of all food product selling to children on television. The evidence seems to be that the FTC wished to see the industry regulate itself. In addition to the revised NAB guidelines mentioned above, the National Advertising Division (NAD) of the Council of Better Business Bureaus Inc. set up Children's Advertising Guidelines in 1975.

Taken together, these guidelines should restrain television advertising of products to children quite considerably. (A list of these can be found in Appendix C of Adler *et al.*, 1980). For example, not only must the appearance and performance of toys be realistic for the child but the accompanying footage should be restrained and avoid 'overglamorization' [*sic*] such as dazzling visual effects. Commercials for breakfast-type products 'shall include at least one audio reference to and one video depiction of the role of a product within the framework of a balanced regimen'. This latter limitation meant that television commercials for heavily sugared breakfast cereals were inevitably presented with the ubiquitous glass of milk and the voice-over trailing '. . . part of a balanced breakfast'. Guideline NAB 10 states that 'It [broadcast advertising to children] shall also avoid employing irritating, obtrusive or strident audio techniques or video devices such as cuts of less than one second in length, a series of fast cuts, special effects of a psychedelic nature (e.g. flashing colors, flashing lights, flashing supered copy, or other effects which could over-glamorize or mislead)'.

When the author made an analysis of British television advertising to children (details can be found in Chapter 6), one of the categories of analysis was known as 'whizz', which referred partly to television commercials that employed fast cuts. The spirit of NAB 10 is not found in television advertising in the UK.

The movement towards self-regulation was encouraged by the FTC whose chairman, Lewis Engman, announced in 1973 that a committee composed of advertising, broadcasting and consumer representatives had been formed. Its brief was to devise a voluntary code for children's television advertising that was acceptable to all parties. By 1974 the committee had abandoned this task. It looked as if the interests of consumer groups and the interests of broadcasters and advertisers were incompatible and that no mutual agreement was possible. Later that year the Federal Communications Commission finally issued a report on its investigations which were instigated as a consequence of ACT's petitions. This concluded rather lamely that 'broadcasters have a special responsibility to children' but neglected to adopt any of the ACT proposals. In fact, the FCC decided against requiring any specific changes in children's programming or advertising practices.

By the middle of that decade it would appear that the FTC, although full of good intentions, was unable or unwilling to take any decisive action on issues concerning television advertising to children. What were these issues? Adler *et al.* (1977) in a later review noted that they were based on certain fundamental concerns. These were: that children are exposed to advertising for products or categories of products (such as drugs or heavily sugared foods) which may be hazardous if misused; that any advertising directed at children is *ipso facto* 'bad' because it exploits their vulnerability; that specific techniques used in television advertising may be deceptive or misleading to children, who lack the skills to evaluate them properly; and that long-term, cumulative exposure to television advertising may have adverse consequences on the development of children's values, attitudes and behaviour.

It should be noted that, if these four concerns accurately reflect the tone of research in the first half of the 1970s, they all presume a particular form of the relationship where advertising has some influence or effect to which the child is or is not susceptible. There is also a deeper concern derived from the way people see advertising as a threat and the images they have of the child as a species in need of protection. Advertising as an 'influence' and the nature of the child–advertiser relationship are discussed in Chapter 1. It should be noted that these images and metaphors helped set the agenda and define the problem in much of the research which is examined in more detail later in Chapters 3 and 4.

THE RISE AND FALL OF THE FEDERAL TRADE COMMISSION

The election of a Democratic president in the person of Jimmy Carter to the White House heralded a new toughness in the FTC's treatment of the children and television advertising issue. The new FTC chairman, Michael Pertschuk, was well known as an advocate for a better deal for children from advertisers. A fresh influx of petitions by ACT and a body called Center for Science in the Public Interest (CSPI) in 1977 requested that 'the Commission commence a rule-making procedure to explore whether the advertising of candy or sugared food products to children should be restricted because of its possible adverse effect on their nutritional and dental well-being' (Elliott *et al.*, 1981, p. 10). Another petition was filed in 1978 by Consumers Union of the United States Inc. and the Committee on Children's Television Inc. Their petition stated that 'the issue is whether commercial advertisements which, by definition include persuasive techniques and exaggerated claims, are inherently unfair and deceptive when aimed at young, impressionable children' (Elliott *et al.*, 1981, p. 10).

The details of ACT's and CSPI's petition show an interesting difference in the emphasis given to the definition of the problem area in television advertising. Both of them agreed that 'the great volume of television advertising which urges children to eat sugar is not balanced by a remotely comparable volume of advertising which urges them to consume other foods—or impresses on them the risks they take by eating the advertised products'. (Ratner, *et al.*, 1978, p. 3). ACT's petition was, however, directed at programmes where the advertising was directly aimed at and conceived for children.

The NAB guidelines of 1977 do not apply to those advertisements where, in the creative concept and execution of the commercial, both the audio and video components are clearly designed to appeal to adults and not primarily to children under 12; or, any use of a child is limited to a real-life situation; or, if the child is used other than as an incidental, background character, such use is confined to a situation in which the parent/adult–child relationship is established and the parent/adult remains a principal character; or, the broadcast schedule does not include the placing of the commercial in or adjacent to programmes designed primarily for children (Adler *et al.*, 1980, p. 309).

This is an effective and comprehensive definition of non-child-directed advertising similar to ACT's petition. The 'kidvid ghetto' was the prime target of ACT. This body sought a ban on television 'candy' advertising to children. In particular ACT members wanted this advertising prohibited either before 9.05 p.m. or where the dominant appeal of the advertising is to children or during any periods when children make up at least half of the audience (Ratner *et al.*, 1978, p. 4).

CSPI's petition was much simpler. This group wanted a ban on televised advertising for between-meal snacks which derive more than 10 per cent of their calories from added sugar. Those foods which are allowed to be advertised should have the added sugar content disclosed and the dental health risks faced by eating sugared products disclosed when children make up at least half the viewing audience. According to Choate (1981, p. 334), CCMM also wanted the definition of children's advertising to encompass programmes heavily watched by children seven days a week, no matter for whom they were originally conceived, and they urged the FTC staff to consider including advertising that children watched that was not in the 'kidvid ghetto'.

In February 1978 the Federal Trade Commission issued a report which contained information about the advertising of sugar-related products on television to children and how children understood it. Much of the report dealt with the question of the effects of sugar intake on the child's dental health and detailed legal research which, according to the staff of the Commission, supported the correctness of the FTC's approach in seeking to establish a new Trade Regulation Rule. This was not just another academic review: the report meant business.

Initially, the report recommends that 'the Commission commence rulemaking ... to eliminate harms arising out of television advertising to children' (Ratner *et al.*, 1980, title page). Within this general framework more specific conclusions were reached. These were:

1. All television advertising for any product which is directed to, or seen by, audiences composed of a significant proportion of children who are too young to understand the selling purpose of or otherwise comprehend or evaluate the advertising should be banned.

2. Televised advertising directed to, or seen by, audiences composed of a significant proportion of older children for sugared products, the consumption of which poses the most serious dental health risks, should be banned.

3. Television advertising directed to, or seen by, audiences composed of a significant proportion of older children for sugared food products not included in 2 should be balanced by nutritional and/or health disclosures funded by advertisers. (Ratner *et al.*, 1980, pp. 345–6).

The report's release was accompanied by a request from the FTC for written responses. Feedback from industries that market their products to children, such as food and toy manufacturers, was predictable in its opposition.

They questioned the relationship between sugar or the sugar in food and confectionery to dental caries, extolled the nutritional value of pre-sweetened cereals and of confectionery, denied the allegations of unfair and deceptive advertising, and claimed that the sanctity of the First Amendment, which is concerned with freedom of speech, was under threat.

In spite of this protest, the progress of the proposed FTC rule-making did not appear to be impaired. Legislative hearings, presided over by Judge Needelman, were held. In 1979 he submitted a summary of the testimony provided by expert witnesses to the FTC. Among the facts Needelman believed were adequately established by existing evidence in the record were the following: dental caries is a serious health problem in children and sugar contributes to its formation; advertising directed to children does what it is intended to do—persuade children to ask for products advertised; these purchase requests sometimes cause conflict between parent and child; although the conflicts were not too severe or long, parents yielded to the requests (cited by Shaw, p. 172).

The final chapter in the sad saga of the attempts to regulate child-directed television advertising in the United States was the publication of the *FTC Final Staff Report and Recommendations* in 1981 (Elliott *et al.*) The recommendation printed on the title page of this document was 'That the Commission Terminate Proceedings for the Promulgation of a Trade Regulation Rule on Children's Advertising'.

What had happened in the intervening three years to produce such a dramatic volte-face? It would seem that, when the FTC was issuing its report in 1978, there was considerable lobbying of the Federal government by a coalition of advertising associations, broadcasters and their associations, the US Chamber of Commerce, the Grocery Manufacturers of America, the sugar associations, the chocolate and candy manufacturers, cereal companies and their associations. The group, according to newspaper reports, had access to funds of between $15 million and $30 million to fight the proposed advertising regulations.

By 1980 Congress had voted to subject FTC rule-making to a Congressional veto without presidential intervention. In other words, any new Trade Regulation Rule would become official only if it had not been vetoed by both branches of Congress within 90 days. At one stage all Federal Trade Commission funds had been stopped and officials were contemplating the body's dissolution. The proceedings on television advertising to children were allowed to continue with the provision that any new regulation had to be based on the advertising being deceptive rather than being unfair.

The distinction between deceptive and unfair advertising is an important one. Deceptive advertising consists of communications from sellers to buyers which are false or misleading and which induce purchases. If the FTC found an advertisement false or misleading it could require the seller to cease distribution of the ad, to disclose additional information, or to correct the previous error affirmatively in future ads. Unfair advertising deals with a particular class of advertisement. One cannot prove fairness empirically;

one simply agrees or disagrees depending on one's ethical values. So, for example, both the self-regulatory codes and the FTC regarded it as unfair to allow children's programme characters to serve as product presenters in advertising within or adjacent to the character's own programme although no evidence had ever been submitted showing that this 'host selling' practice resulted in any particular consequences for children. The practice was regarded as unfair *per se* and contrary to the ethical values of both the self-regulatory parties and the FTC (Rossiter, 1980; O'Meara, 1982).

It is reasonable to assume that the three blows to the FTC were intended to reduce its power and influence. The *FTC Final Staff Report* (Elliott *et al.*, 1981) can be considered a state-of-the-art document on various issues of child-directed television advertising with particular reference to sugared products and their relation to dental health, in particular dental caries. Given the history of the FTC's original stance on rule-making and the (apparent) abandonment of its 1978 intentions in 1981, is there any way we can read between the lines of this document to see what led to a U-turn? The most damaging attack on the FTC's power would appear to be the removal from its brief of any consideration of unfair advertising. The authors state, after listing conclusions from the research literature on television advertising and children, that:

Consequently young children do not possess the cognitive ability to evaluate adequately child-oriented television advertising ... the only effective remedy would be a ban on all advertising oriented towards young children, and such a ban, as a practical matter, cannot be implemented. Because of this remedial impediment, there is no need to determine whether or not advertising oriented towards young children is deceptive. Staff's recommendation for this portion of the case is that the proceeding be terminated (Elliott *et al.*, 1981, pp. 2–3).

Having closed the main door, they then dim the lights on other ancillary issues in a rather unconvincing way. They conclude that evidence on the record is inconclusive as to whether advertising sugared products directed to children under 12 years of age may adversely affect their attitudes to nutrition. More importantly, they state (1981, p. 4) that the lack of scientific methodology for determing the cariogenicity of individual products precludes regulation through rule-making of child-oriented advertising for food products on the ground that they contribute to dental caries. It would appear that the scientific evidence was not powerful enough to assist in the judgement of whether or not an ad is deceptive, although all the evidence adduced in the 1970s was certainly adequate for the consideration of whether or not certain advertising was unfair. The FTC staff concluded 'that no further rulemaking procedures are warranted at this time and recommends that the current children's advertising rulemaking be terminated.' (1981, p. 95). The end was very near. Public comments on this recommendation followed for two months after which the commissioners deliberated on their course of action. On 2 October 1981 they published their decision to terminate the rule-making procedure on children's television advertising.

One of the themes that runs through this chapter is the power and control of commercial interests in the US television industry. The history of children's television bears this out. Children are potential clients either on their own merits or by having an effect on members of their family. As clients they constitute an audience for advertisers who form part of the marketing arm of commercial interests. Broadcasters sell audiences to advertisers. Programmes are the bait to attract audiences. Consequently a 'kidvid ghetto' emerges where advertisers can be reasonably sure of catching a demographically pure audience with cheaply produced bait. An initial concern by parents and consumer interests about the quality of programmes beamed at children and the menu offered to them by advertisers soon developed into a matter of public concern. The Federal agencies involved, first the FCC followed by the FTC, attempted to satisfy the interests of advertisers, broadcasters and a concerned public alike. It is in this context that a research boom in the area of television advertising and children has occurred, a growth in research that is essentially concerned with questions that focus on television advertising as a threat and on the child's ability to resist or understand this.

A Democratic president and a series of new appointments within the FTC heralded a change in the attitude of the FTC who came firmly down off the fence with the publication in 1978 of their report on television advertising to children. Within three years, they had been effectively emasculated by being limited to considering only deceptive advertising to children and having their conclusions made subject to a Congressional veto. It would seem that the political influence and financial power of commercial lobbyists have been effective. The FTC 1981 Report states the inevitable: rule-making procedures are terminated.

BRITISH TELEVISION ADVERTISING CONTROL

Britain became the first country in the world to introduce a public television service when the BBC began broadcasting television signals from their studio at Alexandra Palace in London in October 1936. Only a few hundred homes in the London area were equipped to receive this signal but their numbers had risen to between 20,000 and 25,000 by the outbreak of the Second World War. After the war, the government set up a committee to inquire into the future of broadcasting in Britain. Their report, called the Beveridge Report, did not foresee any prospect of the BBC accepting advertising on television but advocated some element of competition for the future. Commercial television was in the offing.

A Television Bill was passed in 1954, much to the disgust of Lord Reith, the BBC pioneer, who compared the coming of advertising to the screen to the introduction of smallpox, the Black Death and bubonic plague into England (cited by Henry, 1986, p. 29). The Television Act of 1954 set up the essential framework within which television advertising in Britain has operated for over thirty years. An advisory committee was to draw up a set of principles that laid out the ground rules.

Children were regarded as a special case from the beginnings of regulations on television advertising in Britain (Henry, 1986). The *Principles for Television Advertising* issued in 1955 by the advisory committee concentrated on two central aspects. One was the need to avoid physical, mental or moral harm to children arising from advertising in association with a programme that was aimed at them or that they were likely to see in large numbers. The second was the avoidance of advertising that took advantage of the child's natural credulity and sense of loyalty. These principles are still maintained in Appendix 1 of the latest *IBA Code of Advertising Standards and Practices* (Independent Broadcasting Authority, 1985) that deals with advertising and children.

Two images of childhood are in the Appendix. One is of the child in need of protection and the other of the child as innocent; the child has not yet abandoned innocent belief and trust and adults should shield the child from the grown-up world of advertising. Although there is an element of truth in these assertions about the nature of children, it is a cultural creation woven into the cultural fabric of our society which includes theories and popular accounts of child development. The various specific provisions of the Code stem from these principles and include the presentation format of toy products (these must be to scale and essential information such as price and whether batteries are included must be shown); matters of health (sweet eating throughout the day or at bedtime is not to be recommended, and sweets or snack products are not to be seen as substitutes for proper meals); portrayal of children in ads (they must not be seen doing dangerous things); and advertising in the context of children's programmes (no ads for alcohol, tobacco, or matches are allowed near children's programmes and no ads of any description are allowed within children's programmes of half-an-hour or less in length).

In 1977 the report of the Annan Committee on the future of broadcasting was published (Home Office, 1977). In section 12.9 and 12.10, members of the committee expressed concern about the effect of advertising in children's programmes. Although it brought income to Independent Television, the majority on the committee believed that it should be banned. They were primarily concerned with the effects on the family. Advertising that persuaded children or their parents to spend money 'encourages a degree of covetousness at a stage when children are unable to exercise sufficient discretion in assessing the merits of such an attitude to life' (Home Office, p. 166). Children would not be able to distinguish between what they were told in a children's programme and what they were told in an advertisement. The child might believe that the branded advertised goods were superior because they were advertised and feel let down when parents 'as prudent housekeepers' bought the retailer's own brand name. Consequently, the committee recommended that 'there should be no advertisements within children's programmes or between two programmes for children; and the Authority should ensure that advertisements promoting products or services of particular interest to children are not shown before 9 p.m.' (Home Office, p. 478).

In 1978 the government issued a White Paper that outlined its plans for broadcasting. The Independent Broadcasting Authority (IBA) had already removed advertising breaks from children's programmes of 30 minutes or less and had thereby gone a little way towards the full Annan recommendations. The government did not, however, accept the report's recommendation that all child-directed advertising be removed from television when children were likely to be watching.

The present control of television advertising in Britain is such that no television commercial can be screened on television unless it has been approved by the IBA. As the production of television commercials is an expensive business, practically all agencies will submit proposed scripts to the IBA before filming begins. The IBA, assisted by committees and independent consultants in specialist fields, checks 11,000 new scripts each year in relation to its Code of Advertising Standards and Practice. In addition, the Independent Television Companies' Association (ITCA) will clear copy on behalf of its members. Consequently, each ad that appears on British television screens will have, in all probability, been scrutinized by two agencies. Any member of the public who still feels distressed about an ad can complain to the IBA who will respond to such individual applications and record them.

That concludes this chapter on the social, historical, and political aspects of issues surrounding children and television advertising. Concern was expressed in the United States at the influence of such advertising on children and this led to research and political lobbying until the prospect of legislation limiting such advertising was imminent. There was no similar coordinated campaign in Britain although those concerned with child health and welfare for instance the dental profession, has been worried about the advertising of sugared products and parents have expressed concern about toy advertising and children putting pressure on parents to purchase. There is often seasonal media interest in the subject just before Christmas, with talk shows and magazine articles discussing children and television advertising. And yet in Britain there was also the prospect of legislation limiting television advertising to children. So far, a blanket ban has not been imposed in either country. Advertising is an important source of revenue for commercial stations and, in the present political climate on both sides of the Atlantic, money seems to be the driving force behind legislation.

3
Understanding Commercials:
The Experimental Evidence

INTRODUCTION

It was shown in Chapter 1 that the combination of advertising as a cultural phenomenon with children as the potential or actual audience generated a host of problems. These emerged as a consequence of the perceived inadequacies of advertising when combined with the real or imagined vulnerability of the child. Chapter 2 demonstrated public and political interest in the problem and highlighted a recent historical dimension to this issue. The climate of opinion on what is good or bad for children and what children should or should not be allowed to see can vary over the space of less than twenty years. It should also be noted that the bulk of academic research into the issue cannot be considered independently of the social and political context. Academic research is never conducted completely separately from the social milieu that spawns it and even so-called pure research will often reflect the commonsense concerns of people in the street. What advertising does to our children is an issue on which many people feel moved to express an opinion, and their views (together with professed answers) can be found in academic research journals or may be presented at learned conferences. The research literature on children and television advertising should not be regarded as a series of detached experimental investigations, each one painstakingly getting one step nearer the goal of truth. Progress has been fitful and centred on particular problem areas. There is much empirical work and dangerously little theory and this has led, as I hope to demonstrate, to some muddled thinking and conceptual confusion during the years when most of the research was published.

A FRAMEWORK FOR RESEARCH

To create order out of the considerable amount of research that has accumulated it is necessary to find a framework that will structure the discussion. Many of the academic investigators have presumed that there are problems when children watch television advertising. For example, in one of the standard texts on the subject, Adler *et al.* (1980) claim that there are four basic concerns:

1. Children are exposed to advertising for products or categories of products (such as drugs and heavily sugared foods) that may be hazardous if misused.
2. Any advertising directed at children is in fact 'bad' because it exploits their vulnerability.
3. Specific techniques used in television advertising may be deceptive or misleading to children, who lack the skills to evaluate them properly.
4. Long-term, cumulative exposure to television advertising may have adverse consequences on the development of children's values, attitudes, and behavior. (Adler *et al.*, 1980, p. 2).

The general assumption is that television advertising is a 'bad influence' on children, rather like a sophisticated, older, and undesirable friend whom you would prefer not to visit or allow your children to play with. This person represents the undesirable, seductive and tempting features of the world 'out there', and this vision of advertising and its role in relation to children set the agenda for much of the research. For example, Adler *et al.* (1980) in their research review of the 1970s state that most of the work has concentrated on specific practices in advertising and the way children understand them. Research on the advertising of particular products, such as foods and non-prescription drugs, is also reviewed. Long-term effects tend to be neglected, not because they are regarded as unimportant but because they require complex, long-term research. In other words, the research agenda is driven by a set of immediate concerns generated by concerned consumer and advertiser alike as opposed to a plan of investigation that stems from interest in fundamental problems of how children understand and behave. Problems are set, funding is made available and results are required within a certain time. In this sense, the research is applied rather than pure.

The one place where one might expect to find more basic issues discussed would be under the second of Adler's four basic concerns, which should include some examination of the child's understanding of advertising in general. The problem that is posed, however, stems from the child's inadequacy. The child is seen as progressing from a state of vulnerability to sophistication, from an earlier lack of skills to a later possession of abilities. Fundamental issues of how advertising is understood that would be found in, for example, a developmental psychology of rhetoric or the development of advertising literacy are not addressed in the literature. There is, however, enough experimental research on what children of different ages know about the purpose and intent of advertising.

One of the first reviews of research was published in 1974 (Sheikh *et al.*). Five areas of activity were identified:

1. The content of children's commercials
2. Children's attention to commercials
3. Their information processing of the commercial message
4. Their attitudes towards TV advertising
5. Their attempts to influence their parents to purchase the advertised products

This segmenting of the work into five major topics reflects an assumption that advertising works on an audience in a sequential manner. The sequence begins with 'what's on'. The child next pays attention to certain parts of this message. The attended information is processed by the child, influencing attitudes and affecting consumer-related behaviour. Although this analysis makes a lot of common sense it does frame the research areas in a particular way that would influence any future analysis of how advertising works with an audience of children.

More recently, Wartella and Hunter (1983) have laid out a similar framework for classifying the research. The distinction between 'what's on' and 'what the child does with it' is maintained as a major division between two different strands of research. The former is concerned with the discourse of television advertising to children and the latter is placed under the heading of 'Children's Processing of Television Advertising' which consists of: attention to commercials; effects of television production factors on children's attention to commercials; programme/commercials separation effects; comprehension of the purpose of advertising; memory for advertising information; persuasive effects of television advertising on children.

McNeal (1987) analyses the research into children and television advertising into three areas that involve processing of the advertised message, cognitions in children, and their consumer behaviour as a result of advertising. The processing of the advertised message can be separated into attention to advertising and understanding of television advertisements. The latter is further subdivided into distinguishing programme from commercial, discerning the intent of television advertising and, lastly, comprehending the content of such advertising. Attention to advertising will depend on personal factors (such as level of motivation, attitudes towards the commercial, influence of parents and peers, lack of knowledge about commercials) and stimulus factors such as the context of the programmes (whether they are boring or interesting), the actual content of the commercial, and the product advertised. Cognitions in children caused by television advertising include attitudes, desires, interests, intentions, and preferences. McNeal considers three types of consumer behaviour caused by advertising: purchase behaviour itself, which is to be distinguished from purchase request behaviour, and antisocial behaviour, such as parent–child conflict.

These are some of the ways in which researchers have attempted to make order out of the different research papers and the host of findings on the question of children and television advertising. Alternative methods of classification could be used to cut across the lines that have been drawn. For example, the methodology used in each study would provide one way of making sense of the literature. It would seem, however, that a classification based on an assumption that the advertising message is processed in sequence, from watching through to buying, is the most popular and will be adopted in this chapter.

Based on the above, we can categorize the research into two main divisions. One is concerned with 'what's on' and various ways of analysing the content of advertising directed at children. Work in this area is reviewed in Chapter 6. The second major research field addresses issues that involve the child and examines how children process the information in advertising, what they do with it, and how their behaviour is influenced by what they see and hear. This second branch effectively consists of two parts, one covering the various cognitive processes activated as a result of watching and listening to television advertising, while the other is concerned with what the child does with the information processed in this way. The first part can be subdivided into several distinct subfields:

1. Attention to commercials
2. Ability to distinguish between commercials and programmes
3. The child's understanding of the intent of the commercial
4. The child's interpretation of the content of the commercial (including consumption symbolism, gender stereotypes)
5. The child's memory for the commercial
6. Other processes invoked (for example, cognitive defences) by viewing

The second part can be divided further into three subfields:

7. The effect on knowledge, attitudes and values (for example, whether exposure to information in ads for junk foods lowers nutritional awareness; what children feel about advertising). This will have short-term and long-term aspects
8. The effect on other people, in particular parents (for example, does the child pester Mum for more?)
9. The effect on choice or consumption behaviour (for example, whether children eat more sweets after watching commercials for that class of product, or

whether they consume more of a particular brand by watching a commercial for that brand?)

A 'miscellaneous' section will include the few studies that cannot be classified. Because the bulk of the work reviewed is from the United States, non-American research will be mentioned with the country specified in the text. If no such mention is made the reader should assume the subjects and researcher were North American. British research is dealt with separately in a later section. The review does not pretend to cover all the work in the field but does discuss the research that has something to say. The last major review of the literature was by Adler *et al.* (1980), but their work is less likely to be mentioned here than subsequent research.

To do justice to the psychological research on children and television advertising, it will be necessary to examine a considerable number of studies in some detail. The rest of this chapter will be devoted to three well-researched areas in the literature. These are: the child's attention to television advertising; the ability of children to distinguish commercials from programmes; and, probably the central issue in children and television advertising research, the child's comprehension of the purpose of television advertising. The remaining literature will be discussed in Chapter 4.

ATTENTION TO COMMERCIALS

Why should researchers be interested in the attention that children give to television commercials? Certainly, selective attention is an important part of any model of information processing in human beings and the mechanism of attention is often regarded as operating like a filter. The amount of information that is potentially available to every one of us is vast and overwhelming and attention can operate only by allowing a selection through for further processing. Consequently, attention can be regarded as the first stage in establishing what television advertisements the child actually sees, hears and understands.

The 'what's on' phase of the sequence can be examined

and analysed and audience researchers can establish from automatic recorders and interviews with viewers when the set is switched on and who is probably 'viewing' in the room at the time. 'Viewing' is deliberately placed in inverted commas because the information presented on the box and the presence of other people in the room do not necessarily constitute the act of watching and listening. We need to know what is being attended to.

Attention has another meaning that is related to the amount of effort involved. In other words, we can be attending and yet be easily distracted or we can be attending with engagement and involvement. The concept of attention has two parts corresponding to direction and strength: what is being attended to and how much attention is being given to it.

One of the main problems in assessing the importance of attention in human information processing is concerned with the meaning of a lack of attention. Basically, the problem reduces to: if I pay little attention to this stimulus is it because I'm not interested or is it because the stimulus is so familiar I don't need to pay attention to it? It is dangerous to assume that 'not paying attention' always reflects a lack of interest. The person could be interested but the familiar first few bars of a tune or first scene of a shot would be enough to activate recall of the whole television commercial. In more technical language, is the information being processed stimulus-driven or schema-driven? A schema is a system of mental representation that sets up expectations of what we probably will see or hear, often based on what has been learnt in the past. Watching a new television commercial for the first time may be stimulus-driven information processing with the viewer paying close attention to what's going on. After several showings, the commercial now familiar, may not receive much attention from the average viewer who is likely to get up and go off to put the kettle on. This does not mean the commercial is not being processed. The schema or system of mental representation that has been activated when the commercial was recognized is driving the processing although the viewer may not be viewing and may not even be in the room.

The interesting research questions (which have not yet been adequately addressed in the literature on advertising and children, let alone answered) are concerned with the nature of these representations of different ads after several viewings and the recognition 'trigger' that will activate them. Does the narrative dominate? Are the events in their original sequence or is it just a jumble of images? Is the basic discourse structure of ads preserved? How much of the affective or emotional 'after-taste' remains? Is music the dominant trigger (in which case, the 'viewer' need not be in the room and the first few bars might be enough to activate the schema)? These questions have a developmental dimension as well as posing theoretically interesting and practically useful problems for the advertising researcher.

Attention is a complex psychological construct with different facets. The assessment of attention should be concerned with establishing those behaviours that can be measured reliably and that have some validity because they have a bearing on an aspect of the construct being looked at. Although experimental psychology has used simple but limited measures of attention such as the length of time a child visually fixates on different types of stimulus displays (for example, Mackworth and Bruner, 1970), or indirect measures that look at the decrement in performance as a result of various distracter stimuli (for instance, Hagen, 1967), there is no reason why a wider range of naturalistic behaviours could not be sampled as possible indicators of aspects of attention. For example, what non-verbal signs denote 'rapt' attention in the sense of engagement with sole attention devoted to what's being shown to the exclusion of all else? Other research questions could be asked. How does the child's attention vary as the commercial is being viewed and what does this mean? Does the change indicate a change from interest to lack of interest or, alternatively, a shift from stimulus-driven to schema-driven processing? Can the indirect methods of assessing attention be used in television advertising research with children and 'distracters' of differing intensity set up to obtain an indirect measure of the pulling power of a commercial? In the general field of psychological research into children watching television these problems and issues in attention have frequently been discussed (Husson, 1982; Anderson and Lorch, 1983).

The developmental sequence of children's attention to television as outlined by Anderson and Lorch (1983) consists of three major stages. The first occurs in infancy and very young children before the age of 2½ years. Attention is sporadic and the child rarely sits oriented towards the television set. By the age of 2½ years, however, the child has adopted what could be called 'a viewing schema'. That is, the concept of 'watching television' emerges as an integrated form of activity which, although often interrupted by the child's playing with toys, has a certain underlying organization and purpose. The child will take up a position in the room oriented towards the television set, playing with toys but also looking up frequently. Visual attention to television increases from this time until school age. During this period, attention is driven by the schema underlying the activity of 'watching television' but the content will also hold the attention of the child. There is some evidence that this level of attention does not increase much into the school years when the child's understanding of the forms and conventions of television becomes more sophisticated as various schemata for television comprehension develop.

Attention to television can be described as the interplay between two sets of processes. One is characteristic of the stimuli 'out there' in the television message and the other, within the growing and developing child, is characteristic of the emergence of more and more sophisticated mental schemata that guide and predict what will come next. There is a third principle that operates within a time scale of less than a minute and is important when attention to commercials is discussed. Looking at or looking away from television is not just the result of something happening on the screen that draws the viewer's attention (stimulus-driven) or of the viewer's decision that more information is needed or that none is required (schema-driven). There are dependencies within the sequence of looking at and looking away from the screen. In short, the longer a viewer looks continuously at television the more likely it is that he or she will continue to do so. Conversely, the longer it has been since the viewer last looked at television, the less probable it is that he or she will resume viewing.

The term 'attentional inertia' has been coined by Anderson, Alwitt, Lorch, and Levin (1979) to describe this phenomenon, although Krull and Husson (1980) claim independently to have discovered a similar effect and have given it the same name. Attentional inertia is relatively independent of content and can be observed in children as young as 12 months and on into adulthood. It would seem to build up as an influence over 15 seconds when it remains as a steady effect. It can be broken, of course, or else we would never start— or stop—watching and it can be overridden by stimulus-driven and schema-driven information inherent in the content or features of what is seen or what is expected.

As more complex and powerful schemata develop as the child grows older, attentional inertia becomes less important as a source of influence. Children can then expect, predict and sample the parts of the television programme they want to instead of relying on the rather crude, content-free process of attentional inertia. For younger children, however, attentional inertia is a useful maintenance process that carries them over the parts of the programme that are uninteresting or incomprehensible when stimuli or schema do not drive attention to the screen.

The researcher interested in a fine-grained analysis of attention to different parts of a single commercial (which will normally last for 30 seconds or less) must consider attentional inertia, especially with young children as subjects. An attention score for a short commercial may be spuriously high as a result of attention to a preceding part of the audiovisual flow, such as the preceding commercial. If the commercial is preceded by a period of non-attention, then a false low attention score for that commercial may be obtained.

When the literature on children's attention to television commercials is examined, it would appear that the most frequent operationalization of the 'attention' construct is simply whether the child looked at the screen or not. Attention is either *on* (looking) or *off* (not looking) and measures are taken by counting over a time base. This is a simple, quick, and easily processed measure that facilitates the rapid publication of results, but there may be other reasons why this technique is preferred.

Academic psychologists would see different measures of attention as indicators of possible cognitive processes and information processing strategies and tactics, but the audience researcher is more concerned with measures that might be useful to the advertiser. Advertisers who use broadcast media are concerned that people watch their advertisement and don't switch channels to watch someone else's. Audience researchers are consequently under pressure to produce measures that provide an index of just this 'watching'. If an easy measure could be made of the numbers of pairs of eyeballs that are glued to the screen for particular programmes at different times for differently defined audiences then this measure might provide a way of rating programmes and selling airtime. The 'attention-grabbing' characteristics of a commercial and the ways the particular audience of children are grabbed by commercials become important goals of measurement in their own right.

One of the earliest studies on the child's attention to television advertising was done by Ward, Levinson, and Wackman (1972). They trained middle-class mothers to act as observers while their children watched commercial television on Saturday mornings. The mothers based their observations primarily on an 'eyes *on* the set/eyes *off* the set' criterion of attention and divided them into various response categories such as 'full attention' and 'partial attention'. The ages of the children sampled ranged from 5 to 12 years.

It was found that younger children have a different attention pattern to programmes and commercials from older children. In particular, younger children tended to pay more attention throughout the commercial, compared with older children. Older children's attention within a series of commercials presented in a block tended to drop towards the end. They also tended to make more critical comments about the commercials than younger children.

For all children, there is a drop in attention when a commercial is shown, compared with attention to previous programmes, and the greatest drop is for the older children. For all children, full attention to commercials is highest for those advertisements shown at the beginning of programmes. It could be that these results support the hypothesis of 'attentional inertia' since younger children's attention is less responsive to obvious structural shifts between commercial and programme or does not drop off so much towards the end of the commercial which is more predictable and hence more likely to be schema-driven.

It is not known whether these structural distinctions between commercial and programme are recognized by younger children or whether they switch from stimulus-driven to schema-driven processing from beginning to end of a commercial presentation. Consequently, the processes of attentional inertia, stimulus-driven attention, and schema-driven attention are confounded. A clearer picture may emerge when the developmental progress of these processes is charted. In addition, data on the relative attention paid to commercials versus programmes as well as cynicism expressed will depend on the programmes and commercials shown and on the degree of novelty and familiarity of both in the eyes of the child.

Wartella and Ettema (1974) used the same measure of attention as Ward, Levinson, and Wackman (1972). That is, attention was measured using mothers' assessment of their viewing child on a three-point scale of full attention, partial attention and no attention. Commercials were placed together in groups of three, four or five and embedded in a 30-minute videotape of a popular situation comedy and shown to 120 upper-middle-class children ranging in age from 3 to 8 years. Measures were taken when the commercial was being shown and at points in the immediately preceding and following programmes.

Wartella and Ettema (1974) were interested in the attention-drawing power of the visual as well as the auditory information in commercials. Some present information in a rapid, changing way so that it is difficult to predict what is coming next. Other commercials are slower in their pacing and predictable in content. It is possible to quantify these characteristics of informativeness or redundancy of information in stimuli and present commercials that differ on an index of informativeness on various channels including separate ratings for visual and auditory channels.

They found that the difference in attention of the youngest, preschool children between the commercials of high complexity and those of low complexity was greater than that of older children, the attention to the high-complexity commercials being greater than to the low complexity ones. For older children, the difference was not so great. It can be argued that the differences in attention to different commercials in the youngest children is best explained by differences in the properties of the stimuli. Most of the information that younger children process is information from out there, in the stimuli. As the child grows older and expectations about the environment become more complex and reliable, schema-based information processing will have a more dominant role to play. Wartella and Ettema (1974) also found that auditory complexity was associated with closer attention by children and that this effect was more powerful than variations in visual complexity.

How much attention do children of different ages pay to television commercials? If attention is regarded as an indicator of different psychological processes, then the question of 'how much' is not particularly important because paying or not paying attention can signify different processes at different ages. This question is important for advertisers and audience researchers who are concerned with quantifying and estimating the size of audiences, and one could say that an audience is not really an audience if the members are not looking or listening to what's on.

The literature does address the issue but no consistent pattern of results emerges. Bechtel, Achelpol, and Akers (1971) observed children ranging from 12 months to 19 years watching television in their own homes. On average, children younger than 11 years watched commercials only 40 per cent of the time they were broadcast but the older children and teenagers averaged 55 per cent. Winick and Winick (1979) observed more than 300 children at home and reported that they regarded commercials as relatively unimportant with children as young as 2 years regularly leaving the room when the commercials came on.

In a study where mothers observed their own children

(Atkin, 1978), they reported that children ranging from preschool age to 9 years paid close attention over half the time whereas only 29 per cent of the mothers of 9-year-old to 11-year-old children reported close attention paid (cited in Wartella and Hunter, 1983, p. 3). In the Wartella and Ettema (1974) study, conducted in a school setting, the 5-year-old to 8-year-old children showed slightly higher overall attention to the integrated ads than the preschoolers.

Zuckerman, Ziegler, and Stevenson (1978) videotaped children's viewing behaviour rather than observer rating as a method of assessing attention. The children ranged from 7 to 10 years and the experiment was conducted in a play-room in a psychology laboratory. Commercials were put together in pairs and placed at different points within a 12-minute programme. In these circumstances, children paid low attention to both programme and commercial with, on average, only 17 per cent of the children attending to the commercials. Their attention dropped dramatically during the time the first commercial appeared and decreased even further during the course of the second commercial.

In contrast to Wartella and Ettema (1974), Zuckerman *et al.* (1978) found that attention to commercials decreased with increasing age of the child. Most importantly, they found that there were important differences in the amount of attention paid to commercials that depended on which commercial was being shown to the child. Some commercials were much more effective at capturing the child's attention than others. This rather obvious finding makes it impossible to formulate a general statement about developmental norms of attention to television commercials and should provoke research into the particular characteristics of different television commercials that determine different forms of attention-based behaviour.

Greer, Potts, Wright, and Huston (1982) varied both the placement of the commercial within a television programme and its perceptual salience. Commercials were either dispersed individually through the programme or were clustered in groups. For preschool children, dispersed high salience commericals maintained attention more than any other combination of experimental variables. They also found a sex difference, with boys being more attentive and maintaining attention across commercials than girls, whose attention tended to decrease after the first five or ten seconds.

Are there any general principles that can be extracted from these results? It would appear that when the child is watching a television commercial several factors will influence the amount of attention he or she gives to what is being shown. Firstly, there's the content and form of the commercial itself. It has been shown that the uncertainty of what is coming will influence attention and that this influence is particularly important with voices, sounds, or music—information that is processed in the auditory channel. Some commercials are intrinsically more interesting than others and this will influence the extent to which children will want to watch a particular commercial, a particular subgenre of commercials, or commercials in general that they have seen before. Commercials will also differ in familiarity depending on whether they have not been seen before or are regulars. This, in turn, will influence the information processing strategy employed. If the commercial is recognized and is well known then a schema-based strategy could be operating and watching or listening can be reduced. A 'sampling' strategy could perhaps be deployed to watch those parts that can be appreciated again and neglect those few seconds that are predictable and uninteresting. If the ad is 'new', processing is more likely to be stimulus-driven and attention will be close.

Secondly, there is the effect of context. Commercials occur with other commercials and the cluster is found in spots in programmes. Commercials are seen on television and sets are most often to be found in the home. There are two context effects, the immediate one of the televisual message, and the 'viewing ecology'. We can call the former the proximal context and the latter the distal context. The proximal context can influence attention because of 'attentional inertia'. Attention may have been focused on an event on screen that occurred ten seconds before and inertia has maintained attention over that period. The recognition of boundaries between categories of events on television such as 'programme' versus 'commercial' can be part of the schemata for understanding that medium and can bring about changes in attention. If the child knows commercials are coming next this may cause a switch in processing strategy or even the onset of some other activity like asking the mother for a snack or doing some homework or leaving the room.

The distal context or 'viewing ecology' has been found to be important because a variation in the context of viewing (home, school or laboratory) is often accompanied by a variation in the amount of attention reported at different ages. A complete specification of the viewing ecology would include accustomed viewing styles (for example, in bed, on the floor, at the breakfast table), alternative activities (such as homework, meals, reading comics), and the presence of other people (including parents, siblings and friends). Attention is frequently distributed across several activities in real life and one of these might be watching commercial television.

Finally, there is a development of age-related abilities in children. When the question of how best to describe changes in a child is asked, one of the ways of answering would be in terms of how adequately a particular description accounts for the observations. The description itself may be a theory of child development in its own right or a model of particular processes or simply an extended metaphor that provides an elegant picture of how parts of the child's mind work.

There are several ways of evaluating adequacy. To what extent does the description cover all observations or are some unaccounted for? Is the explanation parsimonious, using minimal conceptual equipment, or do we have to create many customized concepts for the explanatory job at hand? Are the concepts used universal ones that are appropriate to all areas of growth and development or are they specific to that particular sub-area of investigation? Is the explanation taken from a body of theory relevant to the processes involved in the behaviour observed? Unless a grand theory of development is sought that will unify all observations of most behaviour in many conceivable contexts, the field will be populated with different theories covering differing ranges of behaviour, each having different demands in terms of rigour. When theories are sought of children's developing abilities with regard to the processing and understanding of television advertising, the volume of experimental and survey research produced is not paralleled by a similar amount of work on what might be going on within the growing mind of the child. There are certain areas where this lack of theoretical underwriting is particularly obvious, such as research into the child's understanding of advertising intent.

Perhaps because attention is a popular concept that is well integrated into the body of theory on cognitive psychology, explanations of the child's attention to television advertising appear to be lucid, appropriate and comprehensive in their scope. The main principle is the development of schemata and the gradual incorporation of schema-driven strategies of information processing into the mechanisms underlying attention in the child. There is an age-related drift from attention being based on the perceptual aspects of the commercial to a more conceptual basis. Schemata are conceptual in nature, as they are founded on past experience of the world and produce inferences and predictions of future trains of events.

Another general process can be called the development of attentional control in children. Perhaps this is best described at the level of metaphor or image. Very young children are buffeted by novel and vivid events out there and attention is drawn, held and often stuck by attentional inertia. Older children can decide to allocate attention to particular parts of the world that are considered 'relevant' at the time, or adopt 'sampling' strategies that optimize the amount of attention paid to several attractive and/or important tasks such as watching television, doing homework, and squabbling with brother or sister. What is 'relevant'? The criteria will shift as the child grows older and the direction of shift, from perceptual to conceptual, is predictable from the general principle of the emergence of schema-based processing with age.

These explanations all lean heavily on theories of information processing where the language of description borrows from the discourse of computer software and hardware. Descriptions of the developmental trend from perceptually-based inferences to conceptually founded inferences can be found before computer metaphors, however. For example, Wohlwill (1962) argued that the progress of development can be characterised as the loosening of a reliance on the immediate stimulus field. Younger children are 'perceptually bound' to the extent they are tied to what's going on out there, now, whereas growing older means depending more on what's in here, in the mind, which is not dependent on the here-and-now.

One of the theories that predates computers and is used frequently in the literature on children and television advertising is based on the writings of Jean Piaget. One of the reasons why his work has been adopted with enthusiasm by so many experimenters in this field has to do with the image of childhood that is assumed in the versions of his theories that are culturally transmitted and found in textbooks for teachers and educationists. This image of young children is one of inadequacy that fits with the relationship of seducer and innocent, an emotionally loaded pairing that influences much of the popular visions of what advertising does to children.

The Piagetian concept of 'centration' is relevant and can be used to describe what is known about the development of the child's attention to television advertising. Centration is characteristic of what Piaget has called the 'preoperational' period of development, a stage from about two years to seven years of age. Centration is often found in problem-solving situations where a correct (adult) solution requires taking into account more than one aspect of a situation. The preoperational child will centre on only one aspect and fail to take other, equally important, aspects into account. Often the child will centre on the perceptually salient or dominant part of the perceived situation and disregard other, less salient parts.

For example, one of the classic Piagetian tasks that can distinguish preoperational children from children in the subsequent, concrete operational period of development, involves what is known as conservation of amount. Two identical glasses of the same size (A and B) are filled with lemonade to exactly the same level and shown to the child who agrees, when asked, that each contains the same amount. All the lemonade from one of the glasses (B) is then poured into another differently shaped glass, perhaps a tall, thin container. This new glass with the lemonade in it (C) is then placed beside A and the child is asked if there is the same amount of lemonade in both.

The preoperational child (perhaps aged 5 years) will usually claim that C has more because 'look, the level comes up to here but it's only up to here in that one'. The concrete operational child (perhaps aged 8 years) will look at both A and C and say 'they're the same, there's just as much to drink in this one as in that one'.

The passage from preoperational to concrete operational functioning in the child may be marked by several achievements and the limitations of the preoperational child may be characterized by many inadequacies, and one of these is the existence of centration in young children. Young, preoperational children will attend to just one dimension of that array (the level of the lemonade) and disregard the other dimensions such as the fact that, although C has a higher level, it is a thinner glass than A. Being able to take these dimensions of height and width into account simultaneously is an ability that certainly helps in attaining the concept of conservation of amount. Conserving amount is an' understanding that amount is a property of things that doesn't change when only the shape changes. Amount will change, however, when bits are added or taken away. If a child centres on only one salient perceptual part of the television input and that limited, stimulus-driven information is the main factor determining when to attend and when not to attend, one would expect the switches in attention to the screen to be less sensitive to important changes in content than in the older child who attends to several dimensions. This prediction is confirmed by the results of Ward, Levinson, and Wackman (1972). Attentional shifts between programme and commercial are not as great in younger children as in older children.

In conclusion, the observations and experiments on the

child's attention to television commercials are in accord
with much that is known about theories and models of how
children's attention operates and develops. It should be
added that the data obtained are limited in various ways.
The concept of attention is often operationalized as visual
attention on an *on/off* criterion where the child looks or
doesn't. Data have been collected based on mothers' assessments of their own children's attention, grouped into rated
categories such as 'full', 'partial', and 'none'. It is to be
hoped that future research in this area will explore alternative channels of attention such as auditory attention and use
video-based measures as well as the more conventional rater
scales.

ABILITY TO DISTINGUISH BETWEEN COMMERCIALS
AND PROGRAMMES

The methods and experiments used in one area of research
into children and television advertising often shade into
those used in an adjacent area. For example, in the above
studies of children's attention patterns for programmes
within which commercials are embedded, the variation in
attention could be taken as an operationalization of differentiation between commercial and programme. If the
child perceives the commercial and the programme as no
different from each other then the pattern of attention over
the structural break between the two should not be significantly different from any other measure over the same
time base taken at random in the televisual flow. If a reliable
and significant difference in attention is picked up over these
breaks, then this is strong evidence that some aspect of the
difference between commercial and programme is recognized by the child.

It is possible, of course, that a more primitive recognition
of some difference between television programmes and television commercials exists that is not sensitive to differences
in attention. It would appear likely, though, that attentional
differences are detecting early and basic forms of distinctions
drawn between the two classes of television information.
The measure of attention is based on watching behaviour

and, as the child is not being questioned, no categories of language such as the reference of the word 'television commercial' are brought into use by this method. Before the evidence is examined, it is necessary to clarify what the ability to distinguish between commercials and programmes means. As with much of the work on the subject, many of the research papers are long on experimental findings but short on theory.

The basic cognitive equipment we require for analysing and processing any part of our perceived or conceived worlds consists of classes and relations. The fundamental questions of similarity and difference between events or objects must be put immediately if we are to escape from James's world of 'buzzing, booming confusion' in the immediate here-and-now that was then thought to characterize the mental life of the new born child. Recognition, which James neatly placed in the phrase 'Hollo! thingumbob again!' (1891, p. 417), is the most primitive of operations and presumes an awareness that this-now is similar to that-then. Any mental world consists of classes, sets or groups that are organized in immensely complex and different ways for different purposes.

Recent research in cognitive psychology (Rosch, 1978; Rosch et al., 1976) has established that categories in the mind have an internal organization based on the 'typicality' of particular members of that class. For example, robins and sparrows are more typical members of the class 'bird' than albatrosses or ostriches. A whale is a very atypical sort of a 'mammal' and in common-sense typologies that are used by ordinary people, a whale might be regarded as a 'fish'. This vision of the psychological nature of categories has viewed the boundaries between classes as much less well-defined than logicians would like. There is a 'fuzzy' boundary between sets of things where membership is in dispute and, whereas it is probably more likely that object x belongs to A, there is still a probability that x could lie in class B.

Once a skeleton of classes is laid down, incoming information will be processed using these categories which will develop different ways of processing and will begin to function as specialized agencies within the system of cognitive organization. To use a computer analogy, if a scenario, event or object is recognized as belonging to class A then the appropriate processing module for that class is plugged in. Each module would have rules of inference that may not be the same as the rules for class B. As children mature and learn, we should not expect the structure or function of these classes to remain unchanged but to grow and develop.

What then would we expect from children in terms of the psychological organization of categories concerned with television advertising? Advertising can be distinguished from the rest of television fare by perceptually available features as well as differences in content and intent. Television commercials are short; programmes are longer. Television commercials are repeated in identical form whereas programmes are rarely repeated in exactly the same way although there may be points of dramatic or thematic continuity as in serials and series. Television commercials are persuasive in intent; programmes can be simply entertaining or informative. There are further points of difference that could be mentioned, such as the presence of a brand the child recognizes from kitchen or supermarket shelves in many commercials. The distinctions are not clear and many counter-examples could be used to make the category boundaries more fuzzy. Promotional music videos are structurally very similar to television commercials and public service announcements (PSAs) or programme trailers are often short and succinct although they do not have quite the same commercial intent as advertising.

Advertising is pervasive in contemporary culture and its forms and conventions invade many areas of discourse so that finding disinterested parties in any communication situation is becoming more difficult. Notwithstanding border disputes over what is and is not 'advertising' on television, it is possible to establish lines of distinction that mark off most of television advertising at several different levels of analysis. One of these is based on a simple perceptually-based difference such as the different length of television commercials and programmes. There may be other differences at this level such as the presence of jingles, rapid cuts, or even a difference in range of sound intensity so that commercials sound louder.

The separation between programme and commercial is
enhanced by the use of devices known in the trade as 'separators'. Some years ago, a separator was used at the beginning of a block of advertisements on British commercial
television. It looked like an expanding and rotating star.
This has now fallen into disuse and the 'natural break' is
signalled by a black screen for a brief period of time. On
children's programmes commercial onset is often prefaced
by a logo and signature tune but there are other occasions
when the commercials intrude into children's programmes
frequently with no obvious separator device. In the United
States the National Association of Broadcasters (NAB)
adopted guidelines in 1979. These stated that a separator
device had to be inserted before a commercial during children's programming. The separator had to fulfil the following conditions: a statement had to be made, in both
video and audio, to the effect that the announcer (or the
programme) would return after the separator messages; the
device had to remain on the screen for at least five seconds
but not more than ten seconds; artwork, animation, or still
or motion pictures/title cards could be used in the separators, but if a programme character was depicted it had to
be an 'incidental still shot' that did not detract from the
intent of the separator device; the identification logo of
network or station could be included in the separator provided it did not detract; an announcer, either on-screen or
voice-over, could deliver the separator message, so long as
he or she was not connected with the programme; and a
device had to be inserted on returning from the commercial
to the programme, using a phrase such as 'We now return
to (name of the programme).' The public voiced great concern that commercials should be carefully cordoned off
from programmes and this concern a force behind
much of the research on the child's ability to distinguish
programmes from commercials. Advertising is insidious,
and children are vulnerable, and, as pointed out in Chapter
1, much of the fear and loathing induced when advertising
and children are placed in conjunction is generated by the
mythic relationship of innocent and seducer. It should be
borne in mind, however, that the child's ability to recognize
that television commercials and programmes belong to

different categories is not the same as the more sophisticated skills involved in attributing different intent to television advertising and to television programmes. In one of the standard texts on the subject, Adler *et al.* (1980) investigate the issue in a chapter entitled 'Children's ability to distinguish television commercials from program material' which includes their research. What is now required is some evidence of the earliest age at which the difference between advertising and programming is recognized by the child. Once this is established other differences between the genres of commercials and of programmes can be drawn. One of these would be a difference in intent.

With these comments in mind, the research literature can be examined. Palmer and McDowell (1979) sampled sixty children in two groups, one aged 5 to 6 years and the other 6 to 7 years. They were shown a programme with commercials inserted. At predetermined points within each of the programmes the videotape was stopped and each child was questioned on what he or she had seen—whether it was 'part of the show' or a 'commercial' and how the child could tell. Some of the tapes used separators to define the onset of commercial and programme. The presence or absence of these did not affect results. It would appear from the data, although Palmer and McDowell do not provide significance levels based on a 50 per cent correct recognition on a random basis, that children between 5 and 7 years cannot recognize the difference between commercials and programmes. They were able to identify commercials only 53 per cent of the time. Programmes, however, were correctly identified about 70 per cent of the time.

There were large differences in identification under the different experimental conditions and these were not theoretically predictable. It should be pointed out that, in an actual viewing situation, the distinction between commercials and programmes is carried on other features apart from differences in content. One would expect that young children could draw a distinction on the basis of salient perceptual features but the evidence from the attentional literature is inconsistent. Wartella *et al.* (1981) claim that, in a 1974 study (Wartella and Ettema), children as young as 3 or 4 years were found to make an attentional shift upward at the onset of a commercial; but Huston and Wright cite two studies (National Science Foundation, 1977; Zuckerman *et al.*, 1978), where 5-year-old children continue to attend to commercials at approximately the same level as during the programme. In the Palmer and McDowell (1979) study the child has to know what the verbal labels 'commercial' and 'programme' refer to and be capable of monitoring what was being watched when the tape stopped for correct performance of the researchers' task.

Zuckerman and Gianino (1981) sampled sixty-four children from a middle-class background, with equal groups aged 4 years, 7 years and 10 years. A collection of photographs of animated characters who appear regularly on children's television in programmes or commercials were laid out in front of the child who then identified each character. For example, Tony the Tiger, who appears in Frosted Flakes commercials in the USA and in Sugar Frosties commercials in the UK, is a commercial-only character whereas Bugs Bunny is a programme-only character.

Not surprisingly, recognition and identification of characters increased with age. Two non-verbal tests were performed with the children. Two characters were placed before each child, who was asked which one was in a commercial. This procedure was repeated for ten pairs of different characters, each pair consisting of one programme character and one commercial character. Over half the 4-year-olds correctly identified the photograph of the commercial character in practically all pairs presented. A quarter of the 4-year-olds made significantly incorrect responses; that is, they systematically chose the wrong character as the one in the commercial. This indicated that they were able to discriminate between members of the two classes but failed to apply the correct label to the characters. The 7-year-olds and 10-year-olds performed almost perfectly. Children were asked to point to the character in each pair who 'shows you (product name) on television' and all age groups performed at near perfect levels. Other questions were asked but, as they appear to be concerned with assessing the child's understanding of the concept of a commercial they will be discussed in the next section. The evidence of systematic errors by 4-year-olds on the character choice task demonstrates that an awareness of the difference between commercial and programme is there in the preschool child but the concept of 'programme' and 'commercial' has not developed substantially even to the extent of using the culturally agreed name for the category. What does seem to be part of the concept of a commercial at the preschool age is the relationship between main character and product.

Gaines and Esserman (1981) sampled 104 children ranging in age from 4 years to 8 years. Two 30-second animated commercials for a breakfast cereal aimed at children were embedded in a 6-minute Mighty Mouse cartoon programme for children and the videotape was shown to each child. During the second showing of the commercial the tape was stopped on freeze-frame and children were asked whether it was part of the show about the mouse. Practically all children were able to identify the commercial correctly as separate from the programme with correct identification for 4-year-olds reaching 90 per cent. The methodology here is similar to that used by Palmer and McDowell (1979) with the added refinement that both commercial and programme were animated, thus minimizing differences. In addition, the child had to deny that the commercial was part of 'the show about the mouse' in order to respond correctly. Children often demonstrate an acquiescence tendency to agree with adult interviewers and the good experimenter should be aware of this.

Similar methodologies with variations have been used by other researchers. For example, Stutts, Vance, and Hudleson (1981) were concerned, like Palmer and McDowell (1979), with the ability of children to distinguish between commercials and programmes and whether different kinds of separators would help them make this distinction. They played a videotape of an animated cartoon which was interrupted in the middle by an animated commercial. The 108 children had to keep their hands in their laps until they saw a commercial, when they had to put their hands on a red square. When the show came back on, they had to put their hands back in their laps. Children were timed on both these behaviours. The authors concluded that separators do not appear to influence preschool children's ability to recognize a commercial with greater or lesser speed but that children aged 7 or older may be assisted in speed of commercial recognition by separators. Five-year-olds and 7-year-olds did recognize the commercial as distinct from the programme but 3-year-olds did not.

Butter, Popovich, Stackhouse, and Garner (1981) attempted to assess the extent to which 80 children aged 4 and 5 years were able to distinguish between commercials and programmes by requiring each child to tell the experimenter 'when a commercial comes on'. The children saw a video-tape of a programme with several commercials inserted at different points. If the child did not answer when a commercial was being shown, the experimenter asked if this was still part of the programme. Results demonstrated that the majority of 4-year-olds were capable of discriminating between commercials and programmes as were the 5-year-olds, who discriminated more successfully.

Levin, Petros, and Petrella (1982) used the technique of asking children whether what they had just seen was a 'commercial' or a 'programme' in order to establish when children could differentiate between the two. Segments of programmes and commercials, each lasting 10 seconds, were edited on videotape for this purpose and the child was questioned after each segment. They found that, with seventy-two children ranging from 3 years to 5 years, the percentage of correct identifications was significantly above chance at each age. This result seems to show that children are more capable of discriminating between commercial and programme than the much-cited research of Palmer and McDowell (1979) had found. The fact that commercial and programme segments were the same length meant that children could not use this obvious perceptual cue on which to base their judgements. Unlike Palmer and McDowell, Levin et al. (1982) found that commercials were identified more accurately than programmes but this could be a consequence of the programmes only being shown for the unnatural time of 10 seconds.

There is one piece of research that uses a completely

different methodology from these experimental studies. Jaglom and Gardner (1981) were interested in the more general issue of how children discover the rules that govern the world of television. What sort of knowledge allows them to predict, for example, when a programme will begin or end or when a character will appear or disappear? This study is unusual in that it originated, not from the traditions of consumer psychology, or advertising psychology with its concerns for survey research, experimental intervention and large samples, but from a longitudinal quasi-anthropological investigation of child development. Only three children were studied but they were observed, at regular intervals, over three years.

One developmental thread that is important is concerned with the child's understanding of boundaries that govern the internal world of television; boundaries between types of shows and whether characters were allowed to cross these boundaries. One such boundary is that between commercials and programmes. Jaglom and Gardner (1981) touched on the same issue that concerned many of the researchers in the area of the effects of television advertising on children, but had approached it from a different direction. Their methodology was eclectic, involving parental interviews, the analysis of symbolic play episodes, naturalistic reactions to television viewing, sorting tasks, and specially created guessing games. When results were compared across the three children, one unanticipated finding was that 'advertisements' was the earliest category in the child's developing understanding of the world of television to emerge as distinct from 'the rest' of television. The mean age of emergence was 3 to 3½ years, and in one child a differentiation of commercial versus the rest could be detected as early as 2 years of age.

What general conclusions can be drawn from this body of work on the ability of the child to discriminate television commercials from programmes? It is known, from general psychological research on children watching television, that the class of events which adults call 'television' is differentiated from the rest of the child's world at an early age, often in the first few years of life (Dorr, 1986). There are reasons why this should be so. Television is perceptually very different from the world of real people or things. The medium is full of light and (for most homes now) colour. It comes out of a box and consists of music, sounds, talk, small things, and small people. There is also evidence that the very young child does not separate television from the real world in the same way as adults do. There is anecdotal evidence (Dorr, 1986) that very young children treat people on television like real people. A rudimentary distinction is drawn early but the lines of demarcation between television and real life are based on immediately available, perceptual features of the environment. As the child grows older, the criteria for differentiating between categories will be based on deeper, inferred aspects of the world.

The same applies to the differentiation of television commercials from the rest of the world of television. A rudimentary distinction between commercials and other programmes is made very early, as soon as the child emerges from what has traditionally been regarded as infancy. Why? The reason is that television commercials are perceptually very different from programmes. They are short and programmes are long. There is a variety of other ways of categorizing and classifying commercials as different from programmes. For example, one set of criteria rests on more complex features of form, such as pacing and editing, which are based on the functions and constraints imposed on the commercial by the demands of attention-grabbing within a very short time. There are differences between the content of commercials and programmes, an obvious one being that the commercial remains unchanged over several showings. Differences in intent and style exist too. For the very young child, these will be invisible and only emerge with growth and development. Since distinctions based on more mature features evolve as the child grows up, the line between commercial and 'the rest' will be integrated into a more complex set of differences that separate out funny from serious programmes, persuasive from educational productions and possibly, genre from genre.

There is no one point at which we can say the child recognizes the difference between commercial and programme unless some stance is taken on the social importance of this distinction. The distinction between commercials as persuasive or commercial in intent and programmes as not having this source characteristic, is vital for the child to recognize. The next section looks at this issue in detail.

UNDERSTANDING THE INTENT OF THE COMMERCIAL

What are television commercials? What do they try to do? If children of different ages are asked questions like these, then it soon becomes apparent that their replies vary according to their ages. In particular, older children aged about 9 or 10 years might say that they're there to persuade you or to make you buy things. Younger children, 5 or 6-year-olds, might smile and say they're fun and they're there to make you laugh. Some children, aged 6 or 7 years, may look at you seriously and say that they tell you important things about what's being advertised, things you should know about. There will be many children, of course, who don't say any of these things and look bemused at the question. What does emerge, however, is a difference between those children who are old enough to give a mature reply that an adult would give and those who seem to demonstrate some inadequacy of understanding, an inability to grasp fully that ads are there to persuade you to buy things.

Given the policy context within which much of the research on television advertising and children was conducted, it is not surprising that the question of whether children understand the purpose of advertising is a central one. If researchers can come up with a firm answer to when children are capable of detecting the persuasive and/or commercial intent behind advertising the policy-makers will be better able to make up their minds on the question of whether or not to ban or restrict advertising to children and, if so, the age below which children should be protected. The boffins and back-room boys did, in fact, come up with answers. The problem was that there were several different answers and they were all supposed to be correct. There was, in addition, a lack of theoretical precision about what it means to say the child 'understands' the 'purpose' or 'intent' of advertising and this lack of theory in the field led to much muddled thinking. To examine exactly where these confusions lay and to establish just how the agenda for investigation was created, it is appropriate to look at details of early studies.

The early studies

In 1971 Blatt, Spencer, and Ward published the results of an exploratory investigation into the child's understanding of television advertising. Using a small sample of 20 children ranging from 5 to 12 years and a loosely structured group interview situation they attempted to categorize replies to various questions about the nature and function of television advertisements. The questions the children were asked, included: 'Do you know what a television commercial is?', 'What are they for?', 'What are television programmes for?', 'Who makes television commercials?', 'Do television commercials always tell the truth?', 'Why or why not?', 'How do you know?', and 'What is something you want that you saw in a commercial?' In addition, children were asked to 'make up and act out' a television advertisement of their own.

Responses were collected and analysed within the framework of stage developmental theories of psychological development. These theories often assume that the child progresses through various stages, with qualitative differences between one stage and the next and that the skills and perspectives that are characteristic of one stage are integrated into a different way of thinking in the next. Many developmental psychologists would accept these assumptions that children progress through distinct stages of perceiving and thinking about the world. Consequently, if television advertising is a constant and important part of their reality (and there is no reason to suppose it is not) children should exhibit different levels of perception and understanding of television advertising as they grow older.

The selection of stage developmental theorists in Blatt *et al.* (1972) was eclectic and included Piaget, Kohlberg, and Erikson, all well known in developmental psychology circles. Nine categories of response were established. One of these was the perceived purpose of commercials which was taken to be answers to questions like 'What are commercials for?' Because of the small sample and the generally speculative nature of the conclusions, it is not worthwhile to elaborate on the other eight categories.

Ward, Reale, and Levinson (1972) extended the work of Blatt and others using a sample of sixty-seven children in a similar age range. The methodology was altered slightly. First, standardized questions were asked of each child individually, and the answers were coded and tabulated. Second, the original nine response categories which had emerged in the Blatt study from the group interviews were reduced to seven. Third, the categories were operationally defined as types of answers to a certain question. For example, children were asked 'What is a television commercial?'

Their responses were assigned to three levels of awareness. A 'low awareness' response might be 'a commercial is when they show toys' and typically included children naming specific categories of commercials or products in attempting to explain what a commercial is. 'Medium level' responses exhibited some minimal understanding of the notion of advertising. An example would be 'tells people about things to buy'. A 'high awareness' response was one where the child exhibited a clear understanding of the commercial's intent, for example, 'to get people to buy the product'. The category of 'perceived purpose of commercials' was operationally defined as answers to the question 'Why are commercials shown on television?' A similar three-tier set of responses was defined where level iii was a full demonstration of the selling and profit-seeking motives such as 'get people to buy and they pay for the show'.

When the children were asked 'What is the difference between a television programme and a television commercial?', a very clear difference between younger and older children emerged. Table 3.1 illustrates this. Level i responses refer to concrete differences such as 'commercials are shorter than programmes'. Level ii responses refer to an important functional distinction, an example being 'commercials sell, make money' or 'the programme has a story'.

TABLE 3.1. *Number of children responding to the question 'What is the difference between a television programme and a television commercial?'*

Response category*	Age (in years)	
	5–8	9–12
I	22	6
II	7	24

* See text for explanation of response categories.

Source: Ward, Reale, and Levinson (1972).

Various other questions were asked and responses were coded and tabulated. One interesting result was that about half the children interviewed felt that commercials do not always tell the truth. Such a 'fact', however, should be treated with caution as children of different ages can have different criteria as to what truth is. For younger children, the observation that commercials contain unreal episodes or scenes, such as a man flying through the air, may be adequate to establish that they are not true because men do not really fly through the air. Twenty-four of the thirty-three 9- to 12-year-olds, however, said they felt commercials were not true because the motives were suspect ('They just want to make money'), demonstrating that recognition of the purpose of an advertisement influences the assessment of its truth or falsity.

It is appropriate to pause and ask what changes in direction from Blatt, Spencer, and Ward (1971) to Ward, Reale, and Levinson (1972) can be detected. Blatt's original study was intended to relate the emergence of an understanding of television advertisements to stage-developmental psychological theory. Ward's study is a shift away from studies in cognitive development towards a psychometric or mental measurement approach to individual age-related differences in performance on certain questions. The three-tier response categories of 'low', 'medium', and 'high' levels bear a resemblance to the 'inadequate', 'partially adequate', and 'adequate' response categories in mental tests.

This shift in direction towards a psychometric approach is paralleled by the change in methodology from small-sample, open-ended interviews characteristic of diagnostic and investigative studies to larger-scale, closed, objective measures employing research assistants and which emphasize group data and statistics of significant difference. The shift is from assessing the competence of children to measuring their performance.

One of the advantages of a stage-developmental approach is that a particular period of the child's life can be defined as a self-contained mode of adaptation to a range of possibilities. When the child changes to a higher level of adaptation, this is also self-contained and incorporates the previous level of adaptation. For example, in Piaget's theories, preschool children will employ their own forms of inference on a variety of tasks and as long as appearance and reality coincide, problems need not arise. When appearance conflicts with reality, the preschool child will judge on appearance and make an error from the adult point of view. In Piaget's famous example of rolling a ball of clay into a long sausage and asking if there is more clay now or just the same as before, the preschool child will err by claiming there is more clay in the sausage. The older child will realise that there are certain inferred properties of things (such as amount) that do not change when shape does, but do alter when bits are added to the clay or taken away. The older child will retain the skills that the younger, preschool child possesses but can incorporate them into a more wide-ranging system of mental organization.

In contrast, a psychometric approach implies a criterion of 'adequate performance' or even 'John is better than Jim'. We measure performance to some purpose and often this purpose is to see who has made the grade and who hasn't. Ward *et al.* state that 'our essential concern was whether children could understand that commercials intend to sell goods and services' (1972, pp. 472–3). Consequently their questions were designed to find out how many could understand and how many couldn't. Given the policy context within which the research was carried out this was a reasonable question to ask. So, for example, to be able to state that only a quarter of 11- to 12-year-olds were able to provide an explanation that demonstrated an understanding of selling and profit motives in television commercials (ibid., Table 3) is a useful fact to support a case that children, even at that age, do not completely comprehend advertising.

Ward and Wackman (1973) present data very similar to those of Ward, Reale, and Levinson (1972). The questions are the same and the sample would appear to be the same. The results are similar although most of the tables do not use age as the independent variable but a variable labelled 'cognitive level'. What is 'cognitive level'? Ward and Wackman's argument is as follows. Two questions, 'What is a commercial?' (Q1) and 'What is the difference between a television commercial and a television programme?' (Q2) are asked of the child. It should be noted that in this and other studies and reports by Ward and his associates, questions on the nature of television commercials are presented without showing an example of a television commercial.

Answers are categorized as showing different levels of awareness and differentiation. A low level of awareness to Q1 would be noted if the child's reply demonstrated a reliance on perceptual cues as in 'they show things'. A medium level of awareness would be recorded if the child had the beginnings of a concept of advertising, such as 'it tells people about things to buy'. A high level of awareness would be indicated if the child could identify commercials in terms of persuasion and, in some cases, sponsorship. A low level of differentiation is a reply to Q2 which mentions perceptual differences as in 'A commercial is short and programmes are long.' A high level of differentiation is a reply to Q2 which demonstrates some understanding of the meaning of commercials and programmes as in 'Shows are supposed to entertain, commercials show products.'

Children are then categorized as possessing high, medium or low cognitive levels on the basis of their categorized responses to Q1 and Q2. 'Cognitive level' would appear to be related to the ability of the child to make inferences about the nature of television commercials and to draw distinctions between these and programmes that go beyond the immediate perceptual qualities of the stimulus. The level would also appear to be related to whether the child understands that the interviewer wants to be told about the 'real' as opposed to the 'superficial' and can make the adult distinctions between real and important versus superficial and unimportant. The answer 'Commercials are short and programmes are long' to the question 'What is the difference between a television programme and a television commercial?' is correct because it is in accord with the facts of the matter. If it is the only answer the child can provide to that question (even when this question is asked again) then that is evidence that the child is at a lower cognitive level than the child who would reply 'and commercials show products but programmes are just entertainment'.

These three studies have been described in some detail because early research often sets the stage for later work and many early assumptions are automatically adopted in later studies. One such assumption is that there is a stage-developmental psychology of children's understanding of television advertising and that this is best explained by appealing to Piagetian principles of cognitive development. Although the original study by Blatt et al. (1971) does admit to being exploratory in this direction, the two papers by Ward and Wackman (1973) and Ward, Reale, and Levinson (1972) are more psychometric in nature than cognitive–developmental. Ward and Wackman's tables are, in effect, cross-tabulations of categorized responses to standard questions given to a sample of children of different ages. In this study there is no independent measure of cognitive development such as level of achievement on traditional Piagetian tasks. There is evidence of a developmental dimension in answering questions such as 'What is a commercial?' but an adequate answer must involve a variety of skills and abilities. For example, the ability to infer, beyond perceptual characteristics, an understanding of what interviewers want to know in asking such questions, a confidence in verbal expertise and so on.

The literature on the child's understanding of the intent of commercials was enhanced by the publication of an oft-cited paper by Robertson and Rossiter in 1974. This article, with critical comments and a reply (Ryans and Deutscher, 1975; Robertson and Rossiter, 1976) constitute a significant contribution to the literature. Robertson and Rossiter's aim was to explore children's inferences about the intention of a communicator where the communication is a television commercial. They argue that children should possess other skills in order to understand the purpose of a television commercial. The child should be able to distinguish commercials as separate from regular programmes, recognize a sponsor as the source of the commercial message and perceive the idea of an intended audience for the message. Children must possess the basic capabilities of conceiving of commercials as different from programmes and as having particular source and audience characteristics before they will be able to attribute motives of intent to this message. In addition, a full comprehension of the purposive intent of commercials requires an understanding of the 'symbolic nature of product, character and contextual representation in commercials' (Robertson and Rossiter, 1974, p. 13) and an ability to discriminate, by example, between products as advertised and products as experienced. This analysis of what is required to understand a commercial message is useful and places the comprehension of intent in a sound theoretical framework.

Robertson and Rossiter used a large sample of 289 Catholic boys (no girls were sampled) ranging in social class and age throughout the primary school. They were interviewed and asked six questions designed to assess a variety of cognitive and affective variables, including the abilities described above. The questions were: 'What is a television commercial?'; 'Why are commercials shown on television?'; 'What do commercials try to get you to do?'; 'Do you believe what television commercials tell you?'; 'Do you like television commercials?'; and 'Do you want every toy and game that you see advertised on television?' These abilities were regarded as part of the composite skill of attributing persuasive and commercial intent to a television advertisement. The results of the interviews were coded on these variables and subjected to a multivariate analysis.

The following conclusions were established. There are two types of attribution of intent. One, called assistive, is where the child sees commercials as informative as in 'commercials tell you about things' and the other, called persuasive, is where the child sees commercials as 'trying to make you buy things'. Although both types of attribution of intent can co-exist in a child, there is a trend towards persuasive intent attribution becoming more frequent as the child gets older. By 10 to 11 years of age, practically all children are able to attribute persuasive intent. Also, children of parents with higher educational levels will tend to attribute persuasive intent at an earlier age than children of parents with lower educational levels. Older children will tend to see ads functioning more as persuaders than providing helpful information.

A more striking conclusion to emerge from the results is as follows. Children who were categorized as attributing persuasive intent to television commercials also tended to possess all the antecedent skills that Robertson and Rossiter hypothesized as necessary for the comprehension of persuasive intent. In other words, they could distinguish programme from commercial, they understood about an external source or sponsor, they saw that an audience was intended for the commercial, they were aware of the symbolic nature of commercials and they cited instances of negative discrepancies where the product did not come up to expectations as extolled by the advertisement. Those children who attribute assistive intent to commercials as in 'commercials tell you about things' tended to be capable of perceiving the idea of an intended audience and of seeing a source for the message. There was no significant correlation between the attribution of assistive intent and the other variables, however. Children who attributed assistive intent also tended to trust commercials more compared with children who attributed persuasive intent.

Robertson and Rossiter argue that the attribution of persuasive intent is a vital component when processing advertising messages. Being able to conceive of this purpose behind commercials leads to 'cognitive defences' against advertising where the child can mentally generate counter-claims, is aware that a special plea is being made and can generally adopt a sceptical attitude towards the advertisers' claims. What underlies attribution of persuasive intent? The authors' statistical analysis led them to place symbolic perception as the main determinant of persuasive intent recognition. The 'symbolic' nature of commercials means that advertisements use devices such as idealized settings or dramatized character emotions and that these devices symbolize or represent 'real' situations or 'real' emotions. It can be argued that, although all cultural communication is symbolic, there is a case to be made out for some communications being more symbolic than others. Classical opera is more symbolic in this sense than a story told in a pub, assuming that the latter does not become over-ritualized with wild exaggeration.

Interesting conclusions can be drawn from Robertson and Rossiter's (1974) study. Evidence has been provided to support the idea that understanding a commercial message is at least a two-stage process. First, the child has to be capable of attributing intent to the message. The results from the study show that there are two skills that are common to attributing both assistive and persuasive intent. These are the ability to understand that there is a source to the message, and the ability to understand there is an audience for the message. The message is not 'just there'. It comes from somewhere for some purpose and is designed for certain eyes and ears. Second, extra skills are required to attribute persuasive intent and, as the child grows older, these skills develop and become more important. The skills were identified as awareness of symbolic representation and of possible discrepancies between the message and the product.

The child's understanding of commercials could be affected by long-term exposure. Unfortunately, the variable of cumulative exposure is confounded with age. In other words, the older the child is the more likely he or she is to have been exposed to a greater number of television commercials than a younger child. Hence it is difficult to establish whether the different performance of an older child is due to the fact that he or she has been exposed to more commercials than a younger child, or whether the performance is a result of psychological maturity, or whether it is a result of an interaction between the two.

For example, it is well known that the understanding of the persuasive intent of television advertising develops as the child gets older. In order to establish the relative importance of exposure to advertising as a variable versus age as a variable it is necessary to find groups of children where one variable is held constant and the other varied. Two such groups are heavy and light television viewers. Heavy viewers of the same age as light viewers will have a greater cumulative exposure to television advertising. In fact, Rossiter and Robertson (1974), using several measures of the child's understanding of the general concept of commercials, did not find a significant correlation with television viewing. This is evidence in support of the view that an understanding of television commercials is primarily dependent on cognitive development rather than simple exposure learning.

In 1975 an extensive report supported by the Marketing Science Institute at Harvad was published, describing in detail the results of the programme of research carried out by Ward and his associates (Ward, Wackman, and Wartella, 1975). The report, republished in book form in 1977, aimed to provide a description of how children learn to buy. This goal can be expanded as an elaboration of the processes that operate as the child develops skills that consumers use. Consequently, the extent to which the child is aware of the purpose of television advertisements is but one variable among a large set sampled by Ward et al. One such variable was an independent measure of the level of the child's cognitive development. This was measured as follows. The child was asked to describe the differences between a school and a house, a car and a truck, and a television programme compared with a television commercial. The replies were then used to place the child in one of four categories. The first was 'coincidental reasoning', where the child demonstrated a lack of ability to focus on dimensions differentiating objects. The second was 'perceptual', where the child focused on physical aspects of the objects, such as the size of the house being smaller than the school. The third was 'transitional', with the child differentiating on the basis of the activities objects perform. Finally, the child could be regarded as 'conceptual', focusing on functional differences such as school being where you are educated and home being where you live.

The assessment of the child's understanding of the nature and intent of commercials was measured by the answers to three questions. These were: 'When you watch television you must see a lot of commercials—what is a television commercial?'; 'Why are commercials shown on television?'; and 'What do commercials try to do?' Responses to each of these questions were placed in one of three categories representing high, medium or low awareness. 'High awareness' involved, for example, being able to recognize the selling motive of the advertiser. An example would be 'to get you to buy stuff so they can make money' whereas 'medium awareness' may include a passing reference to buying in 'They show kids where to buy toys.' 'Low awareness' implies that the child does not demonstrate that he or she is capable of making this kind of inference and refers only to the perceptual or emotional characteristics of the stimuli as in 'They're short—they're funny.' The sample size varied, in the results quoted, between 573 and 601.

Tables 3.2, 3.3, and 3.4 are adapted from Ward, Wackman, and Wartella (1975, tables 3.3, 3.4, 3.5) and, taken together, can be regarded as the primary source for US data on this issue of comprehension of advertising intent. It is obvious from this that there is a significant age-related change in awareness. It is difficult, however, to establish an age or even an age band below which it can be stated that most children do not understand and above which we can say that most children do understand. Even by 11 years the majority of children are not yet capable of providing an answer that demonstrated 'high awareness' to any one of the three questions. And yet, almost half of 5- to 6-year-olds are able to show 'medium awareness' of commercial intent in response to 'What do commercials try to do?'

One of the problems with the data obtained from these interviews, and interviews in general, is the difficulty of knowing whether a response or reply that demonstrates,

TABLE 3.2.   *Children's awareness of why commercials are shown on television (%)*

Awareness level	Age (in years)		
	5–6	8–9	11–12
Low	56	12	3
Medium	40	73	59
High	4	15	38

Source: Ward, Wackman, and Wartella (1975).

TABLE 3.3.   *Children's awareness of what a commercial is (%)*

Awareness level	Age (in years)		
	5–6	8–9	11–12
Low	68	18	2
Medium	26	57	57
High	6	25	41

Source: Ward, Wackman, and Wartella (1975).

TABLE 3.4.   *Children's awareness of what commercials try to do (%)*

Awareness level	Age (in years)		
	5–6	8–9	11–12
Low	50	7	1
Medium	46	67	58
High	4	26	41

Source: Ward, Wackman, and Wartella (1975).

say, 'medium awareness' is the *only* response available. Despite the skill of the interviewer in probing to obtain more information, some children are unable or unwilling to express themselves beyond their initial response. Replies to a standard series of questions are tapping the most salient response for that person, in that it is the most probable response from a range of possible responses. The reason for its being the most probable may be that the respondent thinks it is an important response or is an apt and appropriate reply to that question. The range of possible responses or available responses may include what the interviewer would regard as a more sophisticated response were it to be elicited. But if the response is not forthcoming with the standard question or the standard question plus additional permitted probe question, then there may not be any further opportunity for its emergence.

Salient responses are important in psychological investigations that are concerned with performance data, which provide information on what the person does or says as in intelligence tests or attitude surveys. Available responses are concerned with competence information on what the person can or cannot do. The development of the child's understanding of television advertising should be concerned with competence data, as is Piaget's theory of intellectual development upon which Ward and his colleagues rely for theoretical support. The methodology used in these studies, however, is based on performance data.

A major landmark in the literature on children and television advertising was the publication of a report, financed by the National Science Foundation, that dealt with research on the effects of television advertising on children (Adler *et al.*, 1977). Although this was not the first review of the literature on the subject (see Sheikh *et al.*, 1974) nor the only one since that time (for example, Barry, 1977), it was by far the most important and the most frequently cited in important public discussions on the issue such as the Federal Trade Commission hearings.

The report was revised and published as a book (Adler *et al.*, 1980) and the issue of the child's comprehension of advertising intent is discussed in a chapter by Rossiter. He

TABLE 3.5.   *Children showing persuasive intent recognition with two types of question (%)*

Types of question	Age (in years)				
	3	4	5	6	7
Open-ended	5	12	21	42	48
Response choice	90	83	80	73	73

Source: Atkin (1979).

offers a mild criticism of the methods used to measure persuasive intent recognition and claims that closed and non-verbal methods will detect recognition of persuasive intent at a much younger age. He also suggests an alternative methodology where children are asked about the purpose of specific commercials rather than about the purpose of commercials in general in order to establish a concrete context rather than an abstract one.

One study by Atkin (1979) that used closed rather than open-ended questions is reported. He sampled 480 children aged from 3 to 7 years who were shown pictures from cereal commercials. The interviewer then said to the child: 'They show these cereals on television when kids are watching. Why do you think they show these cereals on television?' Responses of the type 'So people will buy' were coded as persuasive intent recognition. The interviewer then asked the child more directly: 'Do they show these cereals so kids will ask for the cereal?' The child could refer to a cue card with the alternatives 'Yes', 'No', and '?'.

The results of both these methods are shown in Table 3.5. The open-ended results are not unexpected. Although the categorization of responses is not the same as the comprehensive system reported in Ward, Wackman, and Wartella (1975), the results would predict a 50 per cent recognition of commercial intent for group aged 7 to 8 years. The results based on a selection of one out of three response alternatives are peculiar to say the least. Not only does a ludicrously large percentage of children aged 3 years apparently demonstrate recognition of persuasive intent but this percentage decreases with age. Obviously something is wrong. First, anyone who has tested or otherwise assessed preschool children would know that if children are asked questions such as 'Do they show these cereals so kids will ask for the cereal?' and the child has to answer 'Yes', 'No' or '?', the child will often produce a 'Yes' response no matter what the question is, as this is suitably acquiescent strategy for the young child to adopt when faced with a relative stranger asking an unexpected question. A methodological improvement would have been to include a question such as 'Do they show these cereals so kids can laugh at them?' where a non-acquiescent response is more appropriate. The second thing wrong, and this is a more general criticism aimed at much of the research reported on the child's comprehension of persuasive intent, is that the question of what it is, theoretically, to understand the intent of a communicator and in particular the persuasive intent of a source, is largely avoided. Although Piaget and theories of information processing in children are brought in to provide theoretical support to the child assessment programmes of Ward and his associates, no psychological theory is laid out that specifically underwrites the development of an understanding of persuasive intent. Indeed, in many of the studies that have already been described, the commercial intent and the persuasive intent of advertising are confounded.

Research after Adler

In 1981, a collection of research papers on children and television advertising was published by Child Research Service in New York (Esserman, 1981*c*). Much of the tone of this book was critical of the research of the 1970s which used an interview methodology that can underestimate the abilities of the child. Children have to express their knowledge through language and have to possess and utilize language-based skills as well as knowing about advertising.

Zuckerman and Gianino's paper in Esserman's collection has already been cited in connection with the development

of children's ability to distinguish programme from commercial. Children were asked *inter alia* to explain what a
commercial was and to describe the difference between
programmes and commercials. This procedure is the same
as the classic verbal methods for assessing the child's comprehension of persuasive intent reported in Ward, Wackman, and Wartella (1975, 1977). Results tended to confirm
Ward's findings but with lower percentages of 'intent to
sell' responses for all age groups than those in Ward's studies. Children were also asked to pick out all the characters
who 'showed you food or drinks' on television (all the
commercial characters were associated with either food or
drink advertisements), and asked to select characters who
'try to make you want to buy something'. Performance
improved with age and correct performance emerged earlier
than with the verbal questions such as 'what is a commercial?' Zuckerman and Gianino (1981) are hesitant to draw
far-reaching conclusions from these results. They prefer to
see them as an alternative method of assessing what children
do or do not perceive and understand about television programmes and commercials. It is important to emphasize,
however, that these non-verbal results tell us little about the
child's understanding of persuasive or commercial intent
and a lot about the child's ability to discriminate between
commercials and programmes. It is the lack of a theoretical
framework of what it means to 'understand a commercial's
intent' that bedevils so much of this research.

The psychometric approach characterizes most of this
research and it is typical of this approach to lay emphasis on
the procedures used in methodology rather than the processes that are occurring within the child. Consequently,
any progress in assessing children's abilities to understand
commercials has been in the direction of criticizing inadequate instruments and replacing them with alternative measures rather than getting to grips with real theoretical issues
concerned with how best to describe what is occurring in
development as the child advances from one stage of understanding to the next.

Gaines and Esserman (1981) challenged the orthodoxy
established in the 1970s that in middle childhood children

TABLE 3.6.   *Responses by children to questioning on the function and purpose of commercials after viewing a programme and a commercial (%)*

Response	Age (in years)	
	4–5	6–8
Showed understanding of commercial purpose	63	85
Answers not related to selling purpose	15	6
Don't know/none	22	9

Source: Gaines and Esserman (1981).

develop an understanding of what a television commercial is. Their paper is an example of an attempt to improve on existing methodology. Details of sampling and other measures taken can be found above in the section on the child's ability to distinguish programme from commercial. Children were asked what a commercial was for and why it was on television. Results are quite startling, as Table 3.6 shows.

A closer examination of the category 'evidenced understanding of purpose of commercial' in Gaines and Esserman's paper reveals that criteria for inclusion are very similar to those employed by Ward and his colleagues (Ward, Wackman, and Wartella, 1975, 1977) so to that extent the methodologies are the same. The difference is the inclusion of an example of a commercial and a previous question on the identification of a commercial. On this evidence almost two-thirds of 4- to 5-year-olds can demonstrate an understanding of commercial intent whereas the Ward figures did not reach this mark even by ages 11 to 12 years. When the videotape stopped children were asked about how they felt about the cereal they had just seen on television. Over half the 4- to 5-year-olds exhibited a sceptical response, such as 'Might not be as good as they say', or

'Can't believe what they say because they want your money.' It is not possible to equate the findings of Gaines and Esserman where they are based on the verbal procedures described above, with other data obtained using verbal procedures in the 1970s. The only conclusion to reach is that, under certain circumstances of presentation, and in one reported study, children can demonstrate an awareness of commercial intent of advertising as early as 4 years of age when they have not, in all probability, reached the concrete operational period of development.

Wartella contributes a chapter to Esserman (1981c) and provides a thoughtful discussion that extends and elaborates some of the work in Ward, Wackman, and Wartella (1977) as well as reporting some new findings. This article had been published elsewhere (Wartella et al., 1981). She makes the important point that Piaget's theory is essentially a theory of deficits. That is, children of a certain cognitive stage are seen as being unable to perform mental operations more characteristic of another, later stage. Consequently, research programmes that use a Piagetian framework (such as Ward's work with his colleagues) tend to account for findings in terms of children's inadequacies or inabilities.

An ability to perform, however, can be a result of various factors. Certainly one set of skills would be the abilities of the child in verbal expression which, in interview formats, is confounded with the underlying cognitive abilities. Another of these factors is the information processing demands of the tasks involved. For example, television watching and choosing products are very different tasks for the child. Viewing does not impose the same information processing demands on the child as purchase decision making. With the possible exception of Christmas time when children are seeking gift ideas, children sitting in front of the television watching an advertisement do not 'intend' to seek information to use in a purchase decision. Deciding what to buy, however, is a decisive act and as such requires information processing concerned with the assessment of alternatives. Children are likely to access information on products when making purchase decisions and one of the sources of such information is what they remember of television advertisements. It is the memory of the television commercial that is influential in product choice rather than the commercial itself acting as a stimulus for a response of buying.

In Wartella's (1981) experiments, 75 children aged 5 to 6 years and 84 aged 8 to 9 years were sampled. Each child was shown two commercials for two sweet products that were specially constructed for the experiment, both commercials being embedded in a half-hour videotaped cartoon show. After presentation, children were asked 'What does this commercial want you to know about [brand name]?' and 'What does this commercial want you to do?' Although the latter question is asked in the context of commercials in general by Ward, Wackman, and Wartella (1977), the former has not been used with children before. The younger group had difficulty in answering the former question; almost half produced no response. When children did answer the question, the most frequent response for both age groups was to mention a particular attribute of the product.

A second main category of response was a general affective response such as, 'This commercial wants you to like [the product].' When children answered the question about what the commercial wanted them to do, about 80 per cent of the 8 to 9-year-olds responded 'Buy the product.' The number of 5- to 6-year-olds giving this response varied between 50 per cent and 65 per cent depending on the type of commercial. Unfortunately, these figures are not directly comparable to Ward, Wackman, and Wartella's (1975) figures because they would classify a simple response of 'buying the product' as demonstrating 'medium understanding'. 'Full understanding' requires the child to recognize a selling motive which includes taking the role of others. Examples would include 'to get you to buy stuff so they can make money'. 'Medium understanding' also contains responses categorized as 'some recognition of information or general teaching function' as in 'to show the people what's good and bad'. It is not possible to recategorize Ward et al.'s data to obtain comparability with Wartella's (1981) data from the published record alone.

Roberts (1982) briefly reviewed the research on children

and commercials, citing the findings of Gaines and Esserman (1981). He also questioned whether simple recognition that a commercial is intended to 'sell a product' was an adequate indicator of understanding the fundamental nature of commercials. His analysis of what the conditions are for ideal adult comprehension is extremely useful and is a welcome attempt to place children's comprehension of television advertising on a firmer theoretical footing than the basis provided by Piagetian theory. An adult would need to recognize at least the following attributes of a commercial: (1) that the source has other perspectives and hence other interests, than those of the receiver; (2) that the source intends to persuade; (3) that persuasive messages are, by definition, biased; and (4) that biased messages demand interpretation strategies that are different from informational, educational or entertainment messages. Roberts (1982) then states that such an adult processing of commercials depends on the development of relatively sophisticated role-taking abilities and what are known as 'meta-cognitive skills'. Such skills would require children to be able to detach themselves mentally from ongoing information processing and effectively monitor messages in order to adopt different strategies where appropriate.

Roberts also discusses an area of recently developed research where children are taught by means of instructional films about the persuasive and selling intent of commercials. For example, Roberts et al. (1980) evaluated two instructional films that were produced in order to show children how television advertising uses various techniques in order to persuade. They concluded that younger children who were initially most susceptible to commercial appeals were most influenced by the instructional films, and that heavy television viewers were also most influenced. It could be said that heavy viewers bring more examples to bear when exposed to the material contained in the instructional film or that they tend to be the less 'critical' thinkers, at least until a critical strategy is spelt out for them.

In any case, it is possible to 'arm' children against commercials and to use various consumer education strategies to reduce their vulnerability to commercial appeals. Two of the most vulnerable groups (heavy viewers and young children) appear to be the ones on whom this type of consumer education works best. Child-oriented 30-second spot commercials designed to teach 'prosocial lessons' such as safe bicycling, the dangers of junk food, cigarette smoking, and so on, as well as public service spots that have tried to teach children about commercials in general have been developed and broadcast in the United States. Christenson (1980) devised a three-minute 'consumer information processing' spot. He inserted this announcement into a longer sequence containing programming and commercials and found that, compared with children not exposed to the announcement, 6- to 12-year-olds who viewed the message were more aware of the commercials and expressed less trust in commercials in general. He developed the theme that children are capable of being taught about commercial intent in a later paper (Christenson, 1982).

Perhaps the inability of the child to take the point of view of another person means that it is impossible to teach the child before a certain age that commercials are designed and produced by people with a point of view that is different from that of the viewer. This ability develops over a long period of middle childhood. Although it is detectable in familiar contexts as early as 6 years, a full understanding may not be available until 11 or 12 years. If television commercials provide the child with a familiar context because the child has watched a lot of television, then it should be easier to devise brief public service announcements (PSAs) that teach the child about the motives of television commercial makers than if the child is unfamiliar with the genre. One would predict that heavy child viewers would be more influenced by these PSAs than children who watched small amounts of television.

Christenson showed children videotaped programmes without commercials, or with commercials only, or with commercials plus PSA, and asked them questions afterwards. Results showed that the presence of the PSA in a videotape led children to express more sceptical opinions about television commercials afterwards and increased the awareness of intent. It should be noted that, although these results present an optimistic picture of the effectiveness of short PSAs in teaching children about advertising, they do not tell us anything about how the child defends himself or herself against advertising in the long term or the strategies a child develops to counteract the advertising message.

Donohue, Henke, and Donohue (1980) were concerned with designing a non-verbal measure that reveals the child's understanding of the intent of television commercials. They devised the following procedure. An old commercial, broadcast in 1972, that used a fantasy spokesman called Toucan Sam to sell a cereal called Froot Loops by discovering the product in a haunted house was shown to 97 children ranging from 2 to 6 years. Each child was then shown two pictures. One was a colour picture of a mother with a child sitting in the seat of a trolley in a supermarket aisle. The mother had a box of Froot Loops in her hand and the picture was made to look as if she had just picked the box off the shelf and was about to put it in the trolley. The other picture showed a child watching a television screen. The child was then asked to point to the picture that best indicated 'what Toucan Sam wants you to do'. All children tended to choose the picture of the supermarket situation rather than the television watching situation. Seventy-five per cent of the 2- to 3-year-olds chose the former picture and 25 per cent selected the latter. It was assumed that the supermarket picture was 'correct' and the television watching picture 'wrong'. The authors concluded that 'the first major implication of this study is that children understand the intent of television commercials at a younger age than has been reported in the literature' (p. 56). Unfortunately, as there is no way of knowing what processes led three-quarters of 2- to 3-year-olds to point to the supermarket picture, this claim should be treated with a certain amount of scepticism.

The fact that children as young as 2 years of age can make an association between a film of a product in one context (a television commercial) with a picture of the same product in another context (the supermarket) is interesting, but the inference required is quite simple as there is the same product in both situations. It is interesting to a developmental psychologist because the child is capable of extracting information from one context (the product from the television commercial) and extracting the same information from a different context (the product from the supermarket picture). It is interesting for that reason only, but not surprising because it would be expected that children who had advanced beyond infancy would be capable of disembedding the same object from different contexts. In a sense the question asked of the child becomes irrelevant because, given two alternatives, one with a product in context and one with no product, the child will probably choose the alternative depicting Froot Loops having just seen the commercial with the product displayed there. There is the danger that this published study enters the body of literature on the subject and could be abstracted and disseminated as evidence that children aged 3 can understand the intentions behind television commercials. There is obviously nothing here that is remotely related to the child's understanding of persuasive or commercial intent in any reasonable sense of the term 'intent'.

Stutts, Vance, and Hudleson (1981) asked children two questions found in Ward, Wackman, and Wartella (1977) on what a commercial is and why commercials are shown on television. They found that the majority of 7-year-olds could explain selling intent adequately, but only a small percentage of younger children was able to. The data from this experiment were further analysed by Stephens and Stutt (1982) using a multivariate predictor model. Age emerged as one of the significant predictors of comprehension of advertising intent.

Faber, Perloff, and Hawkins (1982) were also concerned with the skills that underlie the child's comprehension of the intent of advertising. They argued that this is related to social rather than physical cognition. That is, the understanding of the intent is related to the general ability of children to understand and process information about people rather than things.

Two of the main characteristics of the physical cognition of young children are perceptual boundedness and centration. Perceptual boundedness refers to the tendency to attend to and respond largely on the basis of the immediate perceptual aspects of the environment rather than on relationships or changes from past or to future states. Centration is the tendency to focus on only a limited amount of the available information instead of using it all. Whereas these two inadequacies of the physical cognition of young children may help to explain children's attention to and recall of advertisements, they do not, according to Faber *et al.*, explain adequately the young child's lack of understanding of advertising's intent which is concerned with social cognition.

One important skill that appears to be related to many social cognitive skills is role-taking ability, which enables one to take the position of another person and see situations from his or her perspective. Roberts (1982) had already argued that this skill is important for understanding advertising. The ability to take the role of another is important in many areas of children's psychological development such as solving social problems, communicating with and persuading other people, understanding the feelings of another person and reasoning about moral issues.

Faber *et al.* (1982) sampled 35 children aged 6 to 7 years and 32 aged 8 to 9 years and assessed their role-taking skills. He used open-ended, in-depth questions designed to measure their understanding of the feelings and actions of different characters in a short story that was read to them. In addition they were asked the standard questions on comprehension of commercial intent and cognitive developmental level from Ward, Wackman, and Wartella (1977). They found a significant correlation between comprehension of commercial intent and role-taking ability and cognitive developmental level. Although Faber *et al.* (1982) claim that the larger correlation between comprehension of commercial intent and role-taking ability implies that role-taking ability is a more important determinant of the understanding of commercial intent, it is perhaps safer to conclude that it is an important variable in predicting level of understanding of commercial intent but that level of cognitive development is also important.

Macklin (1982, 1983) interviewed 18 children aged 4 years

and 17 children aged 5 years using various measures designed to assess their understanding of television commercials. Each child was first asked the standard Ward, Wackman, and Wartella (1975) question 'What is a television commercial?' They were then shown three television commercials and were asked after each one to tell the interviewer what had happened in the commercial. All 4-year-olds showed a low level of understanding with only a quarter of the 5-year-olds demonstrating a medium awareness. Recall of the commercials tended to be fragmented and not integrated, and occasionally lapsed into fantasy. However, when a set of non-verbal measures were used with these children their performance improved. The child had to point to different alternatives concerning incidents and information in the commercials and such recognition measures produced a level of correct performance varying between one-third and over two-thirds depending on the commercial and the age of the child.

Macklin (1985) replicated and extended the Donohue et al. (1980) work by adding to the range of pictures the child had to choose from. Sixty children ranging from 3 to 5 years of age were studied. In one condition there were three alternatives, the two used by Donohue et al. (1980), and a picture of the product being shared between a girl and her friend. In the original study by Donohue et al. (1980), there were only two alternatives, one depicting the product and the other depicting television viewing. Macklin's results were very different from Donohue's. Eighty per cent of all the children who were given the extended range of pictures failed to select even one correct picture that would indicate an understanding of intent.

In a similar paper, Macklin (1987) conducted two more experiments. In the first, 120 children aged 3, 4, and 5 years were shown a television commercial and then presented with ten drawings and asked: 'Why are commercials on television? What do they want you to do after you watch them?' The correct picture is a drawing of a family buying goods at a supermarket checkout. There are several distracter items that range in distance from target. Some have absolutely no connection with buying and selling or consuming products. Others involve activities with the product but only one is concerned with buying the product at a supermarket. An insignificant number of 3- and 4-year-olds chose the correct drawing but 20 per cent of the 5-year-olds picked the right one. This is regarded as significantly above chance assuming all the alternatives had an equal probability of selection.

The second study sampled forty-five children and results are reported on a group size of fifteen (three groups aged 3 years, 4 years, and 5 years). Forty per cent of the 5-year-olds are capable of acting out the behaviour that would be an appropriate response to the question '... show me what the elves on television would like you to do after watching them', when suitable props are available in the room. The 'elves on television' refers to cartoon characters as product endorsers in a television commercial that was shown to them. Six out of the fifteen 5-year-olds acted out a scene that was identifiable as shopping for the advertised product.

Understanding the genre

Can any general conclusions be drawn from the ability of the child to comprehend the purpose of advertising from the research described above? Certainly something seems to be happening in middle childhood, since most of the work that has used verbal procedures has established that an awareness of advertising's intent emerges at this time. The norms of when this awareness predominates in a sample of children are difficult to establish with any degree of accuracy, however. To argue that, at some age between 5 and 12 years, children understand the purpose of advertising is probably a true statement but not a very helpful one for advertisers and policy-makers.

Are methods that try to bypass the use of language in an interview situation any better at determining when children understand ads? The research in the studies cited above can be taken as evidence that some awareness of the relationship between 'the television commercial' and the social acts of shopping and buying products is potentially available at an early age, about 5 years. The research, however, that has attempted to establish norms as to when 'most' children 'understand advertising' has not been successful in establishing a consensus among researchers.

What is required is some theoretical foundation upon which to base predictions and against which these predictions can be tested. In particular, the child's comprehension of television advertising's purpose or function needs to be firmly located in a context of a psychological theory of advertising, a theory of the development of an understanding of television discourse and *relevant* theories of the child's understanding of particular aspects of television advertising, such as comprehension of the communicative intent of different media, and the comprehension of various rhetorical forms used in advertising.

The literature on understanding different kinds of television discourse is limited. For example, Blosser and Roberts (1985) did not find any literature that directly examined the development of the child's ability to differentiate between the different intentions or functions of messages, one of the few exceptions being some work on the child's understanding of television commercials. If we take a selection of communicative intentions such as 'to inform', 'to instruct', 'to entertain', 'to persuade', then a particular media form or genre such as advertising could be said to incorporate all of these to some degree. Ads tell you about the product, have an implicit goal of purchase, are fun to watch and employ various rhetorical techniques that present partial and biased information. To establish the dominant intent of advertising, it is necessary to consider various similar forms and decide what are the features of the function of advertising that distinguish it from adjacent activities. In the case of television advertising, we must consider the other types of television such as documentaries, situation comedies, serious drama, sport, news, and so on in order to decide what is the major and distinctive function of television advertising. This would appear to be the commercial and persuasive nature of television advertising. Brands, products and services may appear in other contexts, such as consumer programmes that are designed to inform, so just knowing that ads communicate something about brands is not adequate.

In the more general context of all media communication, even knowing that ads sell products is not enough because classified advertisements do that and they are different from television commercials. Persuasion may also appear in other programmes such as committed documentary, panel discussions on politics or even critical reviews of film or drama.

Commercial function and persuasive intent taken together distinguish television advertising from other television forms. Consequently the child who understands that these two functions are inherent in advertising has taken possession of an important skill that is part of becoming advertising literate.

Blosser and Roberts (1985) showed videotapes of different kinds of television messages to 90 children aged from 4 to 11 years. News broadcasts, television commercials, PSAs, and educational programmes were shown and the children were interviewed on what they had seen, why they thought it was put on television, and what these shows do. Most of the children, at all ages, were able to understand the rudiments of what was going on in each of the different kinds of television shown. They were able to comprehend the content of the television message. The children were less able to label the different types with the conventional word or phrase. Most 6-year-olds were able to name news programmes as 'the news', and about half the 5- to 6-year-olds were able to use the label 'commercial' or 'advertisement' successfully. By 10 years of age, this accuracy of television commercial labelling had risen to 100 per cent.

When it came to understanding intent, the results showed that no child younger than 5 years was able correctly to articulate the intent of any message type and it was not until after 8 years that a majority of children correctly identified the intent of anything apart from the news. By 7 years, only a third of 7-year-olds were able to identify the goal of commercials as persuasion. This had risen to a majority of children by 8 years of age, however. If the criterion of advertising intent is taken as either reference to the selling function of commercials or the persuasive function, then the majority of children was able to articulate this intent by 6 to

7 years of age. These last results demonstrate the importance of keeping commercial intent separate from persuasive intent in any analysis of the child's understanding of the purpose of advertising.

4

The Effects of Advertising:
The Experimental Evidence

The major categories of research outlined at the beginning of Chapter 3 will also structure this chapter. Literature on the effect of television advertising on various cognitive, affective, and behavioural processes within the child are reviewed here. These include: the child's interpretation of advertising content; memory for commercials; the various intermediate processes activated in the child by viewing; the influence of television commercials on the child's knowledge, attitudes, and values; the effect of children's television advertising on other people; and the effect on choice or consumption behaviour. Finally, there is a miscellaneous section of unclassified studies.

THE CHILD'S INTERPRETATION OF THE CONTENT OF THE COMMERCIAL

The content of cultural representations of the world, such as television commercials, can be interpreted at different levels. In other words, different 'readings' can be taken at different depths of analyses. What these levels of analysis are and what interpretations can be made based on the knowledge interpreters are assumed to possess constitute much of the theory of advertising (see Chapter 5 for further details). For example, a simple analysis of 'who did what to whom and when' covering the various acts and actors and the structure of events may be regarded as extracting the bare bones of what's in the ad. The meaning, at this level, is shared by many people who watch it. They can recognize human figures, human emotions and people's actions.

Deeper analyses can be made on the basis of culturally specific knowledge that may not be shared by everyone.

The cultural symbols that denote social class in England may not be understood by someone from North America who may 'read' the ad at that level as representing achievement and status. At another, more profound, level, one can draw inferences about the role of advertising in the social world—that advertisements are symptomatic and reflective of women's role in society, that the stereotypes held by advertisers about women are inherently sexist. Not everyone will agree with this interpretation because it depends on ideological assumptions concerned with beliefs about the way society works.

In addition, interpreting the content of an advertisement will be influenced by the particular and peculiar strategies of interpretation that are designed for understanding that genre. If one is aware of the purpose and function of advertising as rhetorical communication for commercial ends, then the sexual or status-ridden imagery used will be seen for what it is. It is there for the purpose of persuasion. Consequently, children's understanding and interpretation of the content of television advertising will depend very much on the development of an understanding of the intent and function of advertising in general and on the nature of the schemata available for interpreting different types of television discourse.

Early work on the influence of advertising content

The major review of television advertising and children in the 1970s (Adler *et al.*, 1980) addresses quite specific policy issues. For example, the code established by the National Association of Broadcasters (NAB) in the United States specifies that, if toys need to be put together or are sold without batteries, television advertising must announce that fact. This is done by using a voice-over such as 'some assembly required' or a video disclaimer to that effect. Liebert *et al.* (1977) found that if children were exposed to a standard disclaimer such as 'some assembly required', they demonstrated no better understanding that the toy had to be put together than those who saw the same commercial with no disclaimer. If the disclaimer was reworded to the child's own level of comprehension ('You have to put it together'), then the children who heard this version showed greater understanding of what was required. This result applied to older as well as younger children. Feshbach, Dillman, and Jordan (1979) tested a graphic display designed to be presented during the last five seconds of a television commercial. This took the form of a robot eating, with a picture of the product and bar graphs displaying its levels of protein, vitamin, and mineral content and calorie content. Findings with eighty-eight children indicated that they were able to comprehend this symbolic presentation of information.

Chapter 5 of Adler *et al.* (1980) consists of a review of the literature on the role of characters and persons in the advertisement and their influence on the child, and the ways in which commercials appeal to the child personally. There is a useful analysis of the different ways the content of the commercial can influence the communication process between advertiser and child. The role of characters in the ads and their impact on audience are called source effects, whereas the influence of a personal appeal to various aspects of the child's self is called the self-concept effect. Certain characters in commercials, such as programme personalities and cartoon characters, may contribute to children's confusion between programmes and advertisements, and this confusion effect can be heightened when the characters and personalities appear in commercials that are shown within or adjacent to their own programmes. This can be called the adjacency effect. Celebrities can be used to endorse a product, either directly, indirectly, or in fantasy where the celebrity or authority does not appear as in real life, but is portrayed by an actor. In British television advertising, this type of endorsement has a restricted use.

The Code of the Independent Broadcasting Authority (IBA) states that: 'Cartoon characters and puppets featured in ITV or BBC children's programmes must not expressly recommend products or services of special interest to children or be shown using the product. This prohibition does not extend to public service advertisements nor to cartoon characters or puppets especially created for advertisements' (Independent Broadcasting Authority, 1985).

Celebrities frequently endorse non-child products with varying degrees of directness. For example, in 1984 John McEnroe verbally endorsed Bic pens, Sebastian Coe visually endorsed C&A clothes, and Daley Thompson visually endorsed Lucozade. More recently, a popular promotional mix has appeared where the brand is a character toy advertised in television commercials and on child-directed product packages, and the hero's adventures can be followed in comic books, television series, and cinema films. For example, in 1987 and 1988 the Masters of the Universe, My Little Pony, and *Care Bears* ranges of toys have all been marketed with this strategy or variations on the theme. These strategies have caused concern in various countries, including the United States where Action for Children's Television has asked the Federal Trade Commission to bar programmes with characters or devices that are marketed as toys on the grounds that the presentations are programme-length commercials (Comstock and Paik, 1987, p. 46). Some European countries limit and restrict commercial television.

With the development of direct broadcasting by satellite and the creation of private organizations designed to exploit this new technology, broadcasting will transcend national frontiers and state regulations. A press report (*Observer*, 1988) entitled 'Sweden's war on toys' claimed that Brio, a toy company, had been importing Masters of the Universe. A three-man research team was studying the toys and the company on behalf of the Swedish Children's Environment Council, 'a State body responsible for determining which toys are suitable for young Swedes'. What has exacerbated the issue is that the Masters of the Universe toys have become popular in Sweden after being advertised on Rupert Murdoch's Sky Channel satellite television station. Although commercial television is banned in Sweden, the authorities have been unable to block satellite programmes.

In Britain, programmes that feature characters which are also available as toys parents or children can buy, can be acquired and broadcast by the ITV companies or Channel 4 provided they are purchased under normal arrangements. That is, they are bought for reasons of intrinsic merit or appeal and not as part of a marketing package or contra-deal against advertising time. Where the IBA draws the line, however, is at so-called interactive toys. They would not permit Independent Television to screen any programme which contained special effects designed to interact with toys on sale in the United Kingdom (IBA, personal communication).

The characters within the commercial, either actors playing roles or presenters, can contribute to the child acquiring social stereotypes. The effects that Adler *et al.* (1980) called confusion, adjacency, fantasy endorsement, and social stereotype are all source effects stemming from characteristics of the source of the communication. Self-concept effects can also be categorized. If the message promises such benefits as strength, growth, physical proficiency and intelligence, they can be regarded as constituting personal enhancement appeals. Another type of appeal is to social status. The IBA Code treats this as follows:

> No advertisement is allowed which leads children to believe that if they do not own the product advertised they will be inferior in some way to other children or that they are liable to be held in contempt or ridicule for not owning it (Independent Broadcasting Authority, 1985).

In other words, forbidden advertisements would appeal to social status by claiming that if you don't own X you'll be worse off than your peers. The guidelines adopted by the National Association of Broadcasters in the United States states that 'appeals shall not be used which directly or by implication contend that if children have a product they are better than their peers or lacking it will not be accepted by their peers' (quoted in Adler *et al.*, 1980). Another type of influence on the child's self-concept is the portrayal of the usage of the product, and both North American and British codes are aimed at limiting exaggeration in this respect. Both are designed to limit the discrepancy between portrayal and practice; between the product as represented in advertising, and the product as used in real life. The IBA Code is concerned with the portrayal of the product.

The true size and scale of the product must be made easy to judge, preferably by showing it in relation to some common object by which its size and scale can be judged. In any demonstration it must be made clear whether the toy is made to move mechanically or through manual operation. Treatments which reflect the toy or game seen in action through the child's eyes or in which real-life counterparts of a toy are seen working must be used with due restraint. There must be no confusion as to the noise produced by the toy—e.g. a toy racing car and its real-life counterpart. Where advertisements show results from a drawing, construction, craft or modelling toy or kit, the results must be reasonably attainable by the average child and ease of assembly must not be exaggerated (Independent Broadcasting Authority, 1985).

The guidelines issued by the National Association of Broadcasters (NAB) and the National Advertising Division (NAD) of the Council for Better Business Bureaus for United States broadcasting refer to the product, but there is further emphasis which would appear to be on the product as portrayed in the context of the advertisement and the product in relation to the child using it.

Both codes prohibit exaggerated portrayals of play value or performance characteristics: usage demonstrations which 'a child' (NAB) or an 'average child' (NAD) is not reasonably capable of reproducing; settings and contexts which a child cannot reasonably reproduce; and portrayals of children possessing unfair or inequitable numbers of products or premiums (Adler *et al.*, 1980, p. 64).

Finally, a self-concept effect would include the use of overt competitive appeals as in comparison advertising or covert competitive appeals as in claims for brand superiority. In other words, if brand x is claimed to be better than brand y and the child does not use brand x, this can influence the child's self-concept. He or she might feel disappointed with presently owned brands or with brand y. Or if brand x is claimed as the 'best' then children who do not own it can also feel disappointed.

In summary, much of the interest expressed in the 1970s in the content of commercials shown to children was based on a regulatory or restrictive approach to deciding what children should or should not see and the techniques of product presentation that may or may not be used. A recurrent theme that emerges in most of the areas of research on children and television is corralling or separating advertising from programming. Advertising is seen as ominous when it spills over into other, non-commercial media genres. It is the pervasiveness of advertising that is seen as dangerous. Product presentation should be fair and the brand must be shown as real without visual tricks. The child's feelings and motives must not be manipulated and the rhetoric that is permissible for use on children must be limited. Here is the recurring image of the advertiser as seducer, lurking round unexpected corners with an attractive and powerful box of delights. Children, in their innocence, need protection from this sort of influence.

Later work

Recent work has been concerned more with the cognitive capabilities of the developing child in the context of understanding and comprehending some aspects of the content of the television message. Van Auken and Lonial (1985) presented children with cards with pictures of characters children see on television. Some of these characters, such as Cinderella and Charlie Brown, would be found in animated cartoons. Others, such as Larry Hagman as J.R. and Linda Carter as Wonder Woman, were human. There were ten characters in all, five found in animated film and five human.

Van Auken and Lonial were interested in how children discriminated between these characters. Would children use the 'human/animate' difference that was available in this set of stimuli to draw distinctions between them? They presented all possible pairs of stimuli to children individually and asked each child whether that particular picture pair was alike or different.

As adults, we can use various different criteria of similarity and difference to answer that question. Charlie Brown is the same as Larry Hagman as they are both males, but different in that one is a cartoon character and the other is a live actor. If we are forced to decide, however, the decision we make will reflect the dominant or most salient criterion we have used to discriminate. Statistical analysis of the results from groups of people over all possible pairs of comparisons will show how the system of perceptual discrimination is organized. This is a well-tried technique in experimental psychology. Van Auken and Lonial used a computerized analysis known as multidimensional scaling on the data and found that all the American children from 6 to 12 years in their samples had two main dimensions available for organizing characters. One was 'male/female' and the other was 'human/animate', and the evidence suggested that the former was the primary dimension.

The methodology used in this study is particularly sensitive to the content of the stimuli used and, as all possible pairs of stimuli are usually presented, the number of stimuli that can be used is limited. Consequently, different results might have been found if other possible lines of discrimination were available in the stimulus pool. For example, if the experiment had been done with characters seen on British children's television, half the characters could have been drawn from ITV and the other half from programmes shown only on BBC. Nevertheless, this result shows that all children are capable of utilizing the 'animate/human' distinction as a working criterion for differentiating types of characters when placed against the more dominant distinction of gender. They claim that their results suggest 'that children may not be as easily exploitable as detractors of children's advertising would have the discipline believe' (p. 22).

This would appear to be an example of confusing the ability to discriminate between categories with being able to understand the purpose or function of these categories. It is not surprising that children can distinguish between 'animate' and 'human' as these are represented in a very direct perceptual way on the stimulus cards and a drawing of a man looks quite different from a photograph of one. This does not tell us very much about how children of different ages conceive the reality of animated versus human characters. There are other examples, such as the already-cited research by Donohue *et al.* (1980), of a similar confusion between discrimination and understanding in the literature on the child's comprehension of the intent of advertising.

As adults we have pretty well-defined stereotypes about the owners of different types of goods and the consumers of certain products. We know what kind of person owns a Filofax and drives a Porsche, drinks Perrier and prefers *nouvelle cuisine*. We can describe people who drink real ale, read the *Guardian*, and shop at Sainsbury's. Indeed, equipped with psychographics, demographics and geographics, market researchers make a trade out of describing the consumption symbolism of people and their accustomed brands. We know that adolescents are notoriously sensitive to the vagaries of fashion and constantly update their views on different kinds of people according to the clothes they wear.

When does an awareness of this consumption symbolism emerge? Belk, Bahn, and Mayer (1982) examined the child's ability to recognize consumption symbolism. Pairs of photographs of houses and cars were shown to children ranging in age from 5 to 14 years. They were asked to choose the one that was most likely to be owned by a particular type of person, such as a doctor or someone with a lot of money or who was the kind of person they'd like to be. The youngest (preschool) group were unable to do this and their choices were at about the chance level. By 7 or 8 years of age there was a definite agreement on certain kinds of people owning certain kinds of things and this was almost fully developed by adolescence. Children could develop an understanding of the consumption symbolism of products bought by adults. How would they manage with brands that they, as children, used?

In a subsequent study, Belk, Mayer, and Driscoll (1984) tried to answer this question by presenting photographs of products familiar to children in the United States, such as different makes of jeans and bicycles. Each child had to check a list of attributes that described the kind of child who owned that product. For example, how wealthy is the child who wears Levis? The child replied on a scale ranging from 'very poor' to 'very rich'.

Belk *et al.*'s 1984 study confirmed that consumption symbolism grew stronger from 9 to 11 years of age; that it was stronger in girls than boys; and stronger in higher social class children than lower social class children. Personal experience with the product would appear to strengthen the stereotype of the product's owners and, not surprisingly, owners of the product tended to hold a more favourable stereotype than non-owners. The stereotype became 'sharper' as the child grew older in that older children held more extreme or more negative stereotypes of the owner. There was a 'brand name bias'. Some of the photographs (for example, of Levi jeans) were identifiable from markings or names as particular brands whereas others were simply a style of shoe. The mere presence of a brand was enough to cause a more positive stereotype of the owner to emerge!

In school-age children it would appear that the presence of brand names is enough to enhance positively the image of the user of that brand, although it could be the case that this bias was caused by the brand name products being more 'upmarket' anyway. Given the popularity of branded clothes among children, further research into this effect with different ages, cultures and products would be worthwhile.

In summary, the evidence would indicate that middle childhood is another important time when the child develops a symbolic interpretation of the content of the ad. No longer does the child just read it as a series of events or incidents, but the features of these scenes are interpreted as symbols that possess cultural meaning.

THE CHILD'S MEMORY FOR THE COMMERCIAL

At the time of viewing a commercial or listening to one or both, the child may pay attention to certain parts and be capable, to some extent, of discriminating and of understanding what is going on and why it is being screened. We are interested in what happens, as soon as that commercial disappears from the screen, to the information that has been processed during viewing and listening. It is the memory for information extracted and stored during watching and listening that is used when later, behavioural, activities such as pestering or buying occurs. Consequently, the child's memory for the advertisement is of central importance in ascertaining just how the television commercial acts on and influences the child (or, for that matter, the child acts and behaves toward television commercials).

Certainly, memory for commercials has been researched since the beginning of television advertising and children. Probably the first publication in the area was by Brumbaugh (1954). This two-page article referred to a study 'done recently' in which 400 children aged between 6 and 12 years were asked to list as many products advertised on television as they could remember. They were given 15 minutes to do this and the results quoted support the general thesis that television advertising is influencing children to the extent that even 6-year-olds can recall an average of twenty products. The top three classes of products listed were detergents, beer, and cigarettes—not products that are advertised to children directly.

Although the study was not designed as a sophisticated experiment using the methods of the psychology laboratory, the procedure employed can be described as free recall from long-term memory. No restrictions are placed on how the information should be organized at output and no prompts or hints are provided for remembering. The information has been already stored and organized over some time; there is no display of stimulus and immediate recall. The items recalled are retrieved 'off the top' of the memory store and the whole exercise is valid with regard to the real world since it reflects how product names 'come to mind'.

Recall of the whole content of the television commercial from long-term memory was reported in Ward, Wackman, and Wartella (1977). The procedure used was simple. Children ranging from 5 to 12 years of age were asked to recall their favourite television commercial and tell the interviewer what happened in it. An analysis of the content of these verbal records revealed that younger children remembered single elements of the commercial (for example, a boy playing with a toy) whereas older children remembered more information central to the narrative or to the purpose of the commercial, such as product information. This is not unexpected given the general principles of cognitive development such as a shift with age from dependence on salient, stimulus-based features for processing information to processing driven by schemata, which are structures that are based on experience with commercials as a distinct type of communication, and that generate expectations of what will come next.

It would appear that children can recall and recognize certain information from food commercials with some degree of success. Gianino and Zuckerman (1977) presented 64 children aged 4, 7, and 10 years with photographs of animated presenter characters from programmes or from food commercials. Seventeen 4-year-olds out of 20 could recognize these characters and could correctly match the specific product they 'show you' on television. Brand name recognition after a single exposure to a commercial for a food product has been found for primary school children. Gorn and Goldberg (1978) inserted varying numbers of ice-cream commercials in the context of a half-hour cartoon show. With six alternative names of ice cream to choose from, almost half of the 12 children exposed to only one ad correctly identified the name of the product. Haefner, Leckenby, and Goldman (1975) claim a recall figure of over 90 per cent of brand names following a single commercial viewing by primary school children. In one study (Atkin, 1975a) each of 500 children aged 3 to 10 years was randomly assigned to view one of two versions of a cereal commercial which was one of a series of nine inserted in a cartoon programme. Both presentations mentioned that the cereal tasted good and is 'good for you'. Under free recall, about one-third of all children repeated the 'good for you' claim present in both versions of the cereal commercial. In summary, it would appear that the recall and recognition of certain information in a food commercial is high for primary school children. The information that is presented as important (such as the brand name) will be recalled. What is not recalled is information that is secondary in importance and consequently not built in as a central theme in the design of the commercial.

There are several reviews of the literature that include surveys of research on memory for information in commercials. Wartella and Hunter (1983) summarize the evidence on memory for advertising across age bands. It would appear that there is a major change in the type of information recalled from commercials between the ages of 5½ and 8½ years. Younger children tend to recall single elements from the commercial whereas older children tend to remember more product and commercial plot line information. Recognition, measured by selection from a range of alternatives, seems to be uniformly poor, ranging from a level slightly above chance for 5- to 6-year-olds to an average level of 70 per cent for 8- to 9-year-olds, based on a chance recognition score of 33 per cent (Wackman, Wartella, and Ward, 1979). Zuckerman, Ziegler, and Stevenson's (1978) results gave a level of recognition slightly above chance over the age range 7½ to 10½ years. There was a high degree of variability across subjects, indicating that some children were accurate and others performed poorly. The majority of errors were errors of commission where children claimed to have seen or heard material that was not presented. Despite low recognition and recall scores, young children can recall certain kinds of information (such as commercial slogans) better than other information (such as brand names). Gunter (1981), in a general review, examines some literature on memory performance and comprehension which looks at recall and recognition issues.

In an Australian piece of research that had not been cited before (Bednall and Hannaford, 1980), it was found that there was no difference in recall of clustered versus distributed advertising in an hour of television programmes after a delay of three days, although clustered advertising was not recalled as well as distributed advertising if recall occurred immediately after presentation. Subjects were 10- and 11-year-old children. Clustered advertising is where the commercials are placed between programmes; in distributed advertising commercials are located both between and within programmes.

There is already a small literature on the relative effects of clustering versus distributing commercial placements in programmes that is reviewed in Adler *et al.* (1980, pp. 173–4) and this study can be regarded as contributing to it. The fact that television commercials are not found in isolation but nested in various different contexts should influence recall and especially errors and confusion in recall. Researchers have not ignored this. For example, Atkin (1975*a*) showed children a television commercial for a cereal called Pebbles. This featured cartoon characters from *The Flintstones*. The commercial was embedded either in a cartoon depicting the adventures of the Flintstones or a Bugs Bunny cartoon. In one condition the commercial was shown within the Flintstones cartoon and in another condition the commercial was shown with other commercials beside the programme. Children were asked whether they remembered if they saw the Flintstones characters eating cereal and if so, where. Some children demonstrated confusion by claiming they saw these characters eating cereal in the context of the storyline of the programme. This happened, however, when the commercial was presented either alongside or inside the Flintstones cartoon but not when it was placed with the Bugs Bunny cartoon. Younger children were particularly susceptible to this kind of confusion.

It can be concluded that the content of the context rather than the 'distance' of the commercial from the programme is the important determinant of confusion in children here. The precise nature of the parameters of content and proximity that determine confusion is not yet known. In other words, how far apart must the same characters appearing in commercial and programme be placed to avoid confusion? What degree of similarity between programme character and commercial character will trigger off confusion if the programme and commercial are near each other?

Ross *et al.* (1981) provide a good example of experimental research. A group of 100 children aged from 5 to 12 years participated in the study and were assigned randomly to either experimental or control conditions. Each child in the experimental condition viewed television commercials for three types of cereals and beverages: 'real fruit', 'nonfruit', and 'artificially fruit-flavoured' products. Each child then had to answer questions about whether the products advertised had fruit in them or not. The experimental design was complex and balanced and the interesting results that emerged were those that were independent of the age of the child. Showing children these commercials resulted in greater accuracy (regarding the presence of actual fruit) in the 'real fruit' and the 'nonfruit' conditions but greater inaccuracy for the artificially flavoured product condition.

Now the difference between an average 5-year-old and a 12-year-old is such that it would be expected that the former would not comprehend the function of commercial advertising too well and the latter (should) know that ads are there to persuade. This is not helpful, however, when it comes to interpreting and comprehending advertising messages—the knowledge that this message is designed to 'make you buy the product' does not protect the child from the tendency to construct information from the advertiser's message that is not there in a literal reading of the message.

Gorn and Goldberg (1980) were interested in the effects of repeating the same commercial to children and constructed several videotapes, some of which repeated the same commercial at intervals in a half-hour cartoon programme. They found that (as might be expected) recall improved with repetition but that there was no difference in consumption behaviour after repeated exposure.

Soldow (1983) compared how visual versus auditory information presented in different forms of advertising affects recognition of a product. The child was shown either a radio commercial for a cereal (auditory information), a television commercial for the same product (auditory and visual information), or a print ad for the same product (visual information). After presentation of one of these forms the child was asked to select from a series of five boxes of cereal the box that most closely matched the package presented in the advertisement. Children were categorized into preoperational (106) or concrete operational (180) in terms of Piagetian stages of cognitive development according to their response on a number conservation task.

A surprising finding was that preoperational children

(cognitively less mature children) were able to select the correct package equally well in the radio condition as in the print and television conditions. In radio condition information was presented in one mode (auditory) and recognized in another (visual), whereas in the print and television conditions information was both presented and recognized in the same (visual) mode. Cognitive limitations as described as Piaget need not extend to differences in information processing by children of different stages in development.

Faber *et al*. (1984) evaluated the effectiveness of placing health information disclosures in television commercials. One of the concerns voiced by critics and those concerned about the issue of television advertising and children is that television advertising of sugared products can promote unhealthy dietary habits in children. Banning ads is just one way of solving this problem, but, given the present political climate on both sides of the Atlantic, it is an unlikely step that any government would wish to take. Placing public health messages in the same context as advertising would be an alternative strategy which would not offend the current received version of political morality where freedom of action and choice is 'good' and state rules and regulations are seen as interference and hence are 'bad'.

Faber *et al*. sampled 164 children ranging in age from 3 to 14 years and presented commercials inserted in programmes to some. Some children viewed different types of disclaimers concerning the public health aspects of eating sweets. The messages were placed at the end of the commercial. When the children were questioned afterwards it was found that even very young children can recall and understand the health messages. The greatest recall was in the so-called 'fear appeal condition' when the message stated that eating too much candy can cause cavities and be bad for teeth and health.

Stoneman and Brody (1983) showed food commercials, placed in a television programme, to children aged from 3 to 8. Immediately afterwards, they were given a product recognition task where they had to identify the advertised brand from among several other products that had not been shown in the programme. They found that recognition was better when the information was presented visually or au-dio-visually rather than by auditory means only, a result that had already been established with children's entertainment programmes (see, for example, Hayes and Birnbaum, 1980). When the recognition errors were examined it was found that the children were more likely to confuse brands from the same product class than from different product classes and that this applied to even the youngest children.

The results of this research could be used to explore the development in children of hierarchies of product categor-ies. For example, do children classify commercials for sweets as similar to commercials for, say, cakes, and differ-ent from commercials for toys by making more confusion errors in recognition between sweets and cakes than be-tween sweets and toys or cakes and toys? Do children make early distinctions between 'adult' products and 'child' prod-ucts on this measure? How do hierarchies of product and brand categories develop? There is a lack of research pub-lished in the public domain on this fundamental problem.

One isolated comment by Dorr (1986, p. 47) is worth recording. She claims that young children who do not know much about the structure of commercials have been found to increase their recall of commercial content after training about the types of information commercials usually contain. Although no detail on the type of training used is given, this result shows that memory for commercials is not a phenomenon that is solely determined by stage-related development—that children remember better just by be-coming cognitively and socially more experienced. Children can be taught what to expect and this enhances fundamental information processing strategies involved in remembering television commercials.

It is difficult to summarize and form any generalizations from the literature discussed above. Although the general principle would appear to be that children remember more information and relevant information as they get older, contradictory results are obtained from similar experiments. For example, Gorn and Goldberg (1978) claimed that chil-dren recognize important information from a food commer-cial even after only one presentation, whereas Zuckerman

et al. (1978) argue that recognition of commercial cc
poor.

Part of the problem can be derived from the pol
text within which much of the research of the 1970s was
conducted. Health education specialists and advertisers alike
would be interested in the recall and recognition of specific
information from particular kinds of commercials. Commercials for nutritionally inadequate food products and
foods loaded with added sucrose are prime targets for investigation, given the public health interest in them.

It should be pointed out that not all commercials are the
same and, whereas there is a case for the 'commercial' being a well-defined entity in terms of its function and
communicative intent, television advertisements are a
heterogeneous collection of different styles as far as their
attention arousing characteristics and memorability are
concerned. Consequently it is not surprising that different
commercials produce different experimental results.

In addition, experimental psychologists have the ever-
present problem of designing experiments that optimize
two different kinds of validity. The internal validity of an
experiment refers to the extent the results obtained are
true and generalizable within the universe of other, similar
experiments. It is possible to design an experiment that
measures recall or recognition in a highly restricted and
controlled way, using an artificial mode of presentation
involving a single child watching a single television commercial under controlled conditions. One would expect
high internal validity here. External or ecological validity
refers to the extent to which the results obtained are true in
that they are generalizable to real life. Does the experiment
simulate what actually happens when children watch and
remember television commercials as part of the ongoing
stream of television in the complex situation of watching
television in the real world?

Obviously a controlled laboratory experiment is not a
slice of real life and one would not expect high external
validity under these circumstances. But if children discuss
and try to piece together what they remember of half an
hour's home viewing, there is the danger that the results

may not be the same if the situation is repeated with another group on another day and that the processes involved in such recall are different from individual to individual. Although the external validity of this experiment looks high, the internal validity will be low. The problem of balancing these two kinds of validity in research on memory for real-life situations is particularly acute.

Another problem concerns the choice of measures. Should recall be preferred over recognition? As recognition is easier than recall under most circumstances, recognition measures will provide more evidence at an earlier age. The question of remembering to what purpose then arises. If the child is accustomed to purchasing the brand in a supermarket context where the familiar brand has to be distinguished among many other similar products, recognition is the more ecologically valid measure. If, on the other hand, the child is accustomed to buying sweets from a corner shop where the transaction is based on a simple request to the shopkeeper, valid measures should include recall as that is what the child may have to do. Research into memory for television commercials should be integrated into a general programme of research into the development of schemata for understanding television advertising in general. At the moment, the results make up a mixed bag of different findings that have yet to be unified in a general theoretical approach.

OTHER PROCESSES INVOKED BY VIEWING

Being able to understand the purpose and function of a communication implies that the message could then be subject to some kind of evaluation. If we recognize that a person is trying to be funny we will judge his or her comments accordingly and 'read' sarcasm as humour rather than rudeness. In particular, if we perceive the intent behind the communication as persuasive or advocatory or in some way designed to get us to do something, then we will interpret claims and arguments with this in mind. We will search for rhetoric and treat claims with a healthy scepticism. Since we know that only the best side of the case is being presented we would put forward the other side ourselves.

It could be argued that the degree of scepticism we employ when dealing with other people will depend on our experience with others and the extent to which we assume truthfulness or deceit as the norm. If we assume, from experience or as a consequence of cultural values, that most people will try to deceive us or take advantage of us, this will be adopted as a canonical rule of interpersonal communication. Truth-telling or the pursuit of disinterested information will be seen as the figure against a ground of normal advocacy or persuasion, forceful or otherwise. On the other hand, experience and socialization may lead us to believe that the default value to apply to everyday conversations is truth and other forms of non-truthful communication should be interpreted as examples of deviant, rule-breaking communication.

It has been assumed that, when children develop an understanding of the purpose behind advertising, they are then capable of resisting its appeal because they perceive the purpose behind the message. Often this is described using an extended metaphor where advertising is seen as 'an attack' with younger children being 'defenceless' and older children erecting 'cognitive defences'. For Rossiter and Robertson (1974), cognitive defence is the ability to understand selling intent of advertisements. Attitudinal defence, for them, is indexed by disbelief, dislike, and lack of inclination to buy advertised products. These three aspects reflect the traditional tripartite structure of attitudes into cognitive, affective and conative components dealing with thought, feelings, and motives respectively. There is an assumption that cognitive mediation occurs between comprehension and action or the well-springs of action however they be conceptualized. The questions that then arise are concerned with the sort of processes that constitute this cognitive mediation, at what stage of development they emerge, and their role in influencing action and behaviour.

In the cited study by Rossiter and Robertson, children were asked in early November to indicate their preference for a variety of toys and games advertised on television.

They found that children who had strong cognitive and attitudinal defences chose fewer products advertised than children with weaker defences. Under these circumstances the mediators proposed by these authors would appear to influence preference. When the children were interviewed just before Christmas, however, after being exposed to an onslaught of television advertising, they found that the relationship between cognitive/attitudinal defence and toy preference no longer held. To extend the 'defence' metaphor, under an extensive barrage of advertising the defences will be breached.

Is it possible for children to resist television advertising if they are too young to understand its purpose and thus unable to erect cognitive defences against it? Esserman (1981a) reported the results of an experiment with young children which, she claimed, had demonstrated that children are able to resist advertising appeals when they were aware it was in their self interest to do so. The theoretical predictions are based on what is known in social psychology as cognitive dissonance theory. The theory of cognitive dissonance (for example, Brehm and Cohen, 1962) holds that attitude change can be driven by a state of cognitive dissonance when non-trivial and emotionally valued thoughts contradict each other. This process operates in adults and children. To use a consumer example, if a child has to decide between two attractive toys, A and B, and chooses A, dissonance will exist because the child still likes B and yet didn't choose it. This state of mental discomfort will cause attitude change to occur in various predictable ways. The child may devalue the rejected alternative ('I didn't really like it anyway'), overvalue the chosen one (thus contributing to brand loyalty) or selectively seek out information that is favourable to A and reject any information that extols the virtue of B (again contributing to brand loyalty).

From observations of children based on her experience in market research, Esserman (1981a) suggested that if a product is appealing to the child and the child knows that his or her parents disapprove of that product then dissonance exists. This dissonance is frequently reduced by the child perceiving the product as less attractive, thus devaluing the importance of the cognition 'this product is attractive to me'. In order to test this hypothesis, Esserman used a sample of 215 children aged from 5 years to 8 years, half of whom came from homes where the mother prohibited the child from chewing sugared gum brands but allowed sugarless gum brands and half of whom came from homes where no such restrictions occurred. Each child was shown a commercial for a sugared chewing-gum that presented the brand in a positive and appealing way. Following this, the child was interviewed and asked a series of questions. Results showed that there was a significant difference between those children who weren't allowed sugared chewing-gum and those who were. The former group, when asked what they thought of the chewing-gum in the commercial, rated it significantly lower than the latter group when they were asked the same question.

Esserman interpreted this finding as support for the hypothesis that dissonance reduction, where the attractiveness of one of the alternatives is devalued, can occur and that 'the findings ... provide evidence of children's ability to defend against the appeals of television commercials' (1981a, p. 51). Although the results of this experiment are important in the context of children being influenced by commercials, they are in no way a demonstration of the child defending against the appeals of television commercials as a result of cognitive dissonance induced by the contradiction between parental injunctions and liking for the product.

What has been shown is that a sample of children from homes where the mother prohibits sugared gum products do not rate sugared chewing-gum very highly. This result is in accord with the predictions of cognitive dissonance. But it is also in accord with the predictions of other *ad hoc* explanations. Homes where sugared chewing-gum is prohibited might be homes where sugared products are regarded as harmful, just because the family shares a core set of values on the subject of diet. Unfortunately this result of Esserman's tells us very little about the capabilities of children to defend against commercials by, for example, counter-arguing in the face of a persuasive communication or by devaluing or derogating the source of the communication.

Is it possible to build cognitive defences for the child against advertising? Instruction and teaching may help and would have advantages over regulation as a way of protecting children. Roberts *et al.* (1980) evaluated two instructional films made to show children how television advertising uses various techniques in order to persuade. They concluded that younger children who were initially most susceptible to commercial appeals and who were heavy viewers were most influenced by the films. It could be said that heavy viewers bring more examples to bear when exposed to the material contained in the instructional film or that they tend to be the less 'critical' thinkers, at least until a critical strategy is spelt out for them.

In any case, it is possible to 'arm' children against commercials and to use various consumer education strategies to reduce their vulnerability to commercial appeals. Also, the two most vulnerable groups (heavy viewers and young children) appear to be the ones on whom this type of consumer education works best. Child-oriented 30-second spot commercials that are designed to teach 'prosocial lessons' such as safe bicycling, the dangers of junk food or of cigarette smoking, as well as public service spots to teach children about commercials in general have been developed and broadcast in the United States. Christenson (1980) devised a three-minute 'consumer information processing' spot. He inserted this announcement into a longer sequence containing programming and commercials and found that 6- to 12-year-olds who viewed the message were more aware of the commercials and expressed less trust in commercials in general than children not exposed to the announcement.

Although the evidence indicates that when children in middle childhood view a television commercial they are aware of the selling intent, they will, after viewing, behave as if they had been influenced by what they had just seen and heard. Roedder, Sternthal, and Calder (1983) found that 9-year-olds ignored their product preferences and responded to the immediate influence of a commercial when making product judgements whereas 13-year-olds were quite capable of sticking with established preferences regardless of the advertising that they had just seen. At these ages both groups of children should have at least a rudimentary knowledge of the purpose of advertising and, according to Rossiter and Robertson definition (1974), be in possession of cognitive defences against advertising.

Initially Roedder *et al.* (1983) assessed product preferences then showed children two different television commercials for a chocolate product called Choco-Nuts. One ad was designed to induce a favourable attitude toward Choco-Nuts whereas the other was intended to produce a less favourable attitude. At the end, they assessed the attitudes and choice preferences of the children. The range of choices included Choco-Nuts. At this point, after exposure to television advertising, differences between the two age groups were found. The older children appeared to consider their attitudes toward the various alternatives and to select the preferred alternative regardless of advertising. The younger children, in contrast, seemed to base their choice on their evaluation of the advertised product and not on a comparison of choice alternatives. They would choose the advertised alternative when exposed to advertising producing a favourable attitude towards it and reject Choco-Nuts when advertising produced a less favourable attitude towards it.

The conclusion from this study should be that knowledge of the intent of advertising is not enough. During late childhood and early adolescence, information processing skills will develop so that the child gradually acquires executive control over relevant information in decision making situations such as product choice. At the early stage of this development however, children will be influenced by immediate, attractive product presentations and will tend to respond accordingly. Adults, of course, are also susceptible to this sort of influence. The difference is that, for most adults, the skills for managing the processing of information should already be developed but, on this occasion, are not being utilised. For the older child, who quite probably knows that advertising is there to try to sell products, advertising will influence already established product preferences. Indeed, Roedder *et al.* regard this as a central problem when considering the influence of advertising on children and argue that 'the potential impact of advertising is not only to persuade children but possibly to make them act inconsistently with attitudes they held previously' (1983, p. 337).

Roedder (1981), in an important theoretical contribution to the literature, proposed that there are three developmental stages in using information. The limited stage is when the child is not capable of using sophisticated storage and retrieval strategies to process information. Roedder claims this holds for children below 6 years of age but Brucks, Armstrong, and Goldberg (1987) argue that such limited processing can be found in children under 8 years. There is an intermediate stage when such strategies can be used if they are cued but are usually not generated spontaneously by the child. Roedder (1981) puts this between 6 and 9 years whereas Brucks *et al.* (1987) determine the age range as 8 to 12 years. Finally the older child and adolescent can process information strategically and independently, Roedder (1981) detecting the onset of this ability at 10 to 11 years and Brucks *et al.* (1987) fixing the latest age at 13 years. Brucks *et al.* provide 'suggested ages for the latest developing activity' (1987, p. 8) which may account for the discrepancy in age norms. Not only must children possess an adequate knowledge base about the purposes and function of advertising but they should be capable of deploying that information when actively processing information from outside, from the ad they are watching.

Brucks has produced two papers (Brucks *et al.*, 1987; Brucks *et al.*, 1986) that are concerned with the child's cognitive response to advertising. They cite Wright (1973) who has laid out three major types of cognitive response that are found in adults in the face of advertising. One is the use of counter-arguments, when prior knowledge is used to 'argue' against explicit and implicit advertising messages. Support arguments, on the other hand, consist of thoughts in favour of advertising messages. Finally, the audience can derogate the source of the communication by generating thoughts that are critical of specific advertisers or advertising in general.

Brucks *et al*. (1986, 1987) were interested in establishing direct measures of the so-called 'cognitive responses' that occur while the child watches a commercial. These were assessed by showing the child a television commercial then asking the probe question 'What were you thinking about during this commercial?' The children wrote down all their thoughts which produced, on average, nine verbalized 'thoughts' per child. Some children were shown films on the persuasive nature of advertising which they then discussed. This condition was designed to activate a high level of advertising knowledge. The cue consisted of a short quiz that measured children's beliefs about advertising. A group of 102 children aged 9 to 10 years were the subjects. It was found that, overall, children who had seen the instructional film produced more sceptical and critical replies when asked a direct question such as whether they thought the commercial made the product seem better than it really was, than children who had not seen the film. This result is consistent with the findings of Roberts *et al*. (1980).

When the results of the cognitive response measures were examined however, it was found that these children do not claim to have had critical thoughts while watching the ad unless they had been cued. In this connection, the direct questions could act as a cue so that cueing works as an activator of the already established knowledge about advertising. This finding is predictable from Roedder's work in that organized retrieval and use of available information are only possible at this stage in the presence of cues.

Brucks *et al*. (1987) explored the policy implications of this finding. Children who are already capable of understanding the advertiser's intent still need more detailed knowledge about the nature of advertising and how it works. This was given in the short instructional films. In addition, this detailed knowledge needs to be cued if it is going to generate counter-arguments and source derogation that characterize sceptical cognitive responses. But although the cue needs to be directive, it can be non-specific, such as a public service announcement to think critically while watching television commercials. There are various agencies that could implement such information and Brucks *et al*. cite teachers, parents as well as broadcasters in this regard.

Wartella (1984) argues that being aware of the purpose of advertising is not enough to prevent children being influenced by it. There is some experimental evidence to show that, although children are equipped with knowledge of advertising techniques, and understanding of advertising's intent, and express a cynicism about advertising in general, they are still influenced by an ad to the extent it will affect their choice of a product. For example, Ross, Campbell, Wright, Huston, Rice, and Turk (1981) found that boys up to the age of 14 years were influenced by a television commercial for a toy racing car that used a racing celebrity and real racing car footage in the ad. They were no different from younger, 8-year-old children in the extent to which this ad positively influenced their product choice. We can add here that, according to Roedder (1981) and Brucks *et al.* (1986, 1987), these older adolescents should be quite capable of processing information in a strategic way. The gulf between knowledge, understanding and decision making is still a yawning chasm. What is missing? Wartella proposes that affect, the emotional qualities in the stimulus and the emotions and feelings in the viewer, has an important role to play in any model of how persuasion works. The rhetoric and discourse of advertising can evoke complex affective processes in adults and children. Certainly the interface between affect and cognition is a place where future research could concentrate its efforts.

In summary, the research on cognitive mediation has shown that knowledge of advertising intent is not the only defence against advertising's influence. Knowledge of advertising and its techniques would constitute the cognitive component of an attitude towards advertising and would help in developing a healthy scepticism toward its claims and rhetoric. There is a developmental dimension to this as well in that the ability to control and manage information processing strategies is necessary to avoid inconsistency between product preference going into the situation of watching the ad and the subsequent preference after watching the ad. Finally, and perhaps most importantly, the feelings and emotions generated while watching as well as the emotional 'after-taste' when the ad is retrieved from memory are important factors in influencing the child's preference and choice.

THE EFFECT ON KNOWLEDGE, ATTITUDES, AND VALUES

It would not be surprising if television advertising contributed to the knowledge, attitudes, and values that gradually evolve in the child. There's certainly plenty of it about. To quote one of those numbing statistics that are frequently found in books on children and television, the average child in the United States will watch some 200,000 commercial messages between the ages of 2 and 12 years (cited by Roberts, 1982, p. 22). No doubt, equipped with viewing figures, commercial logs and a calculator, one could establish similar statistics for the average British child. In addition, ads provide information about foods, toys, snacks, drinks that will interest the child and this information is presented in a glossy, well-crafted, and advocatory or persuasive format. There is also the possibility that the child will develop wrong attitudes and acquire incorrect knowledge from ads when it is important for the sake of health and well-being to maintain a correct stance. For example, much of the research discussed below has dealt with the question of the child's knowledge about nutrition and whether advertising has a detrimental influence on such knowledge.

General questions that have been mooted about the pernicious influence of advertising on people (see Chapter 1) have not been tested, so we do not know whether children hold more materialistic values because of the presence of advertising in their world. Indeed it would be difficult, if not impossible, to put these general questions to test, given the virtually universal presence of advertising from the cradle to the grave. One study does provide a partial glimpse of the situation before and after the arrival of television. Williams (1986) presented a detailed report on a study of a Canadian community who, for geographical reasons, were unable to receive television until recently. It would appear that television negatively affects participation in community activities, and sport in particular, interferes with the acquisition of fluent reading skills and creative thinking by children, negatively affects creative problem solving by adults, increases children's aggressive behaviour, and strengthens sex stereotypes held by children.

Research on the effect of television advertising on the knowledge, attitudes, and values of children centres on several issues. One of these is the attitude of children towards television advertising in general. Do they find it enjoyable and interesting? Or are they bored and sceptical about the claims of advertisers? One of the earliest reviews of the literature on children and television advertising by Sheikh *et al.* (1974) concluded that research demonstrated that, in general, children's attitudes tend to become more negative as they grow older. In other words, older children tend to distrust commercials and find them 'silly'.

Most of the evidence on the relationship in children between television viewing and attitudes towards commercials is correlational and has established that heavy viewers respond more favourably to commercials than their light-viewing peers. Heavy viewers tend to like and trust commercials more and express stronger behavioural intentions towards products advertised on television. Winick and Winick (1979) reported that children as young as 2 years regularly left the room every time a commercial was shown. Although no data on the frequency with which this occurred were provided, they did report that commercials were regarded as relatively unimportant by more than 300 children observed. Bearden, Teel, and Wright (1979) used a test devised by Rossiter (1977) with two samples of 76 children aged 9 to 12 years from medium- to high-income families and 62 children aged 9 to 12 years from low-income families. Rossiter's (1977) original attitude questionnaire consisted of seven items such as 'television commercials tell the truth' and 'television commercials try to make people buy things they don't really need' with children responding on a four-point agree–disagree scale. Bearden *et al.* (1979) found that there was no significant difference between groups on favourableness of attitude toward television advertising but that the lower income group's responses were less consistent than the medium- to high-income group.

Giudicatti and Stening (1980*a*) sampled 165 children in Australia using Rossiter's (1977) instrument to obtain further psychometric data. Riecken and Samli (1981) modified Rossiter's scales to evaluate attitudes towards particular products, including breakfast cereals. They used 152 children between 8 and 12 years of age and derived satisfactory reliability and inter-item correlation coefficients. Barling and Fullager (1983) sampled 545 10- to 11-year-old children using a more extensive attitude questionnaire devised by Schlinger (1979) which was originally designed to measure the attitudes of adults to specific advertisements. This was modified by removing some items that were regarded as inappropriate for children. When the results were statistically analysed using factor analysis, it was found that two main factors emerged which the authors labelled *entertainment* and *irritation–boredom*. This means that children's responses on the attitude questionnaire are structured around these affective components and that the emotional evaluation of ads (for example that 'they're boring' or 'lots of fun to watch') predominates in children's responses to individual television commercials.

Concerning the mother's attitude to television advertising to children, Ward, Wackman, and Wartella (1975) asked 615 mothers with children how strongly they agreed or disagreed with statements concerning television commercials to children and created a composite attitude score from their responses. Almost three-quarters of the sample had a negative opinion of the commercials and these negative attitudes were most pronounced among parents of younger, kindergarten-age children but did not seem to be associated with social class. Wiman (1980) interviewed 122 pairs of mothers and children. The children were aged between 9 and 10 years. Mother and child were assessed on their attitudes towards children's television commercials using Rossiter's (1977) test with slight modifications to obtain the version used with the adults.

The attitudes of parent and child were significantly

related. Even with the restricted age band used, the older children's attitudes were significantly less favourable towards television commercials for children than the younger group. Boys held significantly less favourable attitudes toward these commercials than girls. When the question of banning the commercials was raised during the interview, parents favoured a ban by 58 per cent to 22 per cent whereas children opposed it by 46 per cent to 31 per cent. Attitudes of parents towards television commercials appears to depend on the way they bring up their children. Parents differ in styles of socialization, the way they raise children, and instil cultural values and approved habits.

The varieties of parental influence on children is a large area of research with different practitioners working within different theoretical traditions. Baumrind (1971) has found three patterns or styles of parental authority in the United States which can be called authoritative, authoritarian and permissive.

The authoritative mode is one that encourages communication with the child and considers the child's views and interests. The parent does exert control over the child and monitors the child's environment but restrictions imposed serve as boundaries within which the child can operate with considerable autonomy. For example, authoritative parents would monitor and control the amount of the child's television viewing, but this would be done by discussing the matter with the child and the child expressing his or her opinion. Once the restrictions have been imposed the child would be permitted to watch freely within these constraints.

An authoritarian parent, on the other hand, would limit the child's psychological independence. Any rules on the child's behaviour are imposed without discussion by the parent. Parents of this kind are generally aloof from the child and insist on conformity with their views. They would set limits on the child's television viewing, limits that are not negotiable and have to be obeyed.

Permissive parents impose minimum behavioural restrictions, communicate and discuss extensively with their children and, in general, permit the child extensive rights and demand few responsibilities. It is up to the child to regulate his or her own actions. Consequently, one would expect little control or interference from the parent on the child's television viewing although there may be much discussion about what's on and what's being watched.

Crosby and Grossbart (1984) sampled over 500 mothers of children in a Midwestern state of the United States and, using self-administered questionnaires, found that parents who claimed authoritative characteristics also displayed most concern about television advertising to children. This would be expected. Given the authoritative parental style, much television advertising to children would be seen as potentially subversive to democratic parental control. Crosby and Grossbart, in a message to advertising managers, suggest that parental style might serve as a suitable market segmentation criterion. What this means is that the advertiser may have to pitch differently if the audience consists predominantly of families who are authoritative and consequently concerned about television advertising to children. Permissive families, on the other hand, will not bother so much and a different message can be delivered without the risk of rejection.

Although the conclusion to be drawn from these studies on children's attitudes toward commercials is quite clear, the results should be interpreted with caution. It is to be expected that a growing understanding of the advertiser's commercial intent will breed a certain cynicism with advertising as the child gets older. Negative attitudes towards advertising, however, will be affected by the sample of television commercials the child actually sees and the quality of the pool of advertisements that are shown on television. For instance the general quality of television advertising in Britain in the late 1980s was quite high using humorous situations and visually exciting and fashionable scenarios. Older children, in an attempt to distance themselves from younger children, may scoff at ads designed for younger children as 'childish' or 'for babies' but identify with commercials aimed at adolescents. It is not possible to come to the universal conclusion that older children have more negative attitudes towards television advertising than younger children as these attitudes will depend on what television commercials are watched and the quality of advertising in the culture in general. In the United States, however, older children have less favourable attitudes towards television commercials than younger children.

Effects on health-related knowledge

It has been shown that, in the United States, television advertising to children presents a range of food products that in no way constitutes a healthy diet (see Chapter 6 for details). Food that is low in nutritional value and high in added sugar is the diet children are exposed to in the world of television advertising. The question arises: to what extent does this biased picture influence the knowledge children have of what constitutes a healthy diet? There is a basic assumption here that concerns learning from television advertising. This is that the world as portrayed in the advertisement moulds or influences the picture of the real world that is constructed through childhood. In particular, there is a quantitative aspect to this comparison in that if the world-in-ad portrays a lot of junk food then the child believes that junk food is the norm in the real world.

This quantitative comparison is frequently drawn in popular discussion of media. For example, (American) tele-vision shows a lot of violence. Children watch this, therefore they will grow up thinking that the real world is violent too. There are at least two kinds of mental processes assumed in the transfer from the world-in-television to the world-out-there. One is concerned with the assumed statistical nature of the real world and how this is influenced by the skewed and biased portrayal on television. In this sense, if a content analysis of the world-in-television shows that there's an abnormally high preponderance of violent acts, will the child create a picture of the real world as a place where such acts are accustomed and to be expected? The child may perceive the world as a 'mean and scary' place (Singer and Singer, 1984).

The other process would be concerned with the extent to which children regard what's happening on television as a legitimate portrayal of the real world. If violence is the norm on television, how does this influence the child's opinion of the use of violence in the world of real people as a legitimate means of gratification, or solving problems, or as an end in itself?

To return to the advertising of junk food, the main concern should be with the legitimacy of the portrayal. If the child sees ads for junk food only does he or she assume that junk food is good for you 'because the ads say so'? This will depend on the extent to which the world-in-ad is seen as separate and distinct from the real world and subject to different rules of interpretation and different standards of evaluation. It should also depend on the discrepancy between products as portrayed in the ad and products as found in the world. If children are brought up in an environment where nutritious and non-advertised foods are widely available, on kitchen shelves and in High Street shops, then the discrepancy could provoke an awareness that the content of ads is not the same as real life.

Certain theories of transfer of the content of television to knowledge of the world rely on an extended metaphor of 'cultivation' (see, for example, Dorr, 1986, pp. 90–1). The continual presence of a particular portrayal of a normative world is presumed to cultivate or nourish mental representations of the world as-it-is in the child and, conversely, the absence of certain portrayals will erode or starve these mental images. Of course these may not be the only processes that operate in such a transfer, and the cognitive separation between television as 'unreal', and the world as 'real', or the emotional identification with characters on television, will also have an important role to play.

If we look at the child's general knowledge of food and nutrition an interesting picture of misinformation is found. A survey by market researchers (Reilly Group Inc., 1973) asked children to list 'the kinds of things you call snacks'. Seventy-eight per cent of children cited heavily sugared products such as cookies (biscuits), candy (sweets), cake, and ice cream as snacks. The other food identified as snacks were, in order of frequency: salty chip(crisp)-type products, fruit, sandwiches, and milk. The same study by the Reilly

Group revealed that one out of four children mentioned that these heavily sugared products (cookies, ice cream, and candy) when categorized as after-school snacks were 'especially good for you or healthy'.

Atkin, Reeves, and Gibson (1979) studied a group of 5- to 12-year-old children. About 60 per cent believed that presweetened cereals could cause tooth decay but heavy television viewers were less likely to hold this view. In addition, heavy viewers of food ads on television were twice as likely as light viewers to say that sugared cereals and candies (sweets) were highly nutritious.

Esserman (1981b) described a study designed to assess the nutritional views of 708 children aged 5 to 8 years. Nonverbal procedures were used. For example, the child was asked to select the foods and drinks that would be 'good for you' by choosing from a range of cut-out pictures of foods and drinks. A range of pictures was available to the child as response alternatives. For example, a picture of a worried child with bad teeth represented the alternative 'bad for teeth and gives you cavities'. It would appear from the results of the survey that children in this age range know about the basics of nutrition. For example, 89 per cent of 5- to 6-year-olds thought that candy (sweets) was 'bad for teeth and gave you cavities' by pointing to the appropriate picture. The sample used was geographically representative and took in lower socio-economic levels as well as middle-class households. There appeared to be no differences in children's opinions about food by sex, race, socio-economic status, or amount of television watched.

These results of Esserman can be compared with the state-of-the-art report by Adler et al. in 1980, which concluded that 'children exhibit mixed knowledge about the healthfulness of advertised foods' (p. 137). Adler also states that the nutritional knowledge about advertised foods appeared to vary on the basis of such factors as child's age, family income, and mother's educational level, citing evidence from four studies.

Barry and Gunst (1982) created two television commercials identical in every respect except that one commercial extolled the virtues of the product by the line 'it's chocolatey, rich, and sweet' while the other claimed it was 'healthful, vitaminey, and nutritious'. One hundred and seventy-two children ranging in age from 5 to 9 years were randomly assigned to view either the nutritional or traditional versions of the commercial embedded in a videotape of children's programmes and another commercial. They were then interviewed with a questionnaire. It was found that the ones who had seen the nutritional commercial rated the product high on the attributes mentioned in the commercial such as 'nutritious' and also expressed an intention to purchase it. Barry and Gunst claim that 'children will respond favourably to a healthy nutritious snack bar message' (1982, p. 123).

Scammon and Christopher (1981) reviewed nine experimental studies of the impact of television nutrition messages on children and concluded that different messages had different effects. Exposure to commercials for sugared products led to greater consumption of sugared products, greater preference for sugared foods, including foods that were not advertised, and lower nutritional knowledge. Exposure to commercials for healthy foods (or non-sugared foods) influenced consumption by dampening any increased consumption of sugared foods. Messages combining a sugared product commercial with a disclaimer, or a sugared product commercial shown with a message recommending reduced consumption of sugar, had an intermediate impact on food choice and on nutritional knowledge. The most effective methods tested in terms of children's verbal snack selections and their nutritional knowledge used separate spot messages on nutrition. Studies that used nutrition education programmes found them to be even more effective than short spots. Seven out of these nine studies, however, use the experimental methodology of a short treatment with a videotape followed by an immediate assessment. It is doubtful if this type of research simulates the real-life acquisition of nutritional knowledge and consumer choice behaviour, especially as the 'cultivation' model presumes a long-term process of change.

Lambo (1981) sampled 120 children and assessed their dental health knowledge by their responses to a question on the relationship of sugar to dental caries. Each child was interviewed about the dental health qualities of two television commercials for sugared products. For example, they were asked if this product was good for their teeth. It was found that younger children were less able to evaluate the dental caries risk of sugared products shown in television commercials and that there was a weak relationship between the level of dental health knowledge and ability to evaluate the dental health qualities of the product. Although these results are not exactly unexpected it was the null result that is surprising. No differences between socio-economic status groups were found in a child's ability to evaluate products.

Wiman and Newman's (1987) study looked at the impact of exposure to television advertising on nutritional knowledge in children. In particular they were concerned with one aspect of that knowledge. This they called 'nutritional awareness' which was defined as 'the level of understanding of the nutritional value of foods and the benefits of good eating habits' (p. 3). They wanted to know if there was a relationship between viewing television commercials and nutritional awareness. They gave a questionnaire to a sample of over 300 school children aged from 8 to 12 years in order to establish when the children watched television programmes, to assess their general level of knowledge about nutrition and diet, and to ascertain their understanding of certain words and phrases used in nutrition (such as 'a balanced diet'). This showed there was a relationship between nutritional awareness and television viewing but it was not a simple one. The more children watched Saturday morning television, the lower their scores on nutritional awareness were likely to be. Weekday evening viewing, however, was positively related to one part of the nutritional awareness assessment, that which dealt with nutritional knowledge.

These two results, if taken together, support the idea that exposure to child-oriented advertising has a negative relationship with nutritional awareness. Saturday morning television, in the United States, is saturated with commercials directed at children. They predominantly advertise products heavily loaded with sugar (Barcus and McLaughlin, 1978).

Weekday evening programmes, on the other hand, do not contain advertising that is primarily aimed at the child segment of the viewing population. Nevertheless, Wiman and Newman (1987) have provided clear evidence that heavy child viewers of child-oriented commercials, many of which are for sugared products, tend to have a low level of nutritional awareness. We still do not know the causes underlying this relationship. It could be that children who watch a lot of Saturday morning television constitute a particular group with its own characteristics, certain of which would mediate between television viewing and nutritional awareness. Perhaps these children eat a lot of sweets or are generally inactive.

This type of study is a useful contribution to answering questions concerning the negative influence of television advertising on health education. What is required, however, is a wider-ranging battery of measures used with structured samples in order to provide at least a partial answer to the important question of what goes between watching television and knowing about nutrition.

Miscellaneous studies

Various findings will be described in the rest of this section, results that do not clearly fit into the two main categories established above.

Atkin and Gibson (1978) interviewed children after they had viewed a commercial for a cereal called Honeycombs. The presenter of this brand is a character called Big Boris. A 'substantial proportion' of the children associated Boris's perceived strength with his eating the cereal and, to a lesser extent, inferred that this would also help them grow big and strong. The same children were also shown a commercial for the cereal Cocoa Pebbles that featured Fred Flintstone and Barney Rubble. 'Many' children said they would want to eat the cereal because Fred and Barney liked it. These findings are dependent on socio-economic status as well as age, because younger and lower-class children were more likely to express these beliefs.

Loughlin and Desmond (1981) wanted to know if the

presence of peer interaction in television commercials, where children are depicted playing together with a brand of toy or consuming a snack together, would have an influence on the child's attitude toward that ad or that product. Using a set of questions with 99 children aged from 5 to 8½ years they established that children liked this kind of commercial with peer interaction more, but that the desirability of the product was not affected.

There is evidence from Gorn and Goldberg (1978) that the effects of watching television commercials can operate in a hierarchical way and that the level depends on how many different commercials for the product the child has seen.

'Hierarchy of effects' is a popular concept in advertising psychology and is described in various standard texts on the subject (for example, Rothschild, 1987). There is an assumption that the processes involved between perception and action can be ordered and the traditional three-part division of knowing, feeling, and doing (or variations on that theme) is used to describe the sequence. For example, Lavidge and Steiner (1961) postulate six stages called awareness, knowledge, liking, preference, conviction, and purchase. Awareness and knowledge reflect knowing, liking and preference are aspects of feeling, and conviction and purchase relate to doing. The simple hierarchy of effects model can be modified depending on the involvement of the person watching the advertisement. Buying convenience goods that do not cost much is low-involvement consumer decision-making, whereas a careful decision to buy that car or this house is a high-involvement situation. Generally speaking, high-involvement decisions are modelled by the attitude driving the behaviour but in low-involvement purchases, behaviour in the form of trial purchases can form attitudes that then generate further consumption.

In any case, the issue of whether attitudes precede behaviour or behaviour creates attitudes is a live one in social psychology. Gorn and Goldberg (1978) found that a single commercial exposure can result in a significant gain in information by the child. The brand name is recalled, the flavours of advertised ice cream are remembered. Viewing three different commercials for the same brand embedded in a programme format can result in an increase in brand preference whereas watching five different commercials for the same brand can produce a shift in the children's choice of a snack.

Linn, Benedictis, and DeCucchi (1982) explored the understanding adolescents have of advertisements. They constitute a greatly under-researched segment of the population in the literature. A group of 126 adolescents aged 12 to 14 years was sampled. Interviewing these young people revealed a high degree of scepticism. Almost two-thirds expect that advertisers often or always lie or cheat. This is not unexpected given the adolescent's scepticism with social and political systems in general. However, this general wariness need not lead to a more critical evaluation of particular persuasive messages. For example, some commercials employ product tests in their spots, for instance by demonstrating how spotless floors become with detergent cleaners or how effective shampoos are, compared with the ubiquitous 'brand X'. Although many of the subjects were able to criticize this technique they still believed the adverts reporting the product tests.

Moschis and Moore (1982) sampled 211 adolescents between 12 and 18 years of age and gave them questionnaires on two different occasions, 14 months apart. The questions were designed to assess various aspects of consumer socialization such as how much consumption matters were discussed in the family, the extent to which the adolescent holds materialistic values, and so on. One finding was that television advertising influences the development of materialism and a traditional view of sex-roles in those adolescents whose parents do not discuss consumption matters with their children. This makes sense in that television advertising tends to advocate materialism and depict traditional sex roles and, in those families where consumption matters are not discussed, adolescents would be placed at the mercy of advertising as a source of influence. Families discussing consumption are likely to neutralize such effects.

Rossano and Butter (1987) investigated one category of television commercial that has caused public concern in the United States—that is, proprietary medicine advertising.

The concern is that many children lack the abilities to evaluate the messages that are expressed or implied in such advertisements and that repeated exposure to them is possibly related to drug abuse. What is this message? It has been argued by Berger (1974) that one of the themes found in such advertising is 'pain–pill–pleasure'. The problem is pain. The pill is the solution. Pleasure is the result. This message is then 'cultivated' and may generalize to promote drug taking and drug abuse.

Rossano and Butter attempted to deal with this issue in an experimental setting by showing children aged 8 to 9 and 11–12 years television commercials of proprietary medicines and then questioning them on their attitudes to medicines and medicine use. No effect or influence as a result of watching such commercials could be detected in either of the experimental designs they used. The authors explain this by arguing that little attention is paid to such commercials by children who find such advertisements serious and uneventful. The matter should not be considered closed, however, as the experimental methodology used by Rossano and Butter is not immune to criticism. For example, getting children to watch television and then asking questions immediately afterwards is unlikely to measure any long-term change in opinion or behaviour as a consequence of prolonged exposure to types of television content or the continual repetition of a particular way of coping with pain or discomfort.

Fischer (1985) employed an experimental pre-test–treatment–post-test design to investigate the immediate effect of watching a commercial for toys on choice preference. A measure of the child's preference for various toys was taken. Some children then watched a television programme that included ads for one of the toys. At the end they were asked to make a further ranking of their preference for each toy in the range on display, under the pretext that the original experimenter had made a mistake in recording the initial preferences and 'we would like you to do it over again'. Two groups of 40 children, aged 5 to 6 years and 8 to 9 years, were sampled. It was found that the older children liked the toys more if they viewed ads for them whereas the younger children appeared relatively unaffected by viewing.

Summary

How can the rather disparate body of research examined above be summarized? It would appear that older children in the United States do not like television commercials very much, compared with younger children. This growing dislike, as assessed by attitude questionnaires, can be attributed to at least two causes. One would be the development of an understanding of the commercial and persuasive intent behind advertising and the consequent attitude of cynicism that is induced. Being sceptical and cynical can function as a cognitive defence against the advocacy of one party and is perhaps a natural attribution to make when faced with a communication that one realizes is persuasive and designed to get one to buy the product. The second would be the social desirability of expressing such an attitude. Older children and adolescents, in order to 'distance' themselves from younger children, will claim to be unimpressed and cynical about ads. This does not prevent adolescents being influenced by ads, however, as Linn *et al.* (1982) showed.

When television commercials for foods are examined, it can be concluded that there is evidence that such advertising does influence children's knowledge and attitudes about food and that there is some evidence that the more children watch such advertising, the more they will be so affected. Since most of the food advertising to children on television is for products that are heavily loaded with added sugar and that are not very nutritious, these conclusions are important in the context of policy and public health.

There is also limited evidence that exposure to television advertising influences the values that children possess about the world. In particular, there is a 'sharpening' of social categories where the definition is heightened and the differences are clarified. The classic roles of gender with their associated stereotypes become well defined and clearly distinguished in the child who watches television advertising.

This result is not unusual and would characterize exposure to television and media in general, where characterization tends towards caricature and the brush strokes used to paint the performers are bold.

THE EFFECT OF CHILDREN'S TELEVISION ADVERTISING ON OTHER PEOPLE

The research literature on television advertising and its influence on children has a sense of direction in that there is a presumed sequence of process from attention to behaviour. So far, the processes considered have been intra-individual where the child looks and listens, understands, interprets, remembers, and thinks some more. At some stage in the process, there is a change to action. Exactly what determines, precipitates or drives this action is difficult to establish and we can approach the gulf from either end, examining the roles of affect and thought, and the determinants of preference.

The action, as social or individual behaviour, that is of ultimate interest to the advertiser, parent or child, is related to buying or obtaining and consuming the product or service advertised. Before this occurs, however, there are intermediate stages concerned with the child's role *vis-à-vis* others whether they be grown-ups or peers. A simple model that slots together commercial viewing and product selection is unworkable and, just as various intermediate stages are hypothesized between attention and decision-making, so there should be mediators between individual desires and eventual consumption. Similarly, experiments that attempt to simulate this model and expose children to different commercial viewing conditions and then measure product selection from an array, are naïve. In real life the child's eventual purchase is influenced by and influences other people. Consequently, most contemporary discussions of television advertising and children (see for example Ward *et al.*, 1986) will include discussion of the role of other family members in the decision-making process.

There are other, more practical reasons, why family processes and behaviour are of interest to the researcher. The child wants, but has a limited amount of money to buy. Many of the products advertised on television use rhetoric that is of interest to children and may be aimed solely at children but the brand price is not in the range of 'pocket-money prices'. A marketing strategy that segments the audience on the basis of age bands and aims specifically at these well-defined groups may attract few viewers whereas a more broadly-based, family advertising strategy will show increased viewing figures. The family nexus is a group decision-making arena where the child's interests and desires vie with parental norms on handling children's demands and requests as well as family budgets. Most of the research discussed below looks at the family as the social group mediating between individual preference and purchase behaviour with the emphasis largely on the mother–child relationship. It must be said that there are other social influences at work. Even within the family, father, sisters, and brothers have a role to play and should be incorporated into research on the subject.

Outside the family, children's peers and their various sub-cultures have an influence on what the flavour of the month is, and should be considered as important social influences on decision-making within the context of television advertising. For example, in Britain television advertising is part of the playground culture. Jokes are made about The Man from Del Monte. Three Weetabix and a can of Carling Black Label are culturally mediated symbols denoting special strength or power, but, as they are culturally and historically specific, they will be completely opaque to those readers who know nothing of Britain in the late 1980s. Advertisers will have scaled one of the pinnacles of social influence if some catchphrase or feature of distinction from their ad appears in the form of parody as playground graffiti. Such a social milieu is also important when considering the social antecedents of child consumer behaviour but has received little attention from researchers who are more concerned with intra-familial processes.

Children's influence on parents to purchase advertised products is discussed by Sheikh *et al.* (1974) in an early review of the research on television commercials and children. Ward and Wackman (1973), using a detailed questionnaire on 132 mothers of children aged from 5 to 12 years of age, concluded that mothers had a greater tendency to yield to the requests of older children than to those of younger children. Mothers who spent more time watching television and those who had a positive attitude towards commercials yielded more often to children's attempts to influence purchasing. Mothers saw commercials for food products relevant to children as having the strongest influence on children and mothers were most likely to yield to requests for such products.

This study employs an interview methodology where the answers to questions on children are provided by mothers. Ward, Popper, and Wackman (1977) interviewed and administered questionnaires to 615 mother–child pairs on purchase–request behaviour as part of a larger study on consumer behaviour in children (Ward, Wackman, and Wartella, 1975; 1977). These studies produce useful information on the consumer behaviour of children related to family interaction variables, but the result of most relevance here is that 'the data consistently show that television advertising as a perceived influence on children's requests has little impact on mothers' responses' (Ward, Popper, and Wackman, 1977, p. 57). In other words, mothers in general don't see advertising as particularly influencing children to ask for Frosties. For one group of mothers, however, there was an effect. Mothers were asked to rate their reaction to the child's using reference to television advertising as part of a purchase request (for example, 'The child has just seen a television commercial for a toy and asks you if he/she can have that.'). Mothers who produced a strong negative reaction to such a strategy were less likely to yield to any purchase requests. It could be said that a dislike of the assumed effect of television advertising to get children to ask parents for products means that mothers are less likely to give in to the child's purchase requests in general.

In an exploratory cross-cultural study involving a total of 300 families in the United States, Japan, and Britain (Ward et al., 1984) in which mothers kept television viewing diaries and completed questionnaires on their child-rearing and their children's behaviour, it was found that Japanese children made far fewer purchase requests than their age cohorts in Britain and the USA. Results from all three countries showed that frequency of requests by children decreases with age and that, for the British children, the more attention paid to commercials the more these products are requested by the child.

Wiman (1983) interviewed 222 children and their parents to establish how different forms of parental influence within the family affected children's responses to television advertising. He found that children whose parents see themselves as strictly controlling their child's viewing behaviour have more negative attitudes towards television advertising. Such children tend to come from a higher socio-economic level and have better-educated parents. They make fewer purchase requests to their parents and understand the purpose and nature of advertising better.

Sheikh and Moleski (1977) interviewed 144 children consisting of three groups of 6- to 7-year-olds, 8- to 9-year-olds, and 10- to 11-year-olds. They presented each child with a story which had a basic structure of a child watching a favourite television programme at home that was frequently interrupted by ads for child-related products. Children were questioned at the end on whether they would expect the child in the story to make purchase requests and what the consequence would be. This methodology presumes that the child will project his or her own circumstances into the story and that replies will reflect the child's own experience. Over two-thirds of the children thought that the parents would yield to requests.

What happens if the child receives positive information about a product from one source (the television commercial) and negative information from another (the parent)? Whose advice would they take? Prasad, Rao, and Sheikh (1978) attempted to simulate this kind of conflict in an ingenious experiment. Children watched a video of a television programme which included a toy commercial presented three times. The child's mother (who had been trained to do this without the child guessing the real point of the experiment) then either presented negative information about the product in a power-assertive way (ordering) or presented negative information in a warm and reasoning fashion (reasoning). There was also a control condition where no counter-information was provided. The measure at the end was the child's choice of a 'prize'. Of course one of the items in the range of alternatives was the brand that was advertised in the television commercial the child had watched.

The results seemed to depend on how attractive the child perceived the product to be. If the product was seen as moderately attractive then the child tended to comply with the mother's advice if this advice was presented in reasoning mode. The power-assertive method actually induced the children to choose the brand more than in the control condition, so ordering can be said to work against the mother if the product is seen as moderately attractive. When the product is perceived as highly desirable then all forms of counter-influence fail and the child tends to choose the brand advertised under any condition.

In contrast to the verbal interviews used by Ward, Wackman, and Wartella (1977), the work of Atkin (1975) goes right into the supermarket and looks at what happens there. He observed, unobtrusively, 516 family units in the process of selecting breakfast cereals. The child initiated any interaction (concerned with purchase requests) in two-thirds of the cases. Parents were twice as likely to approve than to refuse proposed purchases. Child activity that was classified as 'demand' was more successful in getting acceptance from the parent than behaviour that was categorized as 'request'. Success in obtaining the desired cereal increased over the age range and about a quarter of all interaction sequences ended in behaviour that was regarded as 'parent–child conflict'. Atkin recorded conflict in 65 per cent of the cases where the request was denied by the parent and unhappiness in 48 per cent of them. There is some tendency for conflict and unhappiness to be highest among 6- to 8-year-olds. However, Atkin noted that conflict was seldom intense or persistent and that displays of child anger or sadness were also short-lived. Thus, from the point of view of an American child in a supermarket, getting what they want will succeed if they demand rather than request, are older rather than younger, and in general is more likely to succeed than fail. If it does fail, then they may or may not be unhappy and will probably have some sort of short-lived conflict with the mother. But don't worry, you won't be sad for long.

In a supermarket observation study Galst and White (1976) found that parents yielded to 45 per cent of children's requests. A study by Stoneman and Brody (1982) also looked at behaviour by mothers and children in the supermarket after watching specially designed television programmes. The families were not aware of the real purpose behind the experiment. Eighteen families watched a television programme with children's food commercials edited in and 18 other similar families watched the programme with no commercials.

Children who were exposed to commercials made significantly more purchase requests to their mother overall and made significantly more purchase requests for advertised products. Mothers who had watched television commercials with their children used power assertion techniques, defined as saying 'no' to requests, telling the child to put the item back on the shelf or putting the item back, and also offered more alternatives in response to children's purchase requests. In Stoneman and Brody's apt phrase 'the food advertisements served to increase the vigor with which the child approached grocery shopping' (1982, p. 374). Consequently, the mother employs control and power strategies. Stoneman and Brody conclude that 'the experience of grocery shopping with their mothers was characterized by increased strife and conflict for those children who viewed food commercials prior to shopping' (1982, p. 374).

Parents seem to be perfectly aware that commercials can cause conflict, although others don't share this opinion. In an opinion survey (Culley et al., 1976) a dramatic difference was found between advertising agency executives and consumers. Whereas fewer than 10 per cent of the former thought television commercials lead to an increase in parent–child conflict, two-thirds of the latter thought they led to an increase.

In a more recent paper, Böcker (1986) discusses the influence children have on their mothers' preferences. The problem is framed within so-called opinion leadership theory in marketing research. In other words, the researcher should not just be interested in the needs, desires and behaviour of the user or consumer of the product but also in the role of other people who will sway the person who buys and uses the brand. Children have an obvious role to play here as it is not difficult to find examples of advertising where the rhetoric would appeal to the child, but where the parent is most likely to buy and the child to use. Examples would include advertising of many sugared cereals, tins of pasta-based products, as well as much of the seasonal advertising of expensive toys and games. Examples of products that appeal to children, but that the parents will buy and use more than their children would use are less obvious. The rhetoric will be utilised to appeal less to the target audience of children and more to a family-based audience. Consequently we may expect to find romanticized versions of family scenes that will appeal to all members of the family, the long-running saga of the Oxo family on British television being a good example.

Böcker's methodology is complex but in essence he was looking at mother and child preferences, both individually and jointly. Mother and child were asked, separately, to rank a list of brands. So, for example, each person would be given twenty chocolate bars and asked to rank them in order according to their preference as regards children's consumption, and using certain attributes such as the price or the ingredients. The same task was also done jointly, with the mother and child discussing the issue.

This methodology will produce numerical results that can be subjected to various statistical analyses. The results are often intuitively obvious (such as children having greater influence on their mothers for certain products such as chocolate bars and children exerting more influence on jointly decided preferences as they get older), but can also be genuinely informative (the greater the number of children living in a household, the more influence they have) even when the result is null (no evidence from this study that girls have more influence on their mothers' preference judgements than boys). It is this kind of research that is grist to the market researcher's mill as the permutation of different products with different family types is endless.

In summary, there is research evidence that children ask for food products advertised on television and that parents will often acquiesce. In addition, there is some evidence that purchase requests by children cause conflict between parent and child although this will depend on the accustomed strategies of the child and ways parents have of handling these. The methodology employed obtains opinions and reported facts from parents and children and uses methods of assessment of child-rearing style that are based on questionnaire responses and structured interviews. Much research still needs to be done in this area and this would benefit from a more intensive, clinically based approach that explored family dynamics and basic values concerning consumerism and materialism.

THE EFFECT ON CHOICE OR CONSUMPTION BEHAVIOUR

If television advertising's effect or influence on people is regarded as a series of processes that can be arranged in (approximate) order, then the end of the line is doing something. Most people would seem to see this as an important area to look at in any programme of research into television advertising. 'Does advertising actually make children eat more sugared sweets, spend too much money, buy toys they don't really need?' This is the kind of common-sense question asked of researchers and they will get short shrift if they answer that they don't really know or that 'it all depends on what you mean by ...'.

Psychologists reared in a behaviourist or functionalist tradition should be interested in behaviour and its antecedents because behaviour is observable, measurable, and suitably sound and reliable for scientists. Consequently research into the effects of advertising on choice or consumption behaviour in children should be driven by interested parties and interested researchers should be willing to tackle this work. There are some investigators who will shy away from this kind of work because they are all too aware of the pitfalls and impossibilities inherent in squeezing a complex social process into the confines of an experimental programme of research.

The gulf between attitude and behaviour, the indeterminacy of decision-making and the uncontrolled and uncontrollable mess of the social world all pose difficult and perhaps insurmountable problems. The astute researcher may prefer to tinker with processes that lie at the interface between major psychological functions. What happens between feeling and deciding, watching and remembering, interpreting and understanding? Ultimately, however, these processes are there and function to one end which is to consume the product or brand advertised. That is what interests the advertiser, health education professional and concerned parent alike. The problem cannot be evaded. It may seem at first sight that the research designed to provide answers to these questions of the influence of advertising on choice or consumption behaviour is naïve and does not simulate what goes on in the real world. Nevertheless, the work is necessary, although it can be criticized and evaluated in terms of its limited external validity.

The behavioural effects of food advertising on children

Goldberg and Gorn (for example, Goldberg and Gorn, 1979; Gorn and Goldberg, 1982) have done much important research that examined the direct behavioural effect of watching television advertising. The typical paradigm can be described as 'watching then choosing' where children are exposed to a videotape of a television programme with commercials edited in. They are required to select from a range of alternative brands or products what they would like with the brand or product advertised included in the range. One novel variation on this theme is to present children with a choice of either playing with the product or playing with friends or parents, thus obtaining a measure of the strength of product attraction. According to Comstock and Paik (1987), this technique was mentioned by Goldberg and Gorn (1977) in an unpublished paper. Goldberg *et al.* (1978) used the first paradigm of choosing from a mixed set of alternative brands and products with 80 children aged 5 to 6 years and found that short-term snack and breakfast food preferences tended to reflect their exposure experience. Children are more likely to select highly sugared foods if they have previously viewed television commercials for them and they are more likely to choose nutritious snack and breakfast foods if they have just seen pro-nutrition public service announcements.

Although it is unlikely that the experimental procedure has much ecological validity in that the results do not simulate real life, these studies can tell us something about the relative effectiveness of different stimulus presentations. For example, in the same paper, Goldberg *et al.* (1978) presented a full television programme called *Fat Albert* that conveyed the message that junk food is bad and fruit and vegetables are good. This programme used animation and comedy and starred the well-known American actor, Bill Cosby. Even when this programme contained ads for sugared foods, it was more effective at reducing the number of sugared foods selected than presenting pro-nutrition public service announcements in the context of a neutral programme.

Gorn and Goldberg (1980) were interested in the effects of repeating the same commercial to children and constructed several videotapes, some of which repeated the same commercial (a new brand of ice cream) at intervals in a half-hour cartoon programme. This procedure has better ecological validity as children in the United States would be exposed to several identical commercials for the same brand in a typical Saturday morning children's television show.

Several groups of up to 40 children between 8 and 10 years of age participated in different versions of the same basic experiment. The children were all Cub Scouts and they were shown one of the videotapes at a meeting of the group. Various measures of product preference and recognition were taken. The child's brand choice was assessed from a range of ice creams including the advertised brand and actual consumption behaviour was measured by allowing the child to eat the chosen brand and, afterwards, weighing what was left! Exposure to a television commercial for the brand influenced choice of that brand in the expected direction and there was also evidence that exposure to more than one commercial for that brand increased the probability that the brand would be chosen from the array of different brands of ice cream at the end. There was no effect on actual consumption behaviour, though. That is, with this procedure, more commercials does not mean the child eats more of the product at a single sitting.

Interestingly, there is evidence that viewing five commercials in the cartoon programme affected the child's second choice of the product they would prefer. They would much prefer ice cream than, say, bubble gum. Given that a central plank in much of the argument for advertising potentially unhealthy products is that exposure to an advertisement for that brand only increases its consumption at the expense of other brands and does not increase consumption of the generic product as a whole, then this finding could be taken as evidence against that position.

Gorn and Goldberg (1982) pursued the issue of behavioural change as a function of viewing commercials and reported on a study they had conducted with 72 children aged 5 to 8 years. This study is discussed in a conference paper (Goldberg and Gorn, 1979) but the cited source is more available to the interested reader. The study was set in a summer camp and it was possible, with the cooperation of the camp supervisors, to offer no fresh fruit or candy (sweets) to the children other than that offered experimentally as part of the afternoon snack. The children watched no television apart from the half-hour a day that was the critical part of the experimental treatment. The camp counsellors were unaware of the particular experimental treatment for each group of children and the children were unaware of the experiment, although they may have tried to make sense about why they were being asked these questions.

The study was well designed and provided complete control in the time available over such variables as amount of television viewed and brand and product consumption, factors that often vary in other studies. The basic procedure was watching then choosing a drink and a snack. The choice was between orange juice or Kool Aid and, for the snack, two out of four choices of two candy bars and two fruits.

Food choice was made in a separate room, just after viewing a videotape with commercials for either fruit or candy products. Control groups either watched a video without commercials or one with health messages about a balanced diet and limited sugar intake.

Under these well-controlled conditions, children who were exposed to orange juice commercials selected the most orange juice. Children who were exposed to candy commercials chose the most candy. Children in all conditions indicated that they knew the camp doctor wanted them to eat fruit as opposed to candy. Whether they acted upon this awareness and actually chose fruit seemed to depend on whether or not they had been exposed to commercials for candy. One condition that did not affect consumption behaviour was where the half-hour video contained the health messages. Children under this condition behaved in a similar way to children who had seen no advertisements in their videotape. Although this experiment should be regarded as a classic study of its type, the results do not simulate the complexities of deciding what to buy or what to eat in real life where the time between watching and doing is not a matter of minutes and the events occurring in between contribute to the decision-making process.

A research programme at the University of Montana (Fox et al., 1980; Jeffrey et al., 1980; Jeffrey et al., 1982) is concerned with the impact of commercials on eating behaviour. The researchers have developed a behavioural eating test which involves children selecting and eating for 8 minutes from a range of 6 pro-nutrition and 6 low-nutrition (junk food) alternatives arranged randomly on a standardized tray. The amount of the different foods consumed can then be calculated.

These studies can be seen as working at the end of the line as they are measuring as an output or dependent variable the actual behaviour that is of concern: the consumption by children, albeit in an artificial setting, of food. These measures can then be related to antecedent conditions such as the child's being exposed to different kinds of television commercials embedded in a television programme. Although this kind of functional, experimental approach does not explore any of the processes that mediate between watching and doing and does not pretend to simulate the social activities of consuming and watching ads, it is useful when evaluating different stimulus conditions of commercial types and presentations. It can also be used with very young children. Results with 4- and 5-year-olds indicated that exposure to television commercials for low-nutrition foods significantly increased caloric consumption of low-nutrition foods whereas television commercials for high-nutrition foods such as fruit and vegetables brought about only small increases in high-nutrition foods. It could be argued, however, that this was due to the greater appeal and professional quality of the persuasive commercial for low-nutrition food which constitutes the large majority of foods advertised to children. Similar results were found with 9-year-olds, demonstrating that, although the mediators of understanding and defending will be different between the two groups, the behaviours do not differ much.

Galst (1980) presented 65 children between 3½ and 7 years of age with videotapes of cartoon programmes. These were constructed with different combinations of food commercials and/or pro-nutritional public service announcements edited in. Each child selected a drink and a food from a range of snacks after viewing. The difference with this study was that children viewed and chose each day for four weeks. In addition, one condition was the presence or absence of comments from an adult after the commercial, these comments being designed to promote a pro-nutritional message.

Although there was a tendency for children to select sugared snacks in any case, Galst found that the most effective combination for reducing the children's selection of snacks with added sugar was the presentation of commercials for food products without added sugar together with pro-nutritional public service announcements with accompanying positive evaluative comments by an adult co-observer. Mere exposure to any television presentation, however, did not influence the children to select sugared snacks with greater frequency. This study is important because of the medium-term time scale used. Whereas some of the short-term 'view and choose' studies seem to demonstrate a choice that's a direct function of what the child has previously seen advertised, this medium-term piece of research would suggest that reducing sugared snack consumption requires a high level of counter-propaganda from more than one source.

In an attempt to evaluate the relative effectiveness of different kinds of appeals in ads, Cantor (1981) placed either a humorous or a serious television commercial for oranges just before a commercial for either a sweet dessert or a toy. These were embedded in a videotape of a children's programme and shown to 37 children aged from 3 to 9 years at a child care centre. The behavioural measure was an index of the frequency of choosing a fruit or sweet at lunch over a week. The results were not completely conclusive but suggested that a serious ad for good nutrition would be more effective than a humorous one, at least in the absence of an immediately subsequent counter-advertisement (the ad for the sweet dessert).

Stoneman and Brody (1981) introduced another variable into the experimental literature looking at the effects of television advertising on food choice behaviour. They ingeniously simulated peer pressure on behaviour by getting children (peers) to indicate to other children (experimental subjects) which one out of an array of foods they (the peers) preferred. The peer would stand in front of the group of experimental subjects and point to the food he or she liked on a projected slide of a selection of foods. Unknown to the experimental subjects, their peers had been told to choose a category of food (salty snacks) by the experimenter. Using a similar experimental paradigm to other researchers in this area, that is, a variety of treatment conditions followed by a food choice task, they found that the effect of peer group influence and television commercial influence was additive, that one reinforced the other if the influence was in the same direction. In other words, the strongest social influence was if the ad extolled the virtues of brand X and the peer also stated a preference for brand X. Television advertisers use this technique themselves when they employ young children in significant roles within the commercial to create peer conformity pressure on the viewer.

Scammon and Christopher (1981) reviewed nine experimental studies of the impact of television nutrition messages on children and concluded that there were different effects for different messages. Exposure to commercials for sugared products led to greater consumption of sugared products, greater preference for sugared foods, including those foods that were not advertised, and lower nutritional knowledge. Exposure to commercials for healthy foods or non-sugared foods influenced consumption by dampening any increased consumption of sugared foods. Messages combining a sugared product commercial with a disclaimer, or a sugared product commercial shown with a message recommending reduced consumption of sugar, had an intermediate impact on food choice and on nutritional knowledge. The most effective methods tested in terms of children's verbal snack selections and their nutritional knowledge used separate spot messages on nutrition. Studies that used nutrition education programmes found them to be even more effective than short spots.

One null result should be reported. Heslop and Ryans (1980) sampled 280 children in two groups: 4- to 6-year-olds, and 7- to 8-year-olds. Children viewed a videotape of a cartoon programme with television commercials inserted. Afterwards, children were taken to an area and left alone with their mother. They were told they could choose products as payment for participation in the study. Using this technique, they concluded that the effect of the advertising on behaviour was minimal. There was little relationship between brand advertised and brand selected and taken home.

Bolton (1983) was concerned about the influence of television food advertising on the child's diet. Although there is experimental evidence for an immediate, short-term effect from various studies cited above, the question of the existence of a long-term effect is still open. Bolton identified the key constructs underlying children's dietary behaviour and their relationships. For example, the extent to which the child has been exposed to food commercials, the kind of supervision and behaviour of the parents, the prevailing patterns of diet, and other child-based factors all have a role to play in influencing what the child will eat and the nutritional status of that diet. These variables were operationalized using questionnaires and diaries on diet and television viewing and a selection of households were given them to keep. The sample was made up of 262 children aged from 2 to 11 years. Using multivariate statistical analysis, Bolton found that children's exposure to television food advertising significantly increased the number of their snacks and that such viewing had a subsequent and independent effect on the child's dietary efficiency and caloric intake. The effect was small, however, and Bolton concludes that 'it is unlikely that effects of this magnitude could seriously affect their nutritional and physical well-being' (1983, p. 194).

General behavioural effects after watching

Roedder, Sternthal, and Calder (1983) were concerned about the consistency of the behaviour that follows the viewing of a commercial. For a competent adult, consistent behaviour is conceived of in the following way. A commercial may induce a favourable attitude towards a brand in that the person concerned may possess evaluatively positive affect towards the brand, hold favourable cognitions about it, and be inclined to consume or purchase the product. In other words, the three traditional components of attitude (cognitive, affective and conative) could produce subsequent behaviour. The consumer behaviour will, however, often involve selecting from a range of alternatives and for each of these there will be an associated attitude. Consistent behaviour occurs when each attitude associated with each alternative is evaluated and a reasoned decision is made. Inconsistent behaviour is where the attitude that has been induced immediately previously by watching a commercial for that brand will dominate the decision making at the expense of the previously established attitudes for other alternatives. In other words, inconsistent children are swayed and influenced by recent advertising for a product to the extent where they will choose that product even when they hold stronger and more positive attitudes for one or more of the alternatives.

The experimental paradigm used in this study involves simulating the sequence 'watch–attitude–decide'. That is, the child would watch a specially created television advertisement for a fictitious product. Measures of the attitude of the child towards that product will be taken after the viewing. These measures are often quite ingenious where, for example, the child has to pick one face out of a range varying from happy through neutral to sad in response to the question 'How much would you like [brand X]'? The child would then choose from four prizes, one of which was the fictitious brand. It had already been established before the television viewing that two of these alternatives were preferred to the fictitious brand.

The research question was: Are there age differences in prize selection and, in particular, do younger children tend to select the just-advertised brand although they expressed a preference for the other brands before viewing? The answer was positive. Nine-year-olds based their choice on an evaluation of the advertised product rather than on a comparison of the choice alternatives. Thirteen-year-olds, on the other hand, would weigh up all the alternatives before deciding on their preferred one, regardless of advertising.

It is not really possible to look at children younger than about 9 years because their processing of the advertising itself would be different. If the number of alternative prizes were reduced then the younger children became more consistent in that their behaviour was determined by their initial preference and was not influenced by the recent advertisement. In other words, young children, given a limited range of alternatives, are capable of decision making that is consistently evaluative. When the range of alternatives is increased or where they are difficult to separate in that they are equally valued, the child's abilities of comparison and evaluation can be overtaxed.

What does Roedder's result tell us about children buying or choosing a brand? The wide range of equally valued alternatives might correspond to a cluttered market place occupied with largely similar products. Perhaps a suitable comparison is with all the different kinds of sweets available at the supermarket check-out. Under these circumstances, the most likely determinant of choice will be the immediately available advertisement for a brand. This could, of course, be a representation of the most salient ad for an available brand retrieved from memory rather than the most recent television commercial or other promotion seen or heard.

Given such a cluttered market place, how best can the advertiser establish a distinctive and salient product that will produce attitude-consistent consumer behaviour in the face of immediately recent advertisements? It is possible, as Roedder *et al.* (1983, p. 347) suggest, for children to deploy decision strategies when decision making involves concepts that have an elaborate memory representation, mental objects that have complex roots in a variety of situations and experiences. Under these circumstances an established positive attitude towards that object can be maintained in behaviour over a range of contexts that include other tempting alternatives. One way of establishing a complex memory schema would be to use 'multiple addresses'. That is, rather than a brand being simply stored away under one 'index' that would be provided by the consistent context of that brand-in-ad, the brand is given various addresses in memory; contextual tags that are provided by an advertising strategy that produces a variety of different contextual associations for the brand. Such a strategy of establishing multiple addresses is by no means new and much of the history of creative advertising can be seen as an attempt to locate mundane brands in as many well-established and meaningful conceptual areas as possible. Open the box called 'sex' or 'power' or 'mother's love' and you should find brand X lurking there. The package at the check-out can then function as a cue to trigger the memory representation and subsequently influence choice decisions.

Dawson, Jeffrey, Peterson, Sommers, and Wilson (1985) were interested in the role of television commercials in influencing the ability of the child to delay gratification. Delaying gratification is waiting before acting to obtain a desired goal rather than immediately going through a 'want–act–get' sequence. Television commercials for sugared foods provide an immediate temptation to the child. How will this affect the child? Dawson *et al.* took thirty-nine 6-year-olds and showed some of them a television commercial for a breakfast cereal. A game was devised which involved the child waiting for a while and getting a preferred reward or calling an adult back at any time but getting a non-preferred reward. This game was designed to simulate delay of gratification and the measure would be the length of time the child could wait for the desired reward. It was found that in the presence of a television commercial the child would wait longer. Children with the food in front of them and no television to distract them waited a relatively short time.

Dawson *et al.* concluded that many television commercials provide distraction and that the child can generate 'fun thoughts' that help their delaying. In other words, the television commerical, although it presents a brand in an attractive and tempting light, can function by delaying gratification in that the entertainment provided by the ad can block and distract thoughts about eating! It should be noted that age could be a relevant factor here. Children aged 6 years will perceive an ad as there for entertainment whereas older ones may see it as a rhetorical device designed to promote the product. It would be useful to extend the sample to older children.

In summary, the experimental procedures used in the studies cited above do provide evidence that exposure to television commercials for particular products, notably sugared products aimed at the child market, have an immediate and short-term influence on choice behaviour. Given the limited external validity of these procedures, this does not tell us very much about how children make up their minds to pick and choose in a supermarket or shop as a consequence of having seen ads for products on television. The processes involved in the experiments are probably quite simple where increased exposure to brand X increase the response salience for choosing brand X.

Within the range of experiments themselves, however,

there are interesting differences. For example, presenting pro-nutritional messages in the format of an extended pro-gramme (Goldberg *et al.*, 1978) or reinforcing them with information from another source such as peers (Stoneman and Brody, 1982) or adults (Galst, 1980) is more effective than simply presenting a single health educational spot.

There is one area of research that would extend the range of response alternatives and provide information on the extent to which advertising influences different levels of brand and product categorization in the short-term. Brands do not exist in isolation in the mind of the child. For example, exposure to a particular brand of chocolate in-creases the response salience to that brand but may also increase it (to an unknown extent) to other associated brands, products and sub-classes of products.

We do not know how these concepts are organized into systems of categorization within the child or within groups of children, far less the principles upon which these categor-ies are organized at different ages. For example, Milky Way may have multiple addresses for one child. It is a member of the category 'snacks', it belongs to the group called 'choc-olate items' and it can be found under a large head of 'things to eat'. But does it belong to a category of 'things that children younger than me eat' or 'things that are bad for me' or 'things that are chewy'? It is vital to have answers to these questions because, as mentioned above, the extent to which generalization of increased consumption behaviour beyond the brand itself occurs is an empirical question and not one that should be left to the disputed claims of advert-isers on one hand versus health professionals on the other.

MISCELLANEOUS STUDIES

There are some studies that cannot be classified under the conventional headings laid out above, either because they use a methodology that is unique or because they are ex-ploring border areas adjacent to the main fields of research. An example of the former is a small pocket of investigation that provides an interesting and refreshing alternative methodology to the large-scale survey work that seems prevalent in so much research into advertising's effects on children. This method uses the approach known as symbolic interactionism and results are found in several papers which can be summarized together (Reid, 1979a; Reid, 1979b; Frazer and Reid, 1979; Reid and Frazer, 1980). Symbolic interactionism is an approach to the study of the child–advertiser relationship that provides an alternative to the view prevalent in the literature which sees the media (including advertising) as having an effect on children where the child is conceived as passive and the media is active. There is also a tendency in effects research to conceptualize all television as basically the same and as having a separate influence, distinct from the influence of family, peers, or social situations. This permanence extends to television advertising and the audience in general, both of which are assumed to possess continuing features over time. To a certain extent this construction of the world of television versus the world of the child versus the world of 'other influences' is determined by the metaphors and imagery of effects research which conceives the world in general as an environment of measurable variables predicting measurable dependent responses or having observable effects. Nevertheless it is a world that is very amenable to scientific experiment and measurement.

On the other hand, a fundamental tenet of symbolic interactionism is that social objects do not carry their own objective and constant meaning, but that meaning is created and confirmed through the process of interpretation, definition, and interaction with other people. Consequently, in order to understand the meaning the child has created and confirmed of particular television advertisements it is necessary to enter the child's viewing situation and attempt to understand the child's point of view. This methodology, known as participant observation, makes no pretence at scientific detachment and the observer is a party to the social interaction going on and the social outcome.

Reid and Frazer (1980) used nine family viewing groups and discussed similar cases in their papers cited above. These transcripts, although limited to very few situations and children, are interesting in that there is evidence from observing one child *in vivo* in her natural surroundings that she was capable from the age of 5 years of understanding that television commercials do not always present the realities of everyday life, and that children can display general scepticism about commercials on certain occasions. It should be noted that the child mentioned was from a family whose head was an assistant professor at the local university. One wonders if similar results would be obtained if less privileged families were sampled.

Obviously it is not possible to generalize beyond the cases quoted in these papers but it would appear likely that skills and abilities reflected in everyday conversation and interaction between child, family and television tend to emerge earlier than in the situation of an interviewer questioning a child. This type of approach, which examines the ecology of television viewing and conversations while viewing, is an exciting one and it is to be hoped that further research of this type will emerge.

Feshbach, Feshbach, and Cohen (1982) were concerned with more general issues of developing parts of the school curriculum in order to teach children about commercials. A large sample of 267 children aged 7 to 10 years was used and different training procedures were evaluated. Three 30-minute training sessions, which were standardized for this experiment, took place in school over a week. It was found that training did have an effect on the child's comprehension of television advertising and attitudes towards television advertising but had a lesser effect on choice behaviours. Training is age-dependent to the extent that only simple economic insights can be taught at younger age levels whereas more complex insights into the motivational properties of advertisements can be instilled at older age levels.

Giudicatti and Stening (1980*b*) assessed 165 Australian children, aged from 6 to 12 years, on seven dimensions of their cognitive abilities in relation to television advertisements. These were: knowledge of 'the conceptual nature of commercials'; knowledge of commercial intent; awareness of the sponsor source of commercials; awareness of the symbolic representation techniques in commercials; ability to discriminate between commercials and programmes;

perception of an audience for commercials; and ability to distinguish between the commercial message and the product advertised. No detail is given of the actual instruments used but the references cited lead one to assume that verbal questioning was used. There were differences based on socio-economic status on all these dimensions, except awareness of the symbolic representation techniques in commercials.

Assuming that children of lower socio-economic status are generally less sophisticated in their understanding of television advertising and are less capable of 'dismantling' that cultural communication into source, receiver, rhetoric, and message characteristics, then this suggests that such children are disadvantaged. The observation that children of lower socio-economic status watch more television on average than children from higher socio-economic backgrounds (Schramm *et al.*, 1961) suggests that these children are doubly disadvantaged. Not only do they watch more television and so see more commercials but they could be more susceptible to the influence of television advertising, if part of the cognitive defence against advertising is knowledge of commercials, their intent and general function.

Soldow (1985) was interested in how children understand the package that encloses or surrounds the product. Packages are important motivators at points of purchase but have not been given the same research attention as a determinant of the child's consumer behaviour as television advertising has been accorded. As research has shown, children understand television advertising very differently from adults because of the child's cognitive limitations. Would children show a similar lack of understanding of the package because of their intellectual immaturity?

Although there are many potentially confusing features of a product package, two in particular were examined in this study. Package identity refers to package size as a perceived determinant of the size of the object inside whereas package function refers to the perceived relationship between package size and consumption need. Package identity was simulated by Soldow by first showing one group of children two plastic balls of the same size. After the children had confirmed that the balls were the same size, they were told to close their eyes. One ball was then placed in a box with a Cellophane window and the other ball was put in a similar but larger box. Another group was shown only the balls visible in their boxes without having seen them out of the box. In all cases each child was asked if the balls in the boxes were the same size or different.

Soldow found that those children who were diagnosed as being in Piaget's preoperational period of thought said that the balls were different in size when the balls were in the boxes. The majority of concrete operational children in the next major stage of intellectual development said the balls in the boxes were the same size. Package function was explored experimentally by asking each child to allocate a number of small packs of cereal to three different people who liked a 'little', a 'medium' amount and a 'lot'. The child was also asked to match different-sized boxes of cereal to pictures of families with different numbers of members. A child was 'successful' if the ordinal relations between people and boxes of cereal was preserved. In other words, 'small' box went with 'small' family, 'medium' box went with 'medium'-sized family, and so on. There was a developmental trend here with older children being more successful than younger ones but there was no qualitative difference between preoperational and concrete operational children, several of the former being capable of performing on the task.

The results of these experiments confirm much of what one would predict from a knowledge of developmental psychology. For younger children, object properties such as 'size' are often inextricably wedded to the contexts in which the objects are found. Much of the cognitive work the child does during development will eventually create a world of objects that is freed from immediate perceptual and customary contexts. Younger children have difficulty in mapping the most basic properties of one collection onto another and understanding the equivalence of ordinal relations is a concrete operational achievement. Nevertheless, the findings of

Soldow are of immediate practical relevance in understanding the limitations of children in dealing with consumer matters.

For example, the astute marketer with an Easter egg or toy that is identical in all respects to its competitors' need only package the product in a partially open package display that is bigger than the other ones and the young child should go for the large box. Young children in a supermarket display setting will have difficulty relating the relative size of products to the ordinal properties of another relevant set, such as money, desire or appetite. Soldow acknowledges this and claims that 'many preoperational children are not likely to understand the functional relationship between package size and the amount of money required for purchase' (p. 66).

Macklin (forthcoming) is interested in the role of music in television commercials for children. Macklin discusses its role in processing the information within a commercial. Although music can assist message transmission by, for example, providing a means for rehearsal by humming a jingle, or by enhancing attention, it can also divert attention from the main message. This diversion can occur both in low and high involvement situations. In the former, where it is assumed that information processing is peripheral, music may provide a cue so that people can then divert their attention away from the commercial. In the latter, when it is assumed that more central information processing occurs, music can interfere with the main message. The state of theory in this area is such that either prediction, attention-getting or attention-diverting, could be made.

Macklin's basic paradigm was that the child would watch a television commercial that had been specially constructed for the experiment followed by an interview. The questions were designed to assess brand choice, attitude towards the ad (affective judgement), free recall of brand name, likelihood of asking mother to purchase brand, and understanding of brand attributes. The subjects in this first study were 75 preschool children. In a second study, the child's visual attention to the commercial was monitored by raters and by video recording and various other measures were taken. For example, feelings towards the commercial were measured with professionally drawn faces representing a range of male and female faces which depicted the emotions 'liking', 'exciting', 'understanding', 'fun', and 'funny'. Unfortunately, no statistically significant results were obtained, so the role of music in the information processing of television commercials by young children has not been established. Certainly, music does not have an obvious enhancing effect with this age group as has been commonly assumed.

This concludes the exploration of the psychological literature on the child's processing of the message in television advertising and the affective and behavioural consequences of viewing and listening. As each relevant section has its own introduction and summary, no overall summary is given beyond the general observation that many of the experimental findings are contradicted by other findings and that in some of the studies the methodology leaves a lot to be desired. Many areas in psychology and in social science are like this: the clear, tidy textbook picture is often found, under closer examination, to be imprecise, contradictory and by no means flawless. The danger in this particular field, however, is that the conclusions established are transmitted to policy makers, concerned members of the public, media pundits, health education professionals and advertisers in the textbook version. That is why this chapter and Chapter 3 have been deliberately designed to incorporate as much information from primary sources as possible, in order to give the first line of facts rather than just an interpreted summary of available findings.

5
The Analysis of Advertising:
Breaking the Code

INTRODUCTION

The analysis of advertising has many practitioners with their own methods and particular assumptions about the nature of the subject and its relationship with the cultural world. It is not one of the objectives of this chapter to review the range of analyses and nor is it claimed here that the descriptions of different methods constitute an exhaustive survey of the field. I do not intend to discuss the role of advertising in other important sectors of society such as economics and law. A general discussion of advertising as a contributory factor in the generation and maintenance of society's problems will be found in Chapter 1. It is important, however, that the reader knows something about analysing, 'reading' or 'decoding' ads in order to establish the extent of the task that the child faces when trying to figure out what a television commercial is all about. In other words, any analysis of advertising in the context of a book about children and advertising should have a certain psychological validity in that the concepts used and the processes described could reflect mental categories and processes.

It is not suggested that a model of the analysis of an advertisement should provide, without modification, a model of adult competence in the art of understanding advertising, but it should be possible to adapt the model for this purpose. In addition, the concepts used in the model should have a developmental dimension in that they can be learnt or acquired by a child. Finally, the conceptual equipment utilized in a relevant model for analysing ads should be theoretically suitable so that it fits in with other more general theories of social or physical cognition, theories of psychological development, and of advertising as communication.

In short, the model should be 'friendly' to a developmental psychologist who is interested in the child's comprehension of different varieties of communication. For example, the preferred analysis put forward at the end of this chapter borrows from theories of metaphor and a branch of linguistic theory known as pragmatics. An examination of advertising communication from a pragmatic perspective would look at the ad in its total communicative setting, taking into account the context within which it is found and the intent of the source behind it. The development of an understanding of metaphor and the child's growing understanding of the forces found in context and communicator's intent that shape interpretation are relevant both to this analysis of advertising and to the developmental psychology of understanding advertising. It is only when these two are theoretically compatible that any proper marriage between psychological description and the analysis of cultural products will succeed.

The process of analysis would appear to be driven by two distinct questions that, while not providing two mutually exclusive sets of answers, will set up fundamental and different approaches to analysis. The first is 'What's there?' and the second is 'What does it mean?'. Both questions are within the game of intellectual inquiry and subject to its rules. Hopefully the answers provided might advance our understanding of the phenomenon of advertising or uncover new and different problems that influence other lines of intellectual progress in unknown ways. They need not be questions that the average person in the street asks when watching ads on television or when flicking through a magazine. They need not be questions that lead to a model that has psychological relevance (although we would not be particularly interested in it if it had none).

The first question can lead to consideration of features of the ad that represent its content. What's there? A brand. Some people consuming or not consuming the brand. A male voice-over. A child eats some sweets. The first question can also lead to consideration of features of form. This ad is fast-paced. How fast? An index can then be computed of, for example, mean number of cuts or dissolves per second.

It could be argued that the first question can never be asked without presupposing the second one concerned with meaning, as all perception involves the construction or reproduction of aspects of social reality, and this reality, although often shared by members of a culture, is interpreted through that culture. Considerations of 'meaning' can be minimized in two ways. One is to select perceptual categories that are objective to the extent that there is little disagreement about their boundaries or definition, and second, to collect as much information as possible about what's there and avoid selectivity. In other words, choose objective categories and don't leave anything out.

For example, it should be possible to establish who did what to whom and when and with what in some television commercials in order to establish the structure of events. It should be possible to provide a description of men and women, and tables and chairs in a magazine ad that most people would agree about. If we make certain attributions about the type of people in the ad, however, cultural interpretation is involved and different meanings may be given. A working-class English viewer may see an 'upper-class man' whereas a middle-class viewer may see a middle-class man and an American may just see a high-status person.

In addition, being selective presumes that some features in the ad are more relevant than others, and this in turn presumes some implicit theory of what constitutes an ad or of what certain aspects of society or culture mean. If it is assumed that an ad has the structure of a myth and one component is missing, then one would search for the missing piece of the jigsaw in this or in other similar ads. If we see a man standing above a woman in an ad, looking down into her eyes with his hand on her shoulder, then we will select this because it fits into our understanding of the role of non-verbal symbols in gender dominance in society at large. It may never be possible to avoid this interpretive contamination of objective reality or it may be that reality involves some degree of interpretation anyway. The 'what's there' approach tries to avoid interpretation as much as possible and, in this, it has a respectable refuge in the tenets and methods of the sciences that aspire to objectivity and that place observers and viewers in the remnant category of variance attributed to error.

The 'objective' approach displays a curiosity simply about what's there and is concerned with collecting and counting. Once objective codable categories are established a representative body of examples of advertisements can be sampled and any conclusions drawn from this sample are potentially generalizable to the world of advertisements at large. The advantage of having objective codable categories through which the advertisements are filtered, one by one, in order to obtain measures of how many ads possess this feature or how many ads possess that feature is that the results are reproducible or at least the methods are replicable if, for example, another researcher wishes to sample another body of advertising in a different culture or at a different point in time. It is possible, with help from other coders and research assistants, to sample an extremely large number of advertisements in this way and to compile an extensive data base which can then be analysed.

THE MEANING OF ADVERTISEMENTS

The other kind of approach, concerned with 'what ads mean'; is often unashamedly interpretive. Why? There are at least two reasons for this interpretive enthusiasm. One is the existence of distinctive metaphors that guide discussion of meaning and the other is the extent to which advertising is immersed in and defined by the culture that created its forms. Our thoughts about meaning are constrained by these general metaphors and the object of study, the advertisement, is very definitely a cultural product.

Two important metaphors of meaning are 'deep/shallow' and 'the quest'. If meaning is to be sought for and found then it will not exist at the surface, at the level of apparent reality. Meaning lurks in the depths, where it is hidden, and we need to explore these depths, strip off the layers of meaning, unpack the nuggets of truth, decode the signal, skim off the different messages, and dig down to get at the truth. The metaphors are deliberately mixed and can be found (separated) in many of the writings by ad analysts. For example, one such analysis can be found in Leymore (1975) where one chapter outlining the theoretical study is entitled 'A spade to dig with'. The ad itself is not a neutral thing like the workings of an engine or the movements of the stars. It is a living cultural product and therefore will have different layers of meaning from the obvious to the culturally interpreted. The work required to analyse an ad in this way can be quite considerable and practitioners of this analysis often limit it to a small sample of ads or even just one (Barthes, 1977).

If meaning is conceived of as a process of exploration from shallow to deep then an extension of this vision is to place various stations at different levels in the investigation. For example, in a standard text on the subject (Dyer, 1982, p. 94) the terms denotative, connotative and ideological are used to mark three levels of ad analysis. Barthes (1977) provides a similar three-level analysis. The difference between each level would appear to be dependent on the extent to which knowledge and assumptions about the nature of the social world are relied upon to obtain an interpretation of the meaning of the ad. For example, an analysis in terms of simple events and objects that have relatively objective definitions would constitute an analysis at the denotative level. A particular world of people going about their particular business handling certain objects and occupying specific environments is represented at this level. To go beyond this and ascribe cultural meaning to the concepts will establish a different level of meaning that may be understood only by some members of that culture. The categories could change and the organization of categories may alter to provide a higher level of cultural definition. That car, this after-shave and those clothes can constitute a culturally recognized category called 'a successful, youthful life-style' by certain audiences. But we are still observing the world-in-the-ad, albeit with a carefully tuned ear and sharp eye.

There is another level of analysis where the world that is found in the ad is interpreted as part of the world. That is, ads form part of the social world and the general over-arching principles that guide the workings of that world will be found at work in the ad. These principles can consti-tute an ideology or set of beliefs concerned with the nature of the bourgeois family, the role of women in the power structures in society, or even advertising itself, and how the symbols of advertising operate to produce 'imaginary rela-tionships with real things' (Williamson, 1978, p. 74) that hides the 'real' relationships between people based on their roles in the production process. The so-called ideological level of meaning still requires a cultural interpretation, but from a different vantage point.

In the field of interpersonal communication Stiles (1986) has established different levels of meaning in utterances. Although these were designed to assist interpretation and understanding in a therapeutic context, there are some ideas that are relevant to the analysis of advertising messages.

For example, he claims that there is a distinction between the literal meaning and the 'occasion meaning' of an utter-ance. The literal meaning is timeless, although contextually interpreted. The occasion meaning is the speaker's intended meaning on a particular occasion. There are several assump-tions underlying the use of the concept of 'occasion mean-ing' which can be rephrased into a set of assumptions where the speaker is the promoter of an advertising message and the hearer is the intended audience. These are: the promoter is aware of what is being promoted; the promoter intends the audience to become aware of the content of the message; the promoter intends the audience to recognize the intent of the promoter; the promoter intends the audience to recog-nize that the promoter intends the audience to recognize the intent of the promoter. Equipped with these assumptions, the meaning dug out of the advertising message may differ considerably from a meaning established simply on the basis of the text as it is, extant.

The question of the 'meaning of meaning' in advertising

still needs to be tackled. From a common-sense point of view it would seem that the best way of understanding something or getting at the meaning of a communication is to ask the person who said it or who constructed that communication. In conventional terminology, it should be the source of the message that provides the criterion of meaning. There are several criticisms of this approach which are particularly relevant if the subject matter is advertising. The main one is that the intentions of the source are not available for inspection in the same way as the product is, the product in this case being the thirty seconds or less of complex sound, music, speech, and vision that constitute the television commercial. If the intentions of the source are not available, they have to be drawn out by asking questions and the answers, of course, may not reflect what was actually 'at the back of the creator's mind' when the ad was put together.

Creative people can be notoriously inarticulate and defensive when asked about their work, preferring to send the inquirer off to look at the work of art or creative end-result rather than permitting an interview concerning their motives. In any case, when the intentions behind the communication are made available to all they are the end product of a process just as much as the end product called the television commercial. The process is one of recall and trying to put feelings into words that can distort and transform the original motives.

The problems in taking the source as the criterion of meaning peculiar to advertising are concerned with the process of producing an advert. The eventual form of a television commercial does not stem from the inspiration of a single source; it is the result of a process where there is much discussion involving information from various sources. The wishes of the client are an important factor and it is known within the trade that certain clients are more 'conservative' than others and will rely on tried and trusted images rather than adopt novel approaches that are put up by the creative department in the agency. Market researchers have a role to play, and if consumers do not like a version of a commercial their input might influence decisions on whether to scrap or retain it. Financial considerations can also affect the commercial that is eventually made.

Asking the source of the ad what they're up to is not a good place to start when analysing the meaning of television commercials, although this is not to say that information about the source (for instance, that they function as persuaders and attention-seekers) is not used in deriving the meaning of an ad. Another place to look for the meaning could be in the receiver's experience of it. Indeed, the audience response to advertising and, in particular, its interpretation by children must be considered, and much of this book is devoted to that purpose. Whether the meaning of a cultural product is in the eye of the beholder or originates in the muse of its creator is an issue that causes much controversy, especially if the product in question is some form of 'art'. 'Art' has painters, authors and creative geniuses at work rather than craftsmen and committees producing it. And yet the cry of the public when confronted with 'art', especially if it is opaque and incomprehensible, is 'I know what I like' (and this is not it). For some members of a culture the meaning of art will lie in the mind that created it, whereas for others the meaning of art is in the interpretation.

The traditional place to start, however, when extracting meaning from commercials is in the text, or corpus, or record of what was seen. With the invention of photography and videotape, this record is freely available for inspection, storage and analysis. Before looking at examples of analyses, it is appropriate to pause and ask the question 'What's the meaning of advertising?' again and see if this question can be separated from the associated question of 'Where's the meaning of advertising?'

A DIFFERENT METAPHOR FOR MEANING

We are accustomed to thinking of the process of communication as a variation on the theme of 'pass-the-parcel' where a source with intent wraps up a message in a text which is transmitted to a receiver who understands by unwrapping or decoding the message. Reddy (1979) has named this mould that constrains our thoughts on human communication the 'conduit' metaphor. Ideas and thoughts are conceived of as objects that are contained in words and sentences. Communication then consists of finding the correct word-container for your idea-object and this filled container is sent along a conduit or through space to the hearer whose job it is to take the idea-object out of the word-container. The problem of meaning in advertising then reduces to finding out where meaning lies. It may be found in the intent of the speaker or communicator or it might be found in the text. Possibly meaning lies in the understanding created by interactions between, say, text and understanding so that a unique *Gestalt* is formed of one play with one audience in a single performance and that's the meaning.

But we need to break the mould. This can be done by conceiving of meaning as a process. A suitable metaphor to aid this conceptualization would be meaning as a quest, made more vivid and concrete (and, as it happens, more fruitful) by considering the voyage as a particular kind of quest. Unfortunately 'meaning as a voyage' tends to lurch into bathos because this particular ancient analogy dominates so much of contemporary culture, from cinema through computer games to science fiction and fantasy. So, we're navigating the ship called 'understanding' in pursuit of meaning. Meaning is the goal of this venture. It's out of sight, over the horizon at the moment, and is generally discussed in hushed or serious tones, for example, 'meaning of this (work of art)'. It can occur in the frame 'the meaning behind this (cultural product)' as if there's more than meets the eye; that meaning has to be extracted, dug out, uncovered. The voyage may end on Treasure Island, but some excavation is required once you arrive there. Meaning also involves the voyager pursuing his or her own interests in the sense that meaning can be attained in terms of the self—the meaning that is eventually attained or conceived of as attainable involves characteristics of the thing-being-understood and the understander.

The goal, and the discovery, involve a union between the object of understanding and the one who understands, and these two can be brought together in the final frame. But voyagers in search of meaning can find enough to their satisfaction before this final stage. Readings are taken at different points during the voyage. Readings can be 'first', 'deeper', and so on. Two important readings mark two identifiable stations on the voyage of understanding. One is comprehension. Comprehension is used here when a reading is based on the semantic components of the elements that constitute the thing-to-be-understood. Semantics is, in this description, an aspect of meaning that is concerned with what these elements refer to in some real world and how the elements are interrelated in some kind of hypothetical dictionary. Often these elements have been codified into texts that are, by and large, context-free and transportable between members of the culture. Traditionally, these texts are codified within a rule-system of writing and the primary chunks of this codification emerge as so-called lexical items that often correspond to words. These lexical items can be decomposed into semantic features that are combined according to another set of rules. Equipped with this analysis, it is possible to obtain a reading which can be called comprehension. 'Comprehending a text' means that a bare-bones reading of 'what happened' can be given. At this level chairs can be differentiated from tables but are analysed as similar when contrasted with love.

But 'understanding the meaning' involves much more than this. At the next major station a reading is assigned that is based on what has gone before, together with contextual considerations and considerations of what the source behind the text intended to mean. In this way, a pragmatic reading is made. Pragmatics is a branch of linguistic theory that can be roughly defined as what remains of meaning when semantics is taken out. Pragmatics will take into consideration the intent of the communicator and the context within which the communication is set. We can call this reading interpretation. So, if a commercial is being watched, an interpretation will take into account both the aims and intentions of the communicator and the setting of the commercial, within the prevailing discourse of television programmes and other commercials.

As soon as one leaves the safety of the text and searches for meaning within the context, one is in the realms of guided or informed inference. Here one interpretation is preferable to another and the preferred interpretation relies on the interpreter's accustomed modes of inference as well as on the schemata induced by contextual information. For example, one of the characteristics of British television commercials is a kind of cross-referencing where features and symbols taken from cinema are transposed into the commercial, the assumption being that these symbols have acquired a certain cultural familiarity and will be recognized and interpreted within the context of the commercial. So the immense revolving spaceship in *Close Encounters of the Third Kind* appears in ads for Maxwell House coffee (1986). In addition, fragments of the style of famous film directors like Steven Spielberg emerge, self-consciously and deliberately, in television ads. A commercial for Zanussi refrigerators (1985) uses a 'white light', over-exposed technique accompanied by a wind of energy that causes hair to be blown back to symbolize the awesome majesty of the brand, rather as Spielberg used this effect to introduce aliens from outer space, or ghosts in *Poltergeist*. Knowledge of the persuasive nature of the source behind these commercials together with contextual information on the genre of cinema is required to produce an inference that one brand being advertised (Zanussi refrigerators) has good qualities associated with modern, scientific technology, whereas the brand of coffee is being promoted in a more entertaining way.

Recognition of this cross-referencing will depend upon the depth of cultural knowledge claimed by the audience. For example, the *Observer* of 28 December 1986, under the heading 'Sex Sell' claimed that one of the 'little gems' of television ads of the past year was a 30-second commercial for Yves Saint Laurent's Opium which possessed elements of two movies: *Shanghai Express* and *The Maltese Falcon*. Presumably, people who had not seen either of these would be unable to assign that interpretation to the perfume ad.

Many less adventurous explorers would stop here and consider that a good job has been done if meaning is claimed as the prize of pragmatically-based interpretation.

Certainly linguists would claim that a full pragmatically-based reading of text-in-context is a difficult enough task to achieve especially if a map of the journey has to be explicated as well. There are further interpretations of text that depend on more knowledge and understanding contributed by the reader. Aesthetic or artistic interpretation, literary appreciation all involve a complex interplay between audience, text and context which involves an appeal to individual intuitions of 'appropriateness' or 'correctness' that cannot, if ever, be explicated and may always remain hidden and vested within the individual rather than be assigned an available cultural representation. Indeed, the best designed texts, although internally organized and positioned within the genre for optimal reading should be 'open' to the extent that the reader provides some of the interpretation from his or her own depth of aesthetic intuition and experience. A well-crafted text will provide enough material to nudge the reader towards a preferred interpretation and still be open enough to allow for individual interpretive contributions from the audience.

Understanding a commercial is a continuous process driven by a fundamental human activity called the search for meaning. It is not necessary ever to achieve this goal. Indeed there are cultural pressures to be satisfied with limited achievements since the television commercial is not high art and 'reading too much into it' is the mark of pseudo-intellectualism, a fate only marginally worse in British society than being called an intellectual. Full pursuit of meaning should be reserved for worthy objects of desire such as God, Art, or Nature. There are also pressures to stop that are based on information processing demands. The depth of inference that is required to obtain a reading that is substantially different from the previous one will influence one's decision to stop, satisfied, or to go on.

THEORIES OF MEANING IN ADVERTISING

Before developing the argument laid out above into a fuller account of a theory of meaning in advertising, it is necessary to sample what other writers have said. If we assume, and most interpreters of ads have made this assumption, that the meaning behind the ad is hidden in the depths and layers of meaning that need to be removed before the 'real' meaning is uncovered then there are two problems facing the ad decoder. An advertisement contains a lot of information which has to be dealt with by reducing it down to a summary form and, secondly, by ignoring some parts and paying attention to others.

The first problem can be called the problem of reduction and the second called the problem of selection. For example, one of Goffman's theses (Goffman, 1979) is that the gender roles men and women occupy imply a difference in power and that this can be detected symbolically in advertising. One ad may have a woman seated beside a standing man who has his hand on her shoulder. To interpret this ad it is necessary to make certain assumptions. These assumptions could be that the inequality between men and women is a general phenomenon, that this inequality is found in power and status aspects of relationships between the sexes and that it can be uncovered, in symbolic forms, in most forms of cultural expression, including advertisements. Given this 'spade to dig with', one can analyse the ad by selecting information such as how men and women are positioned on the page of a magazine, and ignoring information such as the relation between a man and his dog or how red-haired people look at black-haired people. Features such as a man looking down into a woman's eyes can be subsumed with man-with-hand-on woman's shoulder in a general category of symbols of status difference based on gender thus reducing the available information in various ads by finding equivalences.

The constraints imposed upon interpreting and selecting information or features of the advertisements can be classified into two basic types. One would appear to be based on structuralist assumptions and the other on functionalist assumptions. A structural approach would examine a sample from a well-defined universe of ads such as advertisements for toys to children. The assumptions underlying a structural approach would be that the meanings inherent in these commercials are to be found when the relations between parts of different commercials are examined. Like pieces of a jigsaw puzzle, the meaning of one component part can be defined only in relation to the other parts. A functionalist approach would examine the ad in its communicative context. That is, this piece of communication has a particular job to do, either to persuade people or maybe to catch their attention. Therefore the features of the advertisement should be isolated and identified and given meaning as a consequence of the function of the ad. For example, cigarette advertising often places the product in a healthy setting like the great outdoors with a lonesome cowboy, or waterfalls and streams. Why? In the light of the functional knowledge that advertisements are there to persuade, the presence of a healthy context becomes meaningful: it is there to act as a counterweight or antidote to the harsh reality of the product which is that cigarettes are hot and dry and smoking them is often an indoor, unhealthy activity. This need not be the only interpretation. It could be that the 'lonesome cowboy' represents freedom of spirit where governments don't intervene and tell people smoking is dangerous to one's health. The culturally based reading given to an ad by one interpreter may not be the same as another's.

A STRUCTURALIST ANALYSIS

Leymore (1975) provides an example of a structuralist approach to the analysis of advertising. Two hundred and fifty seven television commercials were sampled over a period of four years. In all, six campaigns were chosen for competing products, each product being for standardized, mass-produced, routine, repetitive and low expenditure goods. For example, transcripts of ads were made for different types of packaged foods: beef curry, chop suey, chicken curry, paella, and so on. The products resembled each other closely from the point of view of price, availability, and convenience. Thus advertising was an important factor in the consumer's differentiation of them. Out of the six campaigns four were analysed in detail. Leymore recognized and admitted that all the advertisements for one brand did not constitute a valid sample, while all the advertisements of all competitive brands did.

Structuralists, and Leymore admits to favouring this approach, make certain assumptions about the nature of the world and people's perception of it. Among these assumptions would be the following. First, the perceived world can be structured in binary oppositions of the form 'A/not-A'. Second, there are deep and universal rules that underlie individually occurring incidents or events. Third, these rules and relationships among elements can be studied as a closed whole. These three rather bare descriptions can be examined in more detail.

The binary assumption is based on a characteristic of language emphasized in an approach to linguistics often identified with de Saussure (1915). Meaning in language would appear to be based on opposition. For example in English the difference in meaning between pin and bin is based on a difference in the first speech sound of each word; whether the consonant is voiced or unvoiced. De Saussure argued that meaning emanated from the relationships between elements in language and that meaning, consequently, cannot be considered as a property of unrelated elements. The idea of binary opposition, inherent in Saussurean linguistics, was adopted by other writers in other disciplines such as anthropology (for example Lévi-Strauss, 1968) and is used by Leymore (1975) in her analysis of advertising.

The idea of deep and universal rules underlying events reflects a distinction between individual social acts by people, such as acts of talk, and a system of rules underlying that act and similar acts and independent of the individual characteristics of any user of language. De Saussure (1915) talked of *langue* (language) and *parole* (speech). Chomsky (1965) talked of competence or capabilities for language use and language interpretation versus performance or individual usages. Although these two distinctions are not exactly the same, they do reflect a fundamental difference in two levels of description of a phenomenon, one existing at the level of contextualized social action and the other at a more ideal, abstract level of rules and regularities.

Examining elements of a system and how they are related together and governed by rules can be done in two ways. It can be assumed that the best meaning is obtained only if the interrelations between elements are examined and that, at best an inadequate meaning and at worst no meaning or an invalid meaning is obtained by looking at elements in isolation. The other interpretation of the principle of wholeness is that the elements of the cultural product are like the pieces of a jigsaw puzzle and each has a significant and contributory role to play in defining meaning. Consequently the pieces themselves define the meaning; each piece makes a necessary contribution and all the pieces together make a sufficient contribution. This anticipates a structuralist analysis which is exhaustive in the sense of locating all significant elements (pieces of a jigsaw puzzle) and exclusive in the sense of looking only at those elements within the cultural product for meaning.

These three characteristics of structuralism are given to provide the reader with some of the flavour of this approach to the study of systematic processes in culture. They are by no means descriptive of the whole philosophy of structuralism but they are adequate to distinguish a structuralist orientation from, say, an orientation that emphasizes the message in the total communicative context of who communicates what to whom and when. There is also some evidence that the early optimism concerning, for example, the all-embracing nature of binary oppositions, is unjustified. For example, Leech (1974) has argued that, in the field of the semantics of natural language, opposition is not a simple binary issue of '$A/not\text{-}A$'. The contrasts implied in the pairs red/green, alive/-dead, good/bad are logically dissimilar although there is a case to be made for saying they have binary characteristics. In addition, the extent to which binary opposition pervades our ways of perceiving the world could be more limited than is assumed by structuralists. There is evidence from studies of conversation (Levinson, 1983, chapter 3) and semantics (Leech, 1974) that there is a standard form of communicative behaviour that is basic and fundamental. Deviations from this canonical or unmarked form are recognized as such and treated differently.

So, the distinction between literal and figurative usage is one where figurative usage is flagged as a deviation from the norm by saying, in sarcasm for example, the opposite of what is the case and flouting the rules of 'normal', cooperative discourse. In other words, oppositions need not be symmetrical. Nevertheless, what is important in connection with the three characteristics of structuralism described above is the effect it has on the orientation of structuralist investigation, on the ways structuralists themselves search for meaning.

An example of how Leymore (1975) sets about analysing television commercials should throw further light on the structuralist approach. The example here is a series of commercials for different brands of pre-packaged foods. Each commercial can be described briefly in the sense of 'what's happening'. For example, two children are put to bed and the parents are having a romantic dinner for two which consists of brand R. This dinner is interrupted by the children waking up and demanding attention. From this little tale can be extracted some more formal information which Leymore presents as follows:

Brand R	*Not brand R*
Romantic dinner for two	Looking after the family
Something special	The routine
A touch of Indian magic	Ordinary everyday life

The next strategy for distilling information is to look for a common theme that embraces the oppositions. This theme could be *unusual/usual*. That is, *brand R* versus *not brand R* is as *unusual* is to *usual*. The next strategy would be to put this contrast up as a hypothesis and search through other commercials to see if their structure reflects this contrast. According to Leymore (1975, pp. 76–8), this is the case in several ads in her sample. The hypothesis has been supported.

Leymore then suggests that the *unusual/usual* distinction could be elevated to one which carries more anthropological weight; that between *sacred* and *profane*. In anthropology these terms have a more general sense than in everyday English. 'Sacred' implies abnormal, special, other-worldly, royal, taboo, and sick, while 'profane' implies normal, everyday, of this world, plebeian, permitted, healthy. Supportive evidence for this contrast can be found from the first commercial where the movement of the commercial is from the child being put to bed (= profane), continuing with dinner for two with a touch of Indian magic (= sacred) and ending with the children awakening calling their parents back to profane reality.

The argument and inferences involved here demonstrate the strategy of structuralist interpretation where an initial observation of a commercial creates a hypothesis (*unusual/ usual*) which is then tested against other commercials and confirmed. The hypothesis is then adopted into a body of anthropological theory as applied to advertising-as-myth by elevating *unusual/usual* to *sacred/profane* and selectively perceiving certain features in the first commercial (the sequence of action in this case) as confirmatory of the *sacred/ profane* distinction.

This process of interpretation makes sense when considered as a process starting from some observations and a hypothesis and finishing in a summary statement (phrased in anthropological terminology) on the nature of certain commercials. If the inferences the author makes are considered in isolation, however, they appear quite ludicrous but, taken as part of an argument, they appear reasonable. For example, Leymore (1975) argues that a forkful of brand R represents Cupid's arrow (p. 78). This is reasonable in the context of the argument proposed but silly if taken in isolation.

The bipolar dimensions that can be teased out of commercials are not just restricted to *sacred/profane*. Two other dimensions, *in/out* and *eternal time/profane time* can be extracted and, as further campaigns are explored, the list is extended to include *happiness/misery*, *nature/culture* and *knowledge/ignorance*. Attempts can then be made to look at the interrelationships among these bipolar dimensions in an attempt eventually to provide an analysis of the advertising system.

This approach is useful in analysing ads to the extent that some way of reducing the data is offered that does justice to the themes in individual commercials without reducing them to simple head counts of, for example, the number of times children do or do not appear in the presence of the product. It is, however, to be regarded as just one approach to the problem of analysis. It does seem to suffer from the disadvantage that once the interpretation gets under way, and more and more commercials are brought in for examination, and more oppositions are extracted, there is no principled way of restraining the analysis apart from attempting to fit the jigsaw puzzle together. The theoretical edifice that has been created is all-important and the analysts's attention is focused on that.

The question of whether categories like sacred/profane and happiness/misery are psychologically real in any meaningful sense is not posed and the internal logic of structuralism would suggest it need not be posed. Whether the viewer of ads perceives these contrasts as relevant to the world of the brand-in-the-ad or whether these distinctions structure any cognitive representations of advertising is neither here nor there. Consequently the possibility of meshing together a developmental psychology of the comprehension of advertising with structuralism as an independent description of advertising is quite remote. What is needed is some approach that brings the analysis back to earth in the sense of looking at the commercial as part of a communication process consisting of a source with intent, a message and a receiver or audience.

A FUNCTIONALIST ANALYSIS

One way of taking the intent of the communication into account is to regard the commercial as a form of persuasive communication and to use this knowledge as a way of guiding the search for meaning in the commercial. Instead of looking for binary contrasts and producing a systematic jigsaw puzzle to put together in the manner of a structuralist, the strategy of analysis can be guided by assuming that all television commercials are designed to a rhetorical purpose. Consequently certain assumptions can be made about the object of analysis. Andren, Ericsson, Ohlsson, and

Tannsjo (1978) presented five postulates as rules of interpretation. To quote the first two:

R1 Assign to every commercial advertisement an exhortation to buy and/or use the product or service advertised.

This is called the ad-thesis and can be considered a general rule that characterises all commercial advertisements because of the intentions of the source behind the ad.

R2 Conceive every element emphasised in an advertisement as apt to function, together with some human drive, as a lever in relation to the ad-thesis, either alone or in combination with some other element(s) in the advertisement (or same series of advertisements).

R3 to R5 are guidelines for 'reading' the ad based on the principles of R1 and R2. In particular, the meanings of the words and images, and the implications in the ad are to be considered. The preferred interpretation out of the various possible different interpretations should be the one that is in accord with R1 and R2. The act of analysing an advertisement is considered as an interpretive act designed to extract a meaning beyond the immediately obvious information in the events laid out in the ad. The difference between the approach exemplified by Leymore (1975) and that of Andren *et al.* (1978) lies in the criterion used to select features worthy of interpretation. A structuralist, guided by assumptions which are largely based on beliefs about the design of culture such as its binary basis, will choose features that confirm this view and reduce down to fit in with structuralist theory of, say, mythology. For Andren *et al.* (1978), the assumptions are that different aspects of the ad are there to serve a purpose, the purpose being an appeal to buy or use. Both structuralist and functionalist are searching for meaning but the assumptions that guide the search for sense or coherence have different origins. Another consideration which is explicitly stated by Andren *et al.* is that, although their interpretations are guided by expert knowledge (which is their own), their 'interpretations ought not to be too far-fetched or complicated' and 'should be of a kind that would be acceptable to a normal reader, given that he had read the adverts as carefully as we had and been presented with our interpretations' (1978, p. 19). There is a common-sense appeal here which makes the kind of approach exemplified by Andren *et al.* an attractive one.

Andren *et al.* sampled 300 advertisements from the largest-circulating weekly and monthly magazines in the United States. Consequently, although the rhetorical devices used in those advertisements are not directly relevant to the study of television advertising to children, one of the aims of Leymore's (1975) study which is 'to construct a taxonomy that includes every form of persuasion in advertising' (p. 85) certainly is. The methods laid out, however, do not appear to be particularly reliable according to evidence provided. They quote an index of 'intersubjective reliability' (1975, p. 50) which is a measure of the extent to which the coding of a particular rhetorical device by one judge is the same as the coding by another judge and this figure is usually well below 0.8. Although judges may not agree on how to describe the rhetoric of ads, the list of devices used cover a mixed bag of techniques such as sex appeal, eye-catcher, and paradox.

In summary, Andren *et al.* (1978) attempted to characterize the rhetorical devices used in magazine advertising in the United States. This meant that the mode of analysis or the procedures they used to discover these devices employed in advertising were partly directed by an assumption about the purpose of advertising which is that advertising exists to exhort people to buy goods and services. Consequently the features in ads are there in service of that function. These features, combined with human needs, are designed to fulfil the rhetorical or persuasive goal of advertising. Contrast this with the structuralist view where the end product (the advertisement) is 'disentangled' as part of an intellectual exercise to discover the underlying structure of this particular example of contemporary mythology. Andren *et al.* seemed to be on the right track in that taking into account the purpose of the communication in the search for meaning is a necessary assumption, central to any analysis of advertising.

TOWARDS A PRAGMATIC ANALYSIS OF ADVERTISING

Pateman (1980, 1983) introduced certain concepts from linguistic theory in his analysis of advertisements, 'the speech act' being central to his discussion. Although the idea of speech acts was discussed by Austin (1962), *Speech Acts* is the title of an important book by Searle (1969) who developed a linguistic theory of speech acts in some detail. A speech act has become identified with a particular sense of the act of saying something. An example will make this clear. Suppose that a billboard displays a slogan 'Drink X's best bitter'. This exhortation is not very likely to be used nowadays as the rhetoric of advertising is much less direct than in Victorian or Edwardian times, but it is a possible situation for the purpose of example. The slogan can be examined in three ways. First, there is the propositional content of the sentence, the action referred to, the object and implicit subject with their associated senses and references. Traditionally, this aspect of a speech act has occupied the attention of linguists. Second, there is the conventional force associated with this sentence by virtue of the fact it is emblazoned on a billboard. This conventional force can be described as, for example, a request or forceful persuasion. Third, there is the effect the statement has on the audience if it is uttered, or (in this case) emblazoned on a hoarding. It is the second of these ways of looking at 'Drink X's best bitter' that is the conventional meaning of 'speech act'. How best to describe the speech act that would be involved in the example of 'Drink X's best bitter' is one of the concerns of Searle and he develops a typology of speech acts (1976) that constitute just five basic kinds of action one can perform in speaking:

1. Representatives, committing the speaker to the truth of the expressed proposition (for example, assert, conclude)
2. Directives, which are attempts by the speaker to get the addressee to do something (for example, request, question)

3. Commissives, committing the speaker to some future course of action (for example, promise, threat, offer)
4. Expressives, expressing a psychological state (for example, thinking, apologizing, welcoming)
5. Declarations, resulting in immediate changes in states of affairs within society (for example, declaring war, excommunicating)

These five categories of action performed by speaking need not be the only types of speech acts that are possible. For example Hancher (1979) reviews five of the more interesting typologies including Searle's whereas Levinson (1983, p. 240) claims that Searle's typology was not constructed systematically.

In order for these speech acts to work, a set of felicity conditions have to be satisfied. The term 'felicity condition' was originally introduced by Austin (1962) with reference to the particular class of special sentences called performatives. For example, for the sentence 'I christen this ship the *Queen Mary*' to 'work', a set of accompanying felicity conditions have to be satisfied. These include the bottle of champagne breaking on the bows, the presence of witnesses and various other conventional, institutional arrangements. The original limited idea of felicity conditions applying to performatives was extended by other writers (Austin himself included) to cover all types of utterances. These felicity conditions have been classified into four types by Searle (1969). Pateman (1980) argued that advertisements can be classified as a directive speech act in Searle's typology. In other words, they try to get the addressee to do something. Pateman also examined the felicity conditions in order that advertisements as directive speech acts work and these are as follows:

The first type of condition listed by Searle refers to propositional content. Some speech acts require particular propositional content. For example, a warning should contain information about a future event. Pateman does not mention this type of condition. The second type of condition can be called preparatory conditions. These are (1) that the advertiser and the manufacturer are the same, or that the advertiser is the agent of the manufacturer; (2) that at least one recipient of the advertising message is in a position to buy the product; (3) that the product is available for purchase; and (4) that it is not obvious to both the advertiser and the audience that the audience will perform the action implicit in the directive in any case. These preparatory conditions can be made clearer by imagining examples where each of these felicity conditions had not been met. The following came to mind but the reader might have more.

1. Examples where the advertiser and the manufacturer appear not to be the same, or the advertiser not the agent of the manufacturer would constitute 'free publicity'. Here the advertiser tries not to be seen as the agent of the producer. Promotional activities associated with tobacco provide examples where the specific colours of a brand (red and white, black) are used in settings for sports events.

2. A breach of the requirement of having at least one recipient of the advertising message in a position to buy the product would be advertising travel holidays to long-term prisoners. This would be interpreted as a cruel joke, rather than as a directive.

3. A situation where the product is not available for purchase would be an ad that tried to sell you the moon (literally). It would be predicted that, because one of the preparatory sincerity conditions had not been met, the communicative act called directive was null and void. In this case, it is likely that another intent would be sought and attributed to the source of the communication—as a parody, a fantasy, or a kind of joke.

4. It is difficult to imagine a real example of an advertising situation where it is obvious to both advertiser and audience that the audience will perform the action implicit in the directive in any case. One of the aims of an ad is to change behaviour; to consume more or consume differently, or to maintain consumer behaviour if the absence of advertisement would result in less of the behaviour or in changing direction.

The third type of condition is called the sincerity condition, where it should be apparent to the audience that, indeed, this is a directive; that someone wants them to buy it.

The fourth type is classified under essential conditions. This is where the message must standardly or typically count as an attempt to get the audience to perform the action implicit in the directive. For example, if a message shows a child smiling, biting a chocolate bar, screwing up her face, crying, and spitting out the offending morsel (in sequence), then it is unlikely that the audience would interpret this as a commercial for the chocolate bar. Because one of the essential conditions for the directive speech act has not been met, the directive speech act fails. The audience has to search for meaning; perhaps the intent was humorous, sarcastic, or ironical?

Pateman's (1980) approach looks promising as a theoretical model for advertising as a form of communication with a particular intent. The term 'speech act' can be replaced by 'communicative act' and most of the principles laid out above that are derived from linguistic argument will remain, because the principles themselves are taken from a model of language where there is a person speaking, a setting in which the utterance is produced and someone listening.

It is particularly important, from the point of view of looking at the relationship between the child and television advertising, to find out how amenable this model is to developmental considerations. The audience is interpreting a message—the message has to satisfy certain conditions for the intent to 'work'. Do children infer the same intent as adults? Do children confuse one communicative act with another for different types of advertising? Placing the analysis of advertising in this pragmatic context leads naturally to interesting problems *vis-à-vis* children and television advertising.

It should also be noted that extending the model of pragmatic communication from speech act theory to the theory of communicative acts means that certain felicity conditions become very important. The relationship between the communicative act itself and the source of the communication is important in determining the function of the communicative act. For example 'Drink X's best bitter' emblazoned on a hoarding can be categorized as a form of directive, which could be called a request or a persuasive attempt. One can imagine possible (although unlikely) situations where the same propositional content has the status of an order, if given by an officer to a recruit in the armed forces, for example. Extending from speech act theory to communicative act theory also introduces problems concerned with the meaning of images as well as the meaning of language. Although analyses of the meaning of images are in their infancy, the problem must be tackled if any sense is to be made of television commercials.

Pateman (1980) applies a branch of linguistics (speech act theory) to the analysis of ads. One of the characteristics of his approach is a description of advertising communication as being akin to a particular kind of speech act known as a directive, and then using that knowledge to assign interpretations to ads. Describing the ad is not just an anatomical exercise that labels and identifies one sub-group of media communication called 'advertising communication'. The main function of the description is to provide a set of interpretive strategies that influence any reading made. This seems to make good sense in that knowledge of the context and intent of the communciation should influence understanding and any model of the process of understanding must incorporate this knowledge in some way. It also makes good sense because this kind of model is open to considerations of developmental change. At what age do children acquire knowledge of advertising as a particular class of communication with separate characteristics? How does this affect their understanding of advertising? In the next section we shall look at the general question of the existence of advertising as a separate genre, with its own rules for interpretation.

ADVERTISEMENTS AS PARTICULAR COMMUNICATIVE ACTS

If advertising is to be considered as part of general communication, perhaps sharing some of the rules and characteristics of all human communication but also possessing some special rules for interpretation that are peculiar to advertising, then the nature of human communication must first be explored.

One influential approach to the problem of describing the fundamentals of communication between people has been guided by the writings of Grice (1975, 1978). Grice laid out what he called a cooperative principle that describes a basic tenet of cooperative conversation and which can be extended to all forms of cooperative exchange. This requires one to 'make your contribution such as is required, at the stage at which it occurs, by the accepted purpose or direction of the talk exchange in which you are engaged' (cited in Levinson, 1983, p. 101).

What does this mean? Grice puts forward several maxims that derive from this principle. They can be summarized by saying that participants in a cooperative exchange should communicate with sincerity, being relevant and clear while providing sufficient information. People, of course, often don't do this. So the power of Grice's approach lies in his prediction of what would happen if a maxim was breached.

Imagine I asked you (what I thought was) a straight, sensible, pertinent question and got back (what I thought was) an evasive, irrelevant reply. At this apparent breach of rules of canonical communicative conduct I can make one of several inferences. One could be that you are deliberately being uncooperative and do not wish to talk. Or, I could assume that the principle of cooperative communication is not being abandoned and that you are breaching the rule to some purpose. I then have to do some mental work in order to re-establish your communicative intent. Perhaps you are signalling to me that the topic is a sensitive one and should not be discussed now. Or you are trying to be sarcastic or humorous. The details of the inferences made, the extent to which these inferences are drawn and the conditions limiting them are not important in this context. What is important is that there are two stages in the process. One is a recognition of the breach of the rule, and the other consists of the details of the mental work done to reconstruct communicative intent.

Grice has already appeared sporadically in the literature on advertising. Geis (1982) has argued that an account of how the language of advertising is read should incorporate certain Gricean maxims. The example he gives is the fragment of advertising language consisting of the following exchange: 'Wet feet? Look out for a cold. Gargle with Listerine quick.' The inference which most people would draw from these sentences would be that Listerine prevents colds. This conclusion is not logically entailed by these statements. The conclusion is reached by inference, guided by one of the Gricean maxims, the maxim of relevance. By assuming that the communicator is intending that the third sentence should be relevant to the issues raised by the first two sentences, it can be concluded that Listerine prevents colds. Pateman (1980) had extended his analysis of advertising in terms of speech act theory to include Grice's ideas of conversational implicature, suggesting that not only are there assumptions of relevance and the like in interpreting bits of linguistic discourse but that features of the advertising image should be taken into account when interpreting the communicator's meaning.

Garfinkel (1983) examined television commercials for breakfast cereals and fast food restaurants and explored the implications, carried by both language and imagery, these advertisements possessed. For example, the statement 'You don't know how good it is until you eat someplace else' implies that the advertiser is claiming that his restaurant is the best restaurant. This conclusion is not directly asserted or presupposed within the sentence, however. It is reached by a reasonable process of inference based on pragmatic knowledge about how advertisers communicate, what their intent is and what the basic rules of cooperative conversation are. Another example would be the use of 'new' or maybe 'NEW!' in advertising copy. An analysis of 'new' into semantic features might produce components like 'change of state', 'end-state not recognized as having previously occurred'. A change could, of course, be a change for the worse or for the better, but the reading that is given would depend on knowledge of the context of use. That is, it would depend on pragmatic considerations. Given the cultural context in which 'new' occurred, the preferred reading might be '. . . for the better' in that some vestigial remnants of the idea that progress is inevitable are still with us. If knowledge that the source of 'new' is an advertiser is built into the interpretation, the reading will certainly be 'a change for the better' as it is unlikely that advertisers will extol the virtues of a change for the worst.

Although Grice's ideas are several decades old, they are currently enjoying something of a revival in linguistic and communication circles and the principle, maxims and kinds of inferences drawn should not be regarded as fixed and established assumptions of how communication works. For example, Leech (1983) has postulated a principle of politeness in addition to Grice's cooperative principle. Keenan (1976) has claimed that everyday discourse in a language called Malagasy does not adhere to all Grice's maxims thereby challenging the universality of these maxims. Sperber and Wilson (1986) in an influential book have argued that relevance is of central importance for inferring communicative intent and that the depth of processing involved (a concept taken from cognitive psychology) is also an important variable when communicators try and make sense.

'Gricean pragmatics' is an area where linguists, philosophers, and psychologists who are interested in interpersonal communication or cognitive or social psychology are all working. The ideas that are found there should have a bearing on a theory of the understanding of advertising. Dangers arise, however, when psychologists, linguists, and philosophers work on the same problem and these are to do with the kind of use and validity ascribed to the concepts employed by the different practitioners. Psychologists are accustomed to using concepts that have psychological validity in the sense that people can be said to be using them when thinking, feeling or acting. So, if a principle of politeness is postulated, a natural question might be, 'Are people aware of this?' or 'Can this principle be incorporated into a theory of how communications are understood in individual minds?' Linguists may not be interested in such validity and might simply be concerned whether the introduction of an extra principle provides a more elegant, parsimonious, and wide-ranging account of traditional problems in linguistics. It is important to keep these two traditions distinct in any elaboration of a theory of advertising.

Can advertising be characterized as a particular branch of communication and are there particular rules that are peculiar to advertising? For the moment this question is posed without reference to the psychological validity of such rules, whether they should be part of an account of how people process and understand advertising. Certainly it would be possible to invent some specific ad-rules that would account for some of the linguistic examples cited in the literature. A rule for reading ads that stated, 'Assume that if any problem is implied or stated in the context of an advertisement, the product advertised will solve that problem' would account for the example quoted by Geis (1982) and probably many others. A rule for comprehension that stated 'advertisers tend to exaggerate and are permitted some exaggeration' would account for Garfinkel's (1983) example. But these rules are created on an *ad hoc* basis. What is needed is a principled Gricean description of a category of communication that is similar to advertising.

May (1981) discusses the rules that would have to be established in order to permit cooperative participants in a communication to make inferences that are plausible and useful. The particular communicative situation he is concerned with is where one of the participants is 'Interested' (as opposed to 'Disinterested') in that he or she wishes to generate a preferred response in the other. The advertiser who persuades people to buy certain brands would come into this category, but other sources would also be included, such as advocates, exhorters, and pleaders in various guises. May presents certain maxims for interpreting the messages of Interested participants, one of these being the so-called 'maxim of Best Face'. This maxim requires the reader to treat the case that is put as the strongest that can be made. The type of approach exemplified by May is valuable as it places advertising with other kinds of communicative activities and establishes a firm characteristic.

It should be possible to lay out various maxims on the lines of May (1981) to account for the characteristics of communication by Interested parties. Advertising would then be placed in this category. If the maxim of Best Face is recognized more in the breach than in the observance, and that seems to be characteristic of Gricean rules, then other forms of inference occur. I am assuming now that the maxim of Best Face has some psychological validity. So, if the maxim of Best Face is violated this is recognized implicitly by the reader to the extent that other forms of inference towards an interpretation are brought into play. If an ad is expected and the maxim of Best Face is brought to bear on the situation so that the case that is put is treated as the strongest case that can be made, and it is apparent that the advertiser is understating his case, then the reader has some mental work to do.

In interpersonal communication, such as a conversation, breaches of general communicative maxims can happen often, so that a sudden irrelevant or verbose contribution does not suggest one is being uncooperative but flags a point in the dialogue where the other party has to make inferences as to one's intent. Because there is no such turn-taking between ad and audience, any breach of Best Face must occur at a point within the ad itself relative to the rest of the ad, or will occur with the ad as a whole relative to the genre. In both cases, the understatement would be deliberate. If violation of Best Face occurs within the ad then it could be argued that this is used as a stylistic device, perhaps to highlight or foreground some important part of the message. If violation of Best Face occurs for an ad relative to the genre of ads then it could be argued that the audience for this particular ad will acknowledge this breach to the extent that they will make inferences that go beyond the conventional interpretation of run-of-the-mill ads.

It is to be expected that advertisers would wish to make their own ad as distinctive as possible relative to the backdrop of other ads. Advertising is a competitive communicative business and a distinctive message is retained more effectively by an audience than a conventional one. Consequently, one would expect violation of ad-specific maxims to occur frequently. If the situation arose where rule-violation became the accustomed form then one way of accommodating this change would be to establish a separate sub-genre of ads with a separate set of maxims that specify canonical communicative behaviour for that class.

For example, I can make a case, and will make a case, that a general rule characterizing the discourse of advertising is that the topic of an ad is the brand. If we ascribe Gricean characteristics to this rule then any breach will require further inference on the part of the audience, who will spend more mental time with the ad and do more mental work on it. Advertisers, of course, would welcome this. Some years ago, cigarette advertisements where the brand was apparently missing appeared on British billboards. It was possible, however, to retrieve the brand name without too much difficulty by inferring beyond the immediately available information. One way of highlighting the product is to violate a rule concerning the communication. This violation can be at the level of communication rules in general (so non-literal or figurative representations of cigarette packets appear), or at the level of advertising communication in particular (the apparent non-appearance of brands). If all tobacco advertisers violate this rule, then, it could be argued, billboard tobacco advertising forms a sub-genre in its own right with a separate set of maxims. The presence of this sub-genre would be marked by the setting of a billboard and the Government Health Warning printed at the foot.

THE DISCOURSE OF ADVERTISING: THE INTERNAL STRUCTURE OF AN ADVERTISEMENT

Although advertising is a genre with its own rules for interpretation, it is also a form of discourse with an accustomed topic and various comments and contexts that accompany the topic. The next question to put is concerned with the kind of discourse that occurs in advertising. Kumatoridani (1982) argues that the topic of a commercial is the product. What is the 'topic' in discourse? If the term is to be applied in a general communicative context, as a constant part of all television commercials, it must be defined in a general sense and not tied to aspects of linguistic structure such as subject of a sentence.

Brown and Yule (1983, chapter 3) argue that it is indeed difficult and not possible formally to identify the topic of a bounded piece of discourse, but that sense can be made of notions like 'speaking topically' and 'the speaker's topic' within a 'topic framework'. The 'topic framework' means that both parties in, for example, a conversation have mutual expectations as to what is going to be discussed. Translating this into terms of television as discourse, we expect products when we anticipate commercials. This expectation can be regarded as a Gricean rule of the form 'when a topic is encountered in the ad, assume it is the product' because of the consequences of meeting an ad where there appears to be no identifiable product, such as the ads for cigarettes mentioned above. If the breach of the rule is recognized by the reader then additional inferences should be brought into play. The reader who is unwilling to abandon the general assumption that this really is an ad will search for the product.

It would be useful, however, before constructing more of the argument, to establish a consistent terminology. The term 'product' will be reserved for the generic category and 'brand' will refer to a specific named and packaged product that is marketed by a particular company. 'Brand' can also refer to recognized symbols or signs of the named and packaged product. A packet of Benson and Hedges cigarettes, a pack shot of a packet of Benson and Hedges cigarettes, gold colouring, or the fragments of the characteristic letters of the brand name in a poster ad are all 'brands' in this terminology. A company or political party or private utility like Hanson Trust, the Labour party, or British Rail is a brand. Although we do not buy British Rail we can buy or consume services it provides and the same is true for the other examples. The company has a metonymic relationship with its services in that the company's image stands for or represents its services. The 'product' in the example of Benson and Hedges is either cigarettes or tobacco depending on which particular hierarchy is considered. A basic rule of advertising discourse can then be established stating that 'every ad has a topic which is a brand'.

Kumatoridani then argues that the topic of an ad is found in the expression *'product* has *quality'* (1982, p. 138) which is the central theme. The ad is organized textually around this theme. 'Quality' refers to the virtues, benefits or selling points that the advertiser is extolling. There are three modifications that I would wish to make to this formulation. One is to replace 'product' with 'brand' on terminological grounds. Another is that if the genre of advertising is described using the maxim of Best Face then the accompaniment to 'product' can be neutral. Equipped with this maxim, the inference can be drawn that any description that is associated with the brand will show the brand in its best light or be the characteristic of that brand that the source behind the ad wishes to advertise to an audience.

Finally, the expression *'product* has *quality'* presumes that ads ultimately provide information about the product. Perhaps some ads do and perhaps all ads (historically) did. More recently, particularly in British advertising, there has been a tendency to advertise with the primary aim of altering the image associated with the brand. Recent advertising of large companies, for example, provides little information about their services but a lot about the mood and feel of the company's image as the image-makers conceive it. If a minimal description of the essence of advertising discourse is to be achieved then *'product* has *quality'* is unnecessarily specific. The specification now reduces to *'brand* in *context'* where *context* can be visual, musical, linguistic or a combination of all of these. *'Brand* has *quality'* is a special case of the more general *'brand* in *context'*.

Two rules that are specific to advertising discourse have been established. The first is concerned with the function of advertising and is the maxim of Best Face. 'Treat the case that is put as the strongest case that can be made.' The second is concerned with the discourse structure of advertising and is *'brand* in *context'*. The consequences of adopting this second rule will now be explored.

All objects exist in accustomed contexts. Books are found in libraries and on shelves. Cars are to be found in garages and on roads. Keys are found in locks and pockets and (all too frequently) under piles of papers on desks. Representations of objects are also found in accustomed contexts and the context can influence the interpretation. The content of banner headlines in the tabloid press can be understood only by recognizing the context in which they occur so that 'Sex Romp Dentist in Court Drama' is meaningful just because of the context in which it occurs.

Much of cognitive development can be regarded as a process of a growing understanding that objects are not wedded to their context but can be represented cognitively as independent entities possessing properties that are separate from the context of their occurrence. The marriage between context and object is an emotional one. For example, as a child I was an avid reader of those two classic British comics, *Beano* and *Dandy*. Both had regular characters such as Dennis the Menace, Biffo the Bear, and Desperate Dan and each character had its territory in one comic on a particular page in a set cartoon format with traditional box and balloon presentation. Breaking these rules was unheard of until one day when the cartoonist, in a creative frenzy, decided to put Biffo in the same story as Desperate Dan. This meant that the inhabitants of Cactusville had a new, temporary, resident for that day. This restructuring of my familiar world of comics must have overwhelmed me at the time and the memory of mixed emotions of amazement, excitement, and unease still stays with me. Readers may have had similar childhood experiences when teachers were encountered in town (did we really imagine they lived at school all the time?) or, as adults, when newsreaders were discovered to have legs.

The topic of a commercial, the brand, is embedded in three kinds of context where each context is nested in the other, hierarchically. The brand-in-the-ad is the immediate context within the ad. The ad (which contains the brand-in-the-ad) is embedded in a communicative context. For television advertising, this is the programme within which ads are found. The third context can be called non-communicative and is the physical setting itself, the viewing situation with or without other people, even the television set including the size of the screen and the presence or absence of colour in the image. Each of these contexts will act as a layer that shields the brand from the world.

Readings are filtered through each of these layers and each layer will influence the reading of an ad. Even the physical nature of the medium influences some aspects of the reading. For example, in 1988 the *Guardian* radically altered its presentation with different typeface and layout. As a regular reader, I found this alteration meant my interest, selective attention, and enjoyment of the paper changed and it took several months before 'reading the *Guardian*' was the same experience as it was before the change. The brand is swathed in layers of context and is perceived and understood through these layers. But the brand is also found stripped off, in the world, on shelves, in pockets, in homes. It is this contrast between the brand-in-the-world versus the brand-in-the-ad that will now be explored.

What is the difference between a television commercial the child will watch and the rest of television fare? One striking dissimilarity is that the television commercial shows a brand that quite possibly the child will have touched, examined or consumed, that will probably be available in local shops or supermarkets, and that is possibly on the kitchen shelves in the child's home. The television commercial is an occasion for showing the child parts of his or her familiar world. The rest of television is not. The rest of television is a 'window on the world', a world of people he or she has never met and places he or she has rarely been. The characters may be familiar in that, for example, people can identify with the social situations displayed on *Coronation Street* or *EastEnders* but the actors are not. Indeed, the excitement exhibited on actually meeting in the flesh a television personality or, from the other direction, seeing your mum, dad or next-door neighbour on the telly surely reinforces the idea that, for most people, the rest of television (not-the-commercials) is remote territory.

The television commercial as a display for brands reaches out and grasps the audience via this bond of familiarity in a way programmes cannot do. The difference lies in the context within which the brand is contained. The child does not see on television a Kindersurprise in a box in his local sweet shop or a packet of crisps in the cupboard in his own kitchen. The brand is presented in a context which, given the persuasive nature of commercial advertising, is there for a reason. What is the purpose of this context? It exists to transport the brand from a mundane, everyday context of existence to one where the advertiser thinks it will be presented in its best possible light, where the brand shows its best face.

There are many ways in which this context can be constructed. The context may evoke images that act as an antidote to some of the brand's negative connotations. The context may deliberately blur the distinction between viewers and the object of their perceptions by employing reflexive symbols like mirrors and faces looking back at the camera or by presenting visions of the viewer and his or her ideal life-style. Market researchers will investigate the characteristics of the audience not just to position the brand correctly in the market place but so that advertisers can construct a context that accurately mirrors the viewer, either his or her unconscious desires and motivations, or closely-held values and beliefs. These may have nothing to do with the consumer behaviour relative to the brand but have a lot to do with how the consumer wishes to conduct his or her social affairs in the world of goods and services.

The transition from brand-in-the-world to the brand-in-the-ad involves transforming or moving a representation of an object from one context to another. In addition, the original context of brand-in-the-world would appear to be 'real' or 'more real' than the context of brand-in-the-ad which is a more symbolic representation of reality. It is a representation that changes and distorts the reality of brand-in-the-world, that transforms it to some purpose. If we regard brand-in-the-world as literal reality then the operation of putting the brand in the ad appears to be akin to a metaphorical operation. It is not metaphor in the restricted sense of a particular trope found in language that goes with other words with strange Greek names. It is metaphor in a much more general sense of the term. What is needed now is a theory of metaphor that transcends language and that sees metaphor as a basic mental operation.

METAPHOR IN ADVERTISEMENTS

Fortunately, recent analyses of metaphor have adopted a more general vision of the scope of their enterprise. The interdisciplinary applications of metaphor in science, education and psychology have been described in a collection of articles edited by Ortony (1979) and it is characteristic of this discussion that metaphor is viewed as a general, basic operation that influences human thinking rather than as a particular figure of speech that's encountered in literature. Mac Cormac (1985) has argued that metaphor is a fundamental cognitive operation, and Mark Johnson and George Lakoff, both jointly (Lakoff and Johnson, 1980), and individually (Johnson, 1987; Lakoff, 1987), have examined the pervasiveness of metaphor as a facet of our culture and thought and developed a theory of metaphor as a general and fundamental phenomenon.

What is metaphor? Any attempt to grasp this definitional problem runs into immediate trouble because definitions or elaborations of the nature of metaphor are often themselves metaphorical. A general metaphor for metaphors might be ideas in odd places. This presumes that ideas have accustomed or canonical contexts and that recognizable changes from these standard contexts occur. There is also the assumption that ideas can be conceived of in spatial terms but this is such a pervasive metaphor (Johnson, 1987) that it can be regarded as a root metaphor of much vivid thought. 'Ideas in odd places' would apply to the ad as metaphor as follows. Brands live in accustomed corners of 'real life'. They are found on supermarket shelves, in corner shops, in fridges, and on kitchen shelves. It should be theoretically possible to obtain a normative picture of brands in the non-advertisement context by simply counting where they are to be found. We would find they led a particularly mundane existence with Smarties in kids' schoolbags beside the sandwiches and textbooks and Porsches in car parks in the snow and rain. And yet brands can be found in deliberately attractive positions 'displayed to their best advantage' within a marketing ecology, where their placement and position have been set intentionally by designers of displays or by those who organize supermarket shelves. Stalls are set out and brands are on show to potential purchasers. This shunting of the brand-in-the-world into the brand-in-the-ad is a change of context. But is it a metaphorical shift? In order to answer this, a brief examination of the nature of metaphor is in order.

Metaphor has been seen traditionally as consisting of three parts: a topic, vehicle, and relationship between the two which can be called the 'tension'. Take the sentence 'The tree wept in the wind.' Trees normally do ordinary things in wind like bend, shed leaves and make sounds like people groaning. This cognitive representation of the canonical activity of trees in windy situations can be regarded as the topic. The vehicle is the act of weeping. Placing the vehicle with the topic creates a tension which can be described in creative, aesthetic, or interpersonal terms. In the example of 'The tree wept in the wind', the tension can be regarded as consisting of all three. The weeping embraces much of the characteristic literal features of the activity of trees in windy situations and creates a restructured version of the semantics of this situation. Some users and listeners may derive aesthetic pleasure from the experience, and the sharing by user and listener can create an interpersonal bond generated by mutual participation in the same language game. The listener has to realize that a rule of language use is being broken, that trees do not weep because trees are not human and only humans should be described in literal terms as weeping. Once this breach is recognized, mental work is done and inferences are made in order to establish the meaning intended.

In addition, metaphor is used to some purpose and recognition of this purpose is also required from the listener. Two main functions of metaphor can be called the didactic and the poetic. In the former case abstract or intangible concepts are talked about in familiar or concrete terms, in order to make communication easier. So society is conceived of as an organism, economic abstractions are formulated as the movement of steam engines, human minds are like caverns and so on. Many of these metaphors are culturally and historically moulded but they have the common theme that ideas are moved from *abstract* to *concrete*. In the latter case, ideas are juxtaposed and deliberately set up in association in order to stimulate and give pleasure and to provide a fresh insight into the meaning of concepts. Both functions can co-occur in single communicative acts.

When advertising is considered, there are three shifts to be examined. One is the transposition from brand-in-the-world to brand-in-the-ad. Another is within the genre and is concerned with 'metaphorical ads' versus the rest. Finally, within the ad itself there will be odd movements against the background of that ad.

The first of these is a transition that could be characterized as from *profane* to *sacred* (using these terms in their full anthropological sense) or from *real* to *ideal* or from *mundane* to *sublime* (shading into the *ridiculous*) or from *mutton* to *lamb*. The movement is often the direct opposite of didactic metaphor. Teachers take the abstract and difficult and try to make it concrete and clear, whereas advertisers take the mundane and simple and attempt to put it in a profound place.

Second, within the genre of advertising, the use of metaphor should be considered as an intentional shift of context (within which the brand is embedded) to some purpose against an already established norm of *ideal* or *sacred* context. In other words, we expect the backcloth of advertising discourse to be slightly unreal, for families to be presented as perfect, and babies to be romanticized in ads for disposable nappies. Now, metaphor can be found in some ads where the intent would appear to be predominantly didactic whereas metaphor that is really rather poetic can be found in other ads. The distinction, however, is more difficult to make within advertising discourse although metaphorical intent can be diagnosed and a metaphorical reading given. So, for example, British television commercials for Yorkie chocolate bars (1985, 1986) used broken bridges and steel girders in a fairly loose episodic framework. The metaphor of interest is not the general ad-metaphor common to all ads but it is the use of visual metaphor within this ad. I, as representative of a particular audience, pick up contextual inappropriateness, not necessarily on the first presentation, but perhaps on the third or fourth. So I search for a metaphorical interpretation, which is that the textural quality of this brand has something in common with broken bridges and steel girders: their strength, their solidity, their 'chunkiness'. This intent would seem to be more didactic than poetic whereas ads for Cadbury's Flake, for example use metaphors that are more poetic in intent than didactic. The imagery of escape, sexuality, and sensuality seems designed to achieve that end.

The third kind of metaphorical shift found in advertising is within the ad itself when parts are perceived to be placed in a non-standard setting, when some breach of a communicative rule is recognized, and when some purpose is predicted. For example, a woman speaks with a man's voice or a child sings with a deep voice or grammatical or semantic rules are broken in speech. It is perhaps stretching the traditional notion of metaphor to include these as metaphorical shifts within the ad but they possess some of the features of metaphor. First, a communicative rule has been breached and this is recognized by the viewer. The rule may be operative at various different levels of communication and need not be restricted to the deliberate flouting of restrictions on permissible semantic combinations as in the example of 'The tree wept in the wind'. Second, an intent or purpose lies behind the shift. In this case the effect is known in linguistics as 'foregrounding' (see Van Peer, 1986) where the breach of rules or communicative anomaly is designed to make that part of the text stand out as a figure against a ground of more conventional ordinary text. The goal of foregrounding as a communicative device in advertising must be to increase memorability and to grab the attention of the viewer.

In summary, a version of advertising as metaphor has been proposed. Three kinds of metaphorical operation can be found in advertising. The first is common to all ads and seeks to elevate the ordinary brand-in-the-world to the extraordinary brand-in-the-ad. The direction of this meta-phorical shift is the reverse of the customary didactic direction of *abstract* to *concrete* found in explanatory discourse. The second is found in some ads where the context of the ad functions metaphorically in service of the brand. This can be didactic or poetic. Finally, foregrounding, which can be considered a form of metaphor if the definition of metaphor is suitably wide, can occur within an ad. Foregrounding is essentially an attention-getting device.

That concludes this theoretical chapter on the nature of advertising and advertisements. In the next chapter the question of what children watch will be raised. Although much of the American work on advertising to children does not employ interpretive categories of analysis but looks at simple, objective categories of content, the British analysis does attempt to dig down a little and to use a model for interpreting advertisements.

6

What Children Watch: American and British Television Advertising Compared

INTRODUCTION

What children watch on television is an important question
to ask in the context of television advertising and children.
Answers to the question of the incidence and content of
television advertising to children will be found in this chapter. Another question is concerned with how many children
watch at different times, but this is more difficult to answer.
It is certainly possible to obtain data from a selected sample
of households on whether the television set is on or off and
to find out which channel the set is tuned to. This kind of
data provides limited information. If a television set is
switched on and tuned to BBC1, specially fitted detectors
can transmit the information down the telephone lines to a
computer that can automatically register the information. If
there are no technical faults, the information obtained will
be accurate and the measures reliable. Researchers, however, have to rely on human viewers to obtain further data.
They can be given remote control handsets to press when
they're watching and the data can be recorded and electron-
ically coded and transmitted. Researchers can ask a sample
of households to complete questionnaires on who watches
what and when, how much they like what they see and
what jobs they do, how old they are, and so on, but this
information ultimately relies on the statements of individuals and will incorporate any errors they make. All this
information can be stored, analysed, and sold to interested
parties who are concerned with viewing figures in order to
sell goods and services.

One of the selling points of television as an advertising
medium (as opposed to magazines and billboards, for ex-

ample) is that it is possible to specify in detail the audience that will be watching at a particular time. Advertisers can buy time for their clients at particular points in the day when they know what kind of audience will probably be watching. What they don't know is what the audience is actually doing when the television set is on. Research in the United States has attempted to answer this question by installing video cameras in the home in order to record the behaviour of the family while viewing.

In the most extensive study (Anderson *et al.*, 1985) more than 100 families were observed in this way. Parents kept viewing diaries of their 5-year-old children and were asked questions about each child's viewing habits. The main result of interest is concerned with the validity of viewing diaries. The video record can provide a bottom line of what actually happened against which the diary records can be validated. This visual record was analysed in two ways: the presence of the child in the viewing room gave a criterion for time spent with television and 'whether or not each person was visually oriented toward the TV' (Anderson *et al.*, 1985, p. 1349) was used as a measure of visual attention. Viewing diaries kept by parents provided a valid measure of time spent with television by 5-year-olds but other measures did not.

For example, asking the parent to estimate how long the child watched television in a typical week produced a significant overestimate. When the video record was examined it was found that visual attention to television was present on average for about two-thirds of the time the child was in the room. There were extensive individual differences, however. Anderson *et al.* (1985, p. 1356) cite the example of one child who on the criterion of time spent in the room was a 'heavy viewer'. He spent almost 40 hours a week with television. This is the measure that would also be obtained with diary studies. The video record showed that he spent only 3.4 hours a week looking at television and on that basis he would be ranked among the lightest viewers. Collett in Britain (cited in Root, 1986) used a video camera built into the television set to investigate what happens in the room when the television is on. He has compiled video records that illustrate a wide range of non-viewing activity.

The question of viewing and who watches what is one that bridges the divide between television content and audience. The critical word is 'view' and whether this can be described simply in terms of the availability of television (the box is on and showing a particular programme), and the availability of audience (people in the room), or whether some more dynamic definition of the viewing relationship between audience and television is needed, such as a measure of attention. To return to the question of 'what's on', the next section will examine the research in the United States on what children watch.

AMERICAN RESEARCH ON THE CONTENT OF CHILDREN'S TELEVISION COMMERCIALS

The literature on the content of children's television commercials is not extensive, and this is to be expected in such a specialized area, but it is adequate, at least for the United States. That work has been done in this field is not surprising given the policy interests that surround the issue.

Early research in this area was conducted by Barcus (1971a,b) and Cuozzo (1971). Barcus's work was collected and published in a more available format and will be looked at later. Cuozzo's research consisted of an unpublished MA thesis cited by Winick, Williamson, Chuzmir, and Winick, who claimed (1973, ch. 2 n. 18) that Cuozzo had found that 99 per cent of televised food commercials in the USA emphasized 'sensory pleasure', that about one-third of those commercials was addressed to children, that sugar was the food promoted in 25 per cent of the cases, and that snacks made up the content of nearly half the messages. Choate (1972) reiterated the original findings of Cuozzo (1971), stressing that the content of television advertising of food products to children provided a menu no nutritionist would recommend. At the time he wrote, children's programmes in the United States were interrupted on average twenty times an hour for advertisements. Half of these ads were for edible products and nine out of ten of these promoted the products on the basis of their sugared, sweetened, or 'crisped', (fried) qualities. Gussow (1972, 1973) monitored 388 networked children's television commercials in the United States and found that 82 per cent were for ingestible items like food, drink, candy (sweets), gum (chewing-gum), or vitamin pills. She reckoned that these figures were an under-estimation as they omitted local spot announcements which were heavily weighted towards food. Of these commercials, almost 40 per cent were for cereals.

Winick *et al.* (1973) produced the first book-length study on the content of children's television commercials in the USA. Unlike in previous studies, the incidence of television commercials was not recorded directly off the air. Instead, the authors wrote to advertising agencies to collect copies of commercials of products marketed to children, excluding toys. A total of 236 commercials was included for study this way. Of these, only 15 were classified as miscellaneous. The remainder were for food or food-related products/services (such as restaurants and vitamins) (Winick *et al.*, 1973, table 4.1). The instrument used to code the content of commercials was extremely comprehensive. One hundred and forty-five dimensions were used and each was rated on a four-point scale (none/some/much/very much). For example, under the heading 'Sales Persuasion Techniques' there is a coding dimension called 'Fun Food/Fun Notion'. This is defined as referring '... to a copy reference specifically associating the product with fun, joy, happiness, or pleasure. The dimension also refers to an audio or video representation of fun, joy, happiness, or pleasure that stems from the use of the product. A general fun context would not in itself be sufficient for coding' (Winick *et al.*, 1973, appendix A). A coder would then rate a commercial on this dimension using a number from one to four depending on how intensely that dimension was used in the coder's opinion. The reliability of coders was acceptable by social science standards, a correlation of 0.9 being quoted.

When the commercials for food products to children were studied, it was found that 81 per cent made no reference to sweetness. This statistic should be interpreted with caution, however, as there are certain products (like sweets) which are inherently likely to be sweet and no specific reference would be made to sweetness in the commercial because there is no need to. Reference to sweetness would provide no new information. Reference to physical or oral characteristics, such as crunchiness or smoothness, are found in about one-third of the commercials. The lack of such reference in the majority of commercials is explained by the authors as a consequence of the well-known market research finding that children up to pre-adolescence tend to reject products that have 'bits' in them, coconut and nut chocolate bars, for example.

Eighty-five per cent of the commercials established no relationship between good eating habits and health. Sixty per cent of the commercials emphasized taste and flavour as a selling point. Forty-three per cent associated the product with fun, joy, happiness, or pleasure. Forty-five per cent of the messages employed what the authors call a 'comparative claim'. This occurs when any comparison, not necessarily competitive, is made. For example, the claim that 'chocolate melts in your mouth, not in your hand' is comparative; so is 'No other chocolate tastes quite like it'. Nineteen per cent of commercials made claims of superiority by means of audio or video representation of the superiority of the product or attribute over anything else (for example, use of the word 'best'). Forty-four per cent of commercials used cartoon or fantasy characters as spokespersons, and in 56 per cent of the commercials such characters appeared. Sixty-one per cent of commercials employed fantasy and 59 per cent employed humour. Animation was used in 46 per cent but the use of this technique varied depending on the product. Ninety-one per cent of crunchy snacks, for example, employed animation 'very much'. The language of commercials for children is interesting because only 4 per cent used language which was classified as 'coaxing or prodding', where such language is defined as 'of an imploring, teasing, or persistently provoking nature'. Winick et al. (1973) suggested that the language of commercials is similar to that of fairy tales, and this would appear to apply to many child-directed ads both in terms of language and of setting.

The results cited above suggest that about half of the ads

directed at children involved an unreal context in the sense the product is situated in a cartoon format or associated with cartoon and fantasy characters. Winick *et al.* (1973) attempted to make sense of the vast matrix of data on 236 observations (commercials) of 143 variables (content dimensions) by using the technique of factor analysis. This method would enable the analyst to obtain an indication of which variables 'went with' other variables. A first factor that could be called 'animated/cartoon/fantasy' was extracted. Variables such as the presence of animation as a technique, the presence of fantasy, and the use of animals with added human qualities loaded highly on this factor. Interestingly, 'sweetness' is a variable that loads significantly on this factor, suggesting that those ads that emphasize sweetness tend to use animation and fantasy as techniques.

Winick *et al.*'s (1973) study is extremely comprehensive but the data produced are somewhat indigestible apart from the fantasy/animated cartoon findings, and the few others cited above. It can be considered as providing an extensive data base on the content of advertising to children in the United States at that time, although it must be recognized that Winick's sampling procedure was not 'off-the-air', but rather taken from advertisers. This may limit the validity of the analysis with respect to the child's viewing pattern.

Atkin and Heald (1977) monitored all Saturday morning advertising broadcast on all three United States networks on a pair of comparable days in November 1972 and 1973. Saturday morning had been viewed by broadcasters and advertisers as a time when the child audience was available and could be entertained and sold to. The journalistic phrase, 'kid-vid ghetto', was coined at that time to describe the extent to which advertisers aimed at children on Saturday mornings. Foods comprised 48 per cent of all ads in 1972, and 32 per cent in 1973, the remainder being mainly toys. About half of these food ads were for cereals. All statistics were based on the incident of an advertisement as the unit rather than considering the repetition of a commercial as not contributing to the analysis. So, a version of an ad that was presented three times was counted three times in the analysis, while a single presentation was tabulated once only. Sixty-two per cent of the food commercials used some animation, either totally animated as a cartoon, or mixed with live-action film, whereas 99 per cent of the toy ads used live-action film only. Toy ads also tended to be serious (71 per cent), whereas 92 per cent of the food ads contained some humour. Food ads promoted the product almost exclusively for its fun quality (for example, fun to eat). Ninety-four per cent emphasized this, whereas the corresponding figure for toy ads was 43 per cent. Reference to sweetness, such as a sugary or sweet taste, occurred in 21 per cent of the food ads sampled. Toy products were almost always illustrated in use, either as a photograph of the real product or a portrayal of it. Food products are almost always shown being consumed. Food commercials generally show the characters as highly satisfied with the product.

Doolittle and Pepper (1975) selected one Saturday morning in February 1974 and analysed all network television commercials broadcast then. Sixty separate commercials were logged in 162 separate incidents. It is possible to define an index called the commercial type-token ratio (CTTR), which is the number of different commercials (types) divided by the number of commercial incidents recorded (tokens). The CTTR is a useful metric to estimate the repetitiveness of commercials over time. The CTTR for Doolittle and Pepper's study was 0.37, and a similar study by Barcus and Wolkin (1977) yielded a CTTR of 0.34. Eighty-two per cent of these commercials were analysed using a coding instrument with 28 variables. A statistical analysis yielded five key variables consisting of: product category; minority group membership; general perspective of commercials' presentation (fantasy versus reality); sex (in terms of product use, dominance of presentation and authority figures); and character presence (whether child, teen, or adult in a major or minor role). Reliability of coding was calculated as 94 per cent agreement between raters. The results tend to confirm the earlier findings of Winick *et al.* (1973), thus extending the validity of Winick's (1973) large-scale research to off-the-air samples.

Barcus is probably the most important figure in this small literature dealing with the content of television advertising to children in the United States. A useful summary of his findings will be found in Barcus (1980), while prime sources would be parts of Barcus and Wolkin (1977), and Barcus and McLaughlin (1978). There are earlier studies cited in these later sources. Barcus sampled both weekend television (Saturdays and Sunday mornings), and television during the after-school period when children constituted a significant percentage of the viewing audience. The first study (Barcus, 1971b) sampled television commercials in June 1971 when it was found that, on average, 20 per cent of programme time on Saturday morning was devoted to commercial material, with some stations using 25 per cent of the time for such material. By October 1977 the network-affiliated stations had reduced this figure to 14 per cent for children's television. In the most recent study (Barcus and McLaughlin, 1978), 33 hours of children's programming in Boston, Massachusetts, in 1978 were recorded on video. National and independent networks were both sampled on Saturday mornings and early weekday mornings and afternoons. A total of 495 commercials were broadcast, averaging 19 per cent of total broadcast time. Food products constituted 58 per cent of these. The CTTR ratio was 0.28. This is lower than in previous studies, suggesting that more repetition of the same food commercial occurred than for all commercials. Fifty other different commercials sampled in October 1977 and discussed in Barcus (1978) were added, and the final data base consisted of 133 television commercials for food products to children. All these were different from each other, and statistics are based on type of commercial as the unit rather than on the incident of advertising as the unit (in contrast to Atkin and Heald, 1977). The reliability of coding was established as varying between 80 per cent and 96 per cent agreement between coders. More than half the food products advertised fell into three categories: sugared cereals (24 per cent), candy bars and packaged candies (sweets) (21 per cent), and cakes and cookies (biscuits) (10 per cent). Many food products were never advertised. These included fruits, fruit juices, vegetables, meats, bread, and dairy products.

Barcus and McLaughlin (1978) calculated sugared foods as a percentage of all foods advertised for all Barcus's studies. One-third of all children's television advertising is for sugared food products, food products comprising half of all television advertising for children. When these commercials for children were analysed it was found that some animation was used in 41 per cent and that 47 per cent of the characters in these were engaged in leisure activities (as opposed to work, daily living, adventure, and indeterminable, nonsensical activities). Most advertising tries to associate a product with pleasant or valued activities, and foods are no exception. Seventy-one per cent of commercials associated the product with 'fun, happiness', the most frequent categories being 'energy or sporting ability' (26 per cent), 'adventure' (21 per cent) and 'nature' (20 per cent). Only 7 per cent were coded as using popularity or peer status as a visual association although Barcus and McLaughlin state this coding was made only where the inference was fairly obvious. They calculated that 57 per cent of food commercials employ 'fantasy situations, settings or characterizations' (1978, p. 24), and that these were often used as attention-getting devices. Advertisers frequently make a variety of verbal claims about products and their benefits, and assertions were found in 30 per cent of the food ads studied. There are statements in the ad, however, which refer to some qualities of the product (for example, 'tastes great', 'is new'), and which are often opinion statements and difficult to verify. These were present in 87 per cent of the ads. The most common attributed quality was taste or flavour, in 82 per cent of the ads studied, with novelty second at 11 per cent. Another category of attribution is the physical property of the product (excluding ingredients). This occurred in 71 per cent of the ads studied. The three most frequent types of reference were to the 'texture' (for example, crispy, crunchy, thick, creamy) in 41 per cent; the size, weight, or quantity of the product ('enough to share', 'you get lots') in 20 per cent, and the shape or form ('they're round') in 16 per cent.

The picture in America that emerges from the literature is one of children's programming and advertising found at a particular time within the schedules, a 'kid-vid ghetto' that predominates on Saturday mornings. As well as knowing where to go to find advertising to children in the States, one knows what to expect. About half the ads will be for some form of food and about two-thirds of these will be for foods with added sugar. The content of these ads is less predictable but they possess certain characteristics. Food is fun, fantasy, and sensuality with taste, texture, and shape as the qualities advertised. The next question will be: What is the British scene like?

THE BRITISH STUDY

The author's study reported below on the incidence and content of television advertising to children in Britain was funded at the University of Salford from 1983 to 1985 by what was then the Health Education Council (HEC), now the Health Education Authority. The HEC was concerned with the extent to which sugar-related products were being advertised on television to children and wanted some basic information on how much was being shown as well as some idea of the rhetorical devices used to promote these products. The main public health issue addressed by this work was related to dental caries in children. Dental caries is a multi-factorial disease in that there are several factors that contribute to this problem.

One factor, which can be changed, is the intake of sucrose, usually in the form of sugar added to foods. Many of these are marketed as snacks, and snacking (the intermittent intake of food, with smaller periods of time between one snack and the next than there would be between one meal and the next) with foods loaded with sugar is a very effective route to dental caries. Consequently this British study was primarily concerned with the advertising of sugared foods.

Two methods were used to obtain an assessment of what television advertising was being shown to children. One was quantitative in that some of the available records of commercial spots broadcast in the UK were analysed. This analysis provided breadth, but no information on the content of television advertising apart from the brand advertised. Consequently, a video record of broadcast television commercials was made and the sample was analysed in some detail. This second methodology is qualitative in its approach and complements the statistical analyses of 'what's on'. A picture of what children see in the way of commercials can be compiled from data produced by the Broadcasters' Audience Research Board (BARB) and various published summaries (Smith *et al.*, 1983; Saatchi and Saatchi Compton, 1985; Wober, 1986). Data from BARB provided a complete log of commercials shown in different ITV areas of Britain as well as a percentage index, called TVR (television rating), of the size of the viewing audience, and the published summaries gave an indication of when children watch television. TVR stands for television rating and gives the percentage of the total viewing audience watching a particular channel at a particular time. It is possible from this information to obtain a first picture of the television commercials children watch.

The child market in Britain, in the sense of children buying products rather than putting pressure on parents or others to buy, is worth about £560m a year calculated on the total disposable income of 7- to 12-year-olds (Smith *et al.*, 1983). About 20 per cent of the television viewing population are children and about 8 per cent of broadcast time across the four channels is devoted to what can be categorized as 'children's programming'. Men watch about 21 hours of television a week and women about 24. Girls and boys watch about 16 hours. The highest viewing figures for children, however, are not necessarily of children's programmes.

The patterns of television viewing by adults and children are analysed in detail by Smith *et al.* from BARB tapes. During weekdays the heaviest viewing times for children are late afternoon and early evening. The percentage of child viewers climbs steeply from 4 p.m. and does not fall below a TVR of 30 until 9 p.m. There is a dip between 6 p.m. and 7 p.m., and two peaks at 5.15 p.m. to 5.30 p.m. and 7.30

p.m. to 8 p.m. Another important period of child viewing can be defined as when the proportion of child viewers exceeds that of adult viewers. This occurs from 4 p.m. to 5.45 p.m. and would correspond to the time when the child settles down after school to watch television, until perhaps the rest of the family watches the news. Applying these criteria of absolute number of child viewers and relative proportion of child viewers to Saturday evening viewing it has been found by Smith *et al.* (1983) that the highest child TVR is again obtained in the evening, the rating not falling below 30 between 5.15 p.m. and 9 p.m. In terms of 'demographic purity', however, Saturday morning attracts a relatively larger percentage of child viewers than adults in the proportion of about 3 to 1. On Sundays, adults constitute the majority of viewers after midday. Before midday the viewing audience is negligible. The TVR for children rises above 30 between 7.15 p.m. and 9 p.m. on Sunday evening.

These analyses must be considered when the question of the incidence of television advertising to children in Britain is put. The author decided to videotape television commercials off the air in late afternoon on weekdays and on Saturday mornings. The British evidence was that these were the periods when the child audience was greater than the adult audience and American precedent also favoured these times. This was done, with some days omitted, over a period of seven weeks covering October and November 1983. All recordings were made from Granada television which covers the North West transmission area. By late November the presence of pre-Christmas advertising to children was distorting the profile with an emphasis on toys and other Christmas gifts. Recording resumed in early January 1984.

As was stated above, the question that motivated this British research was concerned with the advertising of sugar-related products to children. A sample of 'child advertising' was taken during the times of recording when the child audience predominated and when programmes directed to children were scheduled. A sample of ads for sugared products was required next. This sub-sample of commercials of 'sugar-related products to children' would be found at the intersection of these two dimensions. A sample of ads for sugared products was obtained by videorecording television commercials one full day a week over seven weeks, sampling a different day each week. A 'staggered week' was thus sampled, again only on Granada, from January to March 1984. The final data base was a full log of every commercial shown on Granada on 47 days in 1983 and 1984, with a videorecord of some commercials shown on each of these days.

Quantitative results

The log of commercials included the product name. From this information it was possible to code whether it was a food product and if it contained sugar. These categories were defined as follows. A food product was 'any article used for food or drink by humans, including chewing gum', a definition used by Kaufman (1980). As the interest in sugared products was from the point of view of their potential cariogenicity, it was decided that any product with a sugar content greater than 10 per cent as listed in Paul and Southgate (1978) would be included. It was found that from a total of over 11,500 commercials, almost 32 per cent were for food products and almost 27 per cent of these were for sugared products. This was calculated where each commercial incident is coded as an event. It can be said that about one-third of the time devoted to commercials in the North-West of England was spent on the advertising of food. Just over a quarter of that time was allocated to sugared foods.

The next stage was to obtain separate figures for the 'child sectors' of the week. Child viewers in the UK predominate on weekday afternoons between 4 p.m. and 5.45 p.m. and on Saturday mornings until 1.15 p.m. in the afternoon. The programming on Granada over the winter of 1983–4 when the commercials were videorecorded confirmed this pattern. On weekdays, an afternoon 'soap' would finish at 4 p.m., to be followed by a block of programmes advertised as *Children's ITV*, followed by a quiz programme for older children until the evening news at 5.45 p.m. On Saturdays, a children's programme (*Data Run*) would begin at 8.40 a.m.

and be followed by children's programming, including the very popular *Saturday Show*, until afternoon sports schedules started at 12.15 p.m. These programmes would be interspersed with commercials occurring in blocks of a few spots up to 6 or 7 at intervals, varying from 10 minutes to 30 minutes apart.

It was decided to sample all ads from the 47 days that lay within the following times: on weekdays from and including the block of commercials immediately preceding the 4 p.m. children's programmes up to and including the last block preceding the 5.45 p.m. news on ITV; and on Saturdays from and including the block immediately preceding children's programmes at 8.40 a.m. up until and including the last block preceding the 12.15 p.m. sports programme on ITV. No ads were videotaped on Sundays because the main ITV channel did not show any on Sunday mornings after the breakfast show. This procedure can be regarded as relating to children's advertising on two criteria: on the grounds of the dominant viewing audience being children, and of the advertising being adjacent to or being inserted in programmes designed to appeal to children. There is no way of knowing whether the rhetoric of the advertising is appealing to children from the product log information alone. Out of the 1,750 ads so sampled, 33 per cent were for food products and 34 per cent of the 573 food product commercials were for sugared foods (within the definitions quoted above for such categories).

This is not directly comparable to the Barcus and McLaughlin (1978) US data, because they based their statistics on a sample of commercials that were not duplicated, but even so the British figures do not show such a preponderance of sugared food products. The difference between television advertising in Britain and in the United States could be a consequence of the definition of 'children's advertising'. There may not be such an identifiable flood of products on British commercial television, designed for consumption by the child, and aimed at the child market, occurring at identifiable times at weekends and weekday afternoons.

It should be possible to identify, from the log-based

information available, which products are for children and which are not. It soon became clear from a cursory examination of the commercials that lay within the boundaries of 'children's television' as defined above, that it was easy to identify products that were of no interest to children, for example double-glazing, perfumes, and washing machines. Consequently it was decided to code and count products that were unsuited to children but that lay in the time periods defined. Although double-glazing and the like can be categorized as not for children there are some products which, although children would not buy them with their pocket money, may be attractive to them and which they may persuade parents to purchase. Cereals are an obvious example and these products were not regarded as unsuitable child products. The product was categorized as definitely not for children if there was evidence that children would have no interest in using the goods or services advertised, either directly, or indirectly by wanting them in the household. So cooking oil fell on the unsuitable side of the dividing line, whereas soups were considered as of potential interest to children. Although cooking oil is consumed by children it is not of interest to children.

The coding was considered unreliable to the extent that some judgement had to be exercised in certain cases as to whether a product was or was not a child product. Because products were coded on the criterion of 'products inappropriate to children' and the ones that did not pass this test were taken to be possibly suitable child products, the size of the inappropriate child product category is probably an underestimate. Forty-eight per cent of the commercials broadcast in the afternoon children's television period were classified as advertising products not of interest to children.

A closer examination of the log data revealed that much of the content of the boundary slots (those at the beginning and the end of the afternoon's children's television period as defined above) contained adult products. Nevertheless, within the children's television period, excluding the boundary slots, a significant number of non-child products were advertised.

It was decided to sample the products advertised on

TABLE 6.1.   *Product categorization of content of children's commercials on Saturday mornings in 1983 and 1984*

Dates	Products advertised (no. of occurrences)				
	Total	Adult	Toys*	Food†	Misc.‡
9 Apr. 83	40	5	26	5	4
9 July 83	38	13	5	13	7
3 Sept. 83	39	12	4	16	7
8 Oct. 83	53	6	39	4	4
15 Oct. 83	54	9	40	4	1
22 Oct. 83	54	6	37	8	3
29 Oct. 83	48	0	38	9	1
5 Nov. 83	55	5	37	9	4
12 Nov. 83	54	4	42	7	1
19 Nov. 83	49	2	39	7	1
26 Nov. 83	48	5	37	4	2
3 Mar. 84	42	13	11	12	6
31 Mar. 84	47	15	14	16	2
TOTAL (%)	100	15	60	18	7

* Includes comics.
† Includes drinks.
‡ Miscellaneous/unfamiliar.

Saturday mornings at other times during the year to see if the content fluctuated seasonally. Accordingly, BARB information on the products advertised on Granada on four Saturday mornings in April, July, September and early October 1983 and 1984 was obtained. The boundaries of Saturday morning children's television were defined as above and the products categorized into adult (defined as above), toys (including comics), food (defined as non-adult and including drinks), and miscellaneous (including product titles that were not known to the author). These statistics for all Saturdays for which product log information was available are given in Table 6.1. It can be seen from these figures that toy advertising is maintained at a very high level of about 75 per cent of all products advertised on Saturday morning children's television in the pre-Christmas period through October and November. There are other seasonal peaks in the incidence of toy advertising (for example, 9 Apr. 1983). A fall in toy advertising entails an increase in the advertising of food products that are not specifically aimed at adults, and coincides with a lack of definition in the Saturday morning children's television market. That is, there are more non-child products advertised at that time (see data for 9 July 1983, 3 Sept. 1983, 3 Mar. 1984, 31 Mar. 1984). In conclusion, when there is a definable Saturday morning children's market place on television the products advertised are predominantly toys.

Food products which may be of interest to children either directly or indirectly will be advertised when there is less competition from toy advertisers. The percentage of products advertised that are food and drink related and that are non-adult fluctuates seasonally and the figure of 18 per cent cited in Table 6.1 is an underestimate given the disproportionate weight of pre-Christmas advertising. An approximate estimate of a quarter of all advertising over the year on Saturday mornings children's television being food and drink related and non-adult oriented can be given.

In summary, it has been established that no 'kid-vid ghetto' of sugared food advertising exists on weekdays afternoons or Saturday mornings in Britain as has been claimed exists in the United States. In order to find out what sugared products are advertised to children it is necessary to adopt a different definition of child-oriented advertising based on the rhetoric of advertising. The criteria employed above (the predominant audience being children and the presence of ads in children's programmes) are not particularly productive in isolating the advertising of these products.

Qualitative analysis

Using the video record of advertisements, it was possible to examine in detail those commercials for sugared products and categorise them with respect to child directedness. A hundred and eight different ads for 78 different products containing more than 10 per cent sugar were identified on the videotape record. Each of these adverts was transcribed so that the following information was retained:

1. the product name
2. the duration of the commercial
3. the spoken and written script
4. any sound or musical effects that were noticeably out-standing
5. a description of each shot summarising 'what's happening' plus camera information (for instance close-up)
6. a list of all shots, numbered in sequence, with the technique employed to get from one shot to another (for example cut, dissolve)
7. the part of the script that coincides with each shot
8. any special techniques used or individual characteristics of the commercial which were noted at the end of the transcription

This pool of 'television commercials for sugared products' was then examined to select those adverts that could be regarded as being directed at children. There was an obvious core of ads in which the brand was of interest to the child and which could be bought by the child (for instance, Smarties). It soon became apparent, however, that any simple criterion based on the extent to which the brand advertised could be purchased by the average child was inadequate. Some ads for sugared cereals were child-directed in terms of rhetoric and style, although it is unlikely that the average child would spend his or her valuable pocket money on a box of Sugar Puffs. Advertising that is child-directed in the sense that the parents may buy but the child may persuade, or put pressure on them to do so, should be considered eligible for selection.

The rest of the commercials were examined and a decision was made, with a colleague, to discard some of them as adult-directed. For example, a small cluster of television commercials for chocolate products uses a particular form of imagery and rhetoric based on the theme of escaping into a fantasy world. They are aimed specifically at housewives watching between soaps in the afternoon. These commercials were regarded as not directed at children. The final pool of child-directed advertisements for sugared products consisted of 58 different commercials. Each was analysed individually using a particular theoretical model. At the time, the theoretical discussion of the nature of advertising that is given in Chapter 5 was not complete, so the model used was only partly based on the principles outlined there. A short description of the analysis follows.

Each commercial provides information which can be classified into three types. First, there is generic information in the sense that it is common to all advertisements. This would include information that the ad is a persuasive message and has persuasive intent; that there is a brand within the ad; and that the ad is a form of discourse whose topic is the brand and whose context frequently functions as a metaphorical system, transposing the mundane reality of brand-in-the-world into the idealized world of brand-in-the-ad. Knowing that the ad is a persuasive message entitles its reader to make certain inferences beyond the formal sense of the linguistic messages. Knowing the function of context suggests that it will be designed to present the product in its best possible light. So, for example, we expect families to be idealized and, if they are more real than ideal, they are presented like this for a purpose. We expect products to be set in contexts that provide an antidote to their negative qualities or define seductive attributes if the product does not possess them. Second, the advertisement provides specific information. This concerns the brand the ad is promoting. Often, it is quite difficult to see if the ad is telling us anything about the brand, but it is assumed that this specific information is there even if it is only the brand name. Third, the advertisement provides rhetorical information. Rhetoric is considered here as those parts of the communication that act as a vehicle or support for the specific information. Rhetorical information is attention-getting. It can be pleasant to watch and listen to. It may involve some of the rhetorical figures that are met in literature, like metaphor, paradox, or hyperbole.

The model described above was then used to provide a description of each of the 58 television commercials. An example of how an analysis proceeds will be given here for a 10-second spot for Dime Bar. The ad starts with a shot of an old-fashioned mountaineer standing beside a rock face in a rather staged setting. He bites into the product and there is a loud crunching sound. An avalanche is shown and the snow covers the mountaineer. A hand emerges from the snow clutching the brand and text on the screen states: 'Sounds like an avalanche'. The voice-over says: 'Is this sound a new crackly, buttery milk chocolate Dime Bar? No. It's an avalanche.'

The first job is to isolate the primary specific information communicated by this ad. A literal reading of this ad might give an interpretation like 'If you eat a Dime Bar it makes a very loud noise.' This, in itself, is a bald bit of information that does not appear to have much relevance in the context of advertising. But it begins to make more sense when combined with generic information that the 10 seconds is providing to the reader because of the fact that it is an advertisement.

For example, a noisy chocolate bar should be a pleasant experience. The full sense of the commercial only becomes apparent when the rhetorical information is also taken into consideration. The quality of loudness provides us with information that is part of a humorous story acting as a rhetorical vehicle carrying specific information. The specific information, inferred from loudness, is the crispy, crunchy texture of the bar itself. Loudness is a surrogate for this textural, oral quality. This inference can be cross-validated by reviewing the content of ads for other food products. In particular, ads such as those for Rice Krispies and Golden Wonder crisps often use this device where the crispiness/crunchiness combination makes a frequent appearance as a brand characteristic. A more confident assertion can be made that crispiness/crunchiness is the textural quality underlying loudness which is the superficial characteristic.

The final confirmation (for this individual analysis) comes when the generic information that 'this is an ad' is put together with the crispy/crunchy quality. Soggy crisps and uncrunchy biscuits are two negative qualities these products can display. They are undesirables. Consequently, advertising promotion in terms of the opposite is an antidote to this potential negative quality. The analysis of this particular ad is now complete. The primary specific information is *crunchiness/crispiness*. Although product information about ingredients is available (contains butter and milk chocolate), this is not carried rhetorically. The rhetorical information consists of *humour* and *hyperbole*.

In this way, individual analyses were made of all the television commercials. These were examined to see if the rhetorical information and the specific information could be characterized and coded and whether there were any other characteristics of children's television commercials that were amenable to some form of coding. The objective of the analysis was to obtain a set of codings that could be applied to each commercial. These coded commercials could then be statistically analysed. The codings used are described below.

1. Product name.
2. Commercial code number and version code.
3. Length in seconds.
4. Number of separate shots.
5. Pace, here defined as commercial length (3) divided by number of separate shots (4).
6. Whether the product is being shown consumed or not. This has only two values: either someone is or is not, eating/drinking what is or can be reasonably inferred to be the product.
7. Whether a child is shown consuming the product or not. This has only two values and it must be that a 'yes' here entails a 'yes' to (6).
8. Whether a family was present in the advert in a participatory role, or not.
9.. Whether the format uses animation or not. This variable had three values corresponding to full animation, partial animation, and no animation.
10. Whether the format uses puppets or people dressed up

in costume to represent animals, non-humans, and non-human creatures in general, or not.

11. Whether the setting involves fantasy or not. Examples of fantasy setting would be spacecraft on the moon's surface with 'cartoon' moon creatures, 'jungly' setting with strange monsters, or a representation of 'nursery-rhyme land'. The moon and jungle can, in other circumstances, be represented quite literally.

12. Whether the action involves fantasy or not. Examples of fantasy action would be cartoon characters (such as Tony the Tiger) falling off cliffs and surviving, or the Milky Bar Kid being able to conjure the brand out of thin air.

13. Whether the setting is an historical one or not. The American West is a popular historical setting.

14. Whether the setting and action are abstract or not. There is no obvious scenic reality in an abstract setting.

15. Whether humour is employed in the script or the action or in neither.

16. Whether any reference to sugar is made in the commercial, either specifically as an ingredient, or by implication, or not.

17. The products were classified into nine categories: chocolate bars, toffee-based products, sweets (sold as items usually in packs), chocolate biscuits, biscuits, cakes, sugared cereals, drinks, and miscellaneous. Each commercial was given a code corresponding to one of the above.

18. Whether the product contains chocolate or not.

19. Whether the commercial contains a child, and whether the child occupies the central role in the commercial, or not. Examples of this were quite obvious in the sample used. For example, a child occupies the centre of the dramatic stage as a majorette in the commercial for Quality Street.

20. Specific information can be categorized into extrinsic and intrinsic information. The latter is characteristic of the product *per se*. It may not be particularly valuable from the viewpoint of a concerned consumer but it is information that is concerned with, for example, the product's texture or perceptual appearance, its prices or ingredients, the brand name or oral qualities (chewy, crispy, or crunchy, or even

all three). Extrinsic information is not part of the nature of the product as such. It may be claims (explicit or inferred) concerning the product's use (this product solves social problems, or is for sharing), or claims about its function (this product is an essential part of a home, or like drinking at a bar) when there is nothing in the product that justifies such claims about use or function. Each commercial can then be coded according to whether specific information provided is intrinsic, extrinsic, both, or neither. It should be noted that this categorization is not objective in the sense that it requires inference and judgement by the observer. Much discussion ensued between the author and colleagues about how best to apply this coding to the different ads.

There are eight remaining categories (excluding humour and fantasy) that deal with rhetorical devices in ads. All are coded as either present or absent and they can be expressed in audio or video. They are defined as follows.

21. *Hyperbole*. A rhetorical device involving overstatement of some other information (for example, specific information).

22. *Adventure*. Specific information can be 'dressed up' in an adventure. The goal can be to attain the specific information related to the product or product use, or the product information can be simply part of the adventure sequence.

23. *Whizz*. This category of rhetoric can involve fast-paced shots and music, and is a general perceptually-based *Gestalt* of excitement.

24. *Romdom*. This label is an abbreviation of 'romantic domestic' and is a representation of a family or household that is highly romanticised, over and above the general idealization one would expect as a consequence of the generic information concerning advertising.

25. *Rompast*. This label is an abbreviation of 'romantic past' and is a presentation of scenes from the past in a romanticized or nostalgic way. The dividing line is drawn between historical settings which involve a depiction of a period which (because of the generic information produced by ads) is likely to be historically attractive or romantic in any case, and those settings in which the romance is used in

a nostalgic fashion to deliver specific information. As with 'romdom', the dividing line is not easy to draw in some cases.

26. *Rhyme.* This category is much easier to establish and consists of the presence or absence of rhyme in the script.

27. *Metaphor.* A metaphor is detected if there is evidence that attributes of the topic of the advertising discourse (the brand) are being extended by metaphorically associating product characteristics with another meaning domain. This can be done visually or with language or both.

28. *Pun.* Any use of language in the commercial that exploits the inherent ambiguity in words or expressions is categorized as pun.

Qualitative results

The first analysis of interest would be to see the frequency of the coded features over the 58 television commercials. These are given below.

Duration: Ten per cent of commercials were 10 seconds long; 34 per cent were 20-second spots, and 55 per cent lasted 30 seconds.

Pace: As the number of shots taken would depend on their length and on the length of the spot, a more appropriate variable is pace, which was computed by dividing the duration by the number of shots. Pace varied from a value of 0.67 to 10 but the higher values tended to be outlying and infrequent and the main distribution lies between 0.67 and 3.33 with a mean of 1.98. In other words, for the average commercial in this sample each shot lasted approximately 2 seconds.

Animation: Sixty-four per cent of commercials employ animation.

Consumption: Fifty-three per cent of commercials do not show the product being consumed. Twenty-nine per cent show the child consuming the product.

Family: Twenty-nine per cent of the commercials portrayed the family in a participatory role.

Puppets: Nine per cent of the commercials used puppets or people dressed up as non-human creatures.

Setting: Forty per cent of the commercials were set in a present day real-life context. Ten per cent were historical settings, 41 per cent involved some element of fantasy and 9 per cent were classified as abstract.

Action: In 62 per cent of the commercials, the action did not deviate significantly from what would be expected in everyday life. Seven per cent were classified as abstract and in the remaining 31 per cent the action involved an element of fantasy or magic.

Humour: Over half the commercials (57 per cent) were humorous.

Sugar: Only nine per cent of the commercials sampled made a reference to sugar.

Product: There were nine product categories, broken down as follows: chocolate bar (11); chocolate biscuits (11); sweets sold as items, usually in packs (9); sugared cereals (8); drinks (6); miscellaneous (5); biscuits (4); cakes (3); toffee-based product (1).

Does the child normally buy the product?: Sixty per cent of the 58 commercials were for products that children would buy.

Does the product contain chocolate?: Sixty-four per cent advertised products that contained chocolate.

Child's role: In 17 per cent of the commercials the child played a central role.

Intrinsic and extrinsic specific information: Each commercial was coded on the number of intrinsic and of extrinsic specific points of information made. Fifty per cent of commercials made at least one extrinsic specific point. Twenty-eight per cent of all ads made at least one extrinsic specific point with no intrinsic specific point.

Hyperbole: Twenty-six per cent used this rhetorical device, either in language, or in the visual message, or both.

Whizz: Twelve per cent were categorized as possessing these features.

Romdom: Nine per cent were categorized as possessing this feature.

Rompast: Sixteen per cent were categorized as possessing this feature.

Rhyme: Forty-one per cent used rhyme in their language.
Metaphor: Metaphor was detected in 29 per cent.
Pun: Twenty-four per cent used puns.
Use of a well-known character: This was found in 21 per cent of all commercials in the sample.

These findings are presented largely without comment as they constitute a small data base on norms for a particular sample of UK television commercials. In order to explore the data further, it is necessary to isolate a sub-set of variables to analyse. This was done by identifying those variables that may contribute to the rhetorical nature or style of the ad. These were the setting (whether normal, historical, fantasy, or abstract), the action (whether normal, fantasy, or abstract), the numbers of intrinsic and of extrinsic specific points made in the ad, humour, the child in a central role, hyperbole, 'whizz', 'romdom', 'rompast', rhyme, metaphor, pun, and the presence of a well-known character.

A statistical technique known as factor analysis was used to investigate the pattern of relationships within this sub-set and this produced three significant factors. The first was identified as a combination of the number of extrinsic specific points, 'whizz', and the child playing a central role in the commercial. The second was a combination of number of extrinsic specific points and rhyme, and the third factor combined humour, hyperbole, and pun. The second factor is difficult to identify but the third can be labelled 'humour'.

The first factor, although difficult to label, constitutes an important finding from the analysis as it shows how three variables that are potentially important to the child audience are interrelated. The number of extrinsic specific points made in an advertisement is an indication of the extent to which it provides specific brand information that is unrelated to the properties of the brand itself. For example, Smarties are similar to drinking, Breakaway is attractive enough to be withheld as a punishment, and McVitie's Home Wheat is an essential part of the family. This characteristic of a commercial goes with (statistically) the feature that children occupy a central role in the advertisement and that the ad uses a jazzy, rapid format called 'whizz'. There is an a priori argument that, if the child in the ad is cast in a central role, children as viewers will identify with the commercial. Extolling the virtues of brand characteristics that are not related to the product *per se* could be regarded as a different and more insidious form of advertising than extolling the virtues of, for example, the price, taste, or texture of the product. It may be an accidental result of the small sample of 58 commercials used that extrinsic, 'whizz', and child-centred role go together. It is a fact or phenomenon, however, and the 58 commercials were reduced from a wide, extensive sample of other commercials.

In summary this chapter has introduced the reader to some of the methods used in the literature to look at the content of advertising directed to children. The question of defining this advertising was raised. What is 'advertising directed to children'? There are various criteria that can be used to establish categories of 'child advertising' and these can inform one's sampling procedure, for example ads within and around programmes directed at children; at certain times of the day or week; that sell products children can buy; that sell products that interest children; that use rhetoric of interest to children. The eventual decision to select certain television commercials and reject others may be based on more than one of the above criteria.

Most of the analyses of advertising to children have been done in the United States and have examined the content of the ads broadcast at certain times on the assumption that this is where the 'kid-vid ghetto' can be found. The depth of analysis has been limited to simple counts of easily coded categories such as types of setting, or qualities of product emphasized. A study of advertising of sugared products to children in Britain has shown that a kid-vid ghetto for these does not exist. At particular times of the year, for instance before Easter and Christmas, Saturday morning commercial spots tend to be monopolized by toy advertising. Outwith these seasonal times, advertising on Saturday mornings in Britain is a mixture of commercials for adult products, and for food and toys for children.

Television commercials for sugared products for children were examined in this same study using a model of advertising that separated out rhetorical information from information about the product and brand. Results demonstrate that such a model is useful and workable. Future research is needed, however, with more sophisticated later versions of advertising analysis on more extensive and varied samples of ads.

7
What Psychologists Know about Children and Advertising

INTRODUCTION

The experimental and psychological literature on the specific issue of television advertising and children was discussed extensively in Chapters 3 and 4. One of the characteristics of this research is a lack of theoretical development in such core issues as the child's understanding of television advertising. Certainly, reference is made to theories of psychological development in the child and the works of Jean Piaget are frequently cited as a kind of theoretical underwriting of the empirical findings that are displayed. It is appropriate to draw together various descriptions of development in children in areas that are germane to the general issue of how children understand advertising in order to understand better how those growing skills and abilities constrain and define their understanding. That is the purpose of this chapter.

If the child is developing and changing so that the five-year-old understands differently and knows less about the worlds of people, things, and culturally represented entities than the nine-year-old, then some model of the end-state of the process of development should be available if only to discover the level of understanding and how much more is still to be acquired at different ages. One has to be wary, however, of mapping achievement at one level onto an 'ideal adult' model.

When we start talking the language of 'acquisition' and 'achievement' at different ages or stages, we tend to presume an image of the child as an intellectually immature or inadequate person who still 'has some way to go' before acquiring the full range of adult skills and abilities. It is quite possible to regard the child at a particular stage of development as being in possession of a set of abilities that are apt and appropriate to the characteristics of the world as construed and constructed by the child at that time. That stage is self-contained because the child has mentally constructed a reality that is in accord with the abilities of that age. The older child will possess a more developed set of abilities and skills but will have constructed a mental world that is more sophisticated and that incorporates the vision of the previous stage. This conception of development is in the spirit of Piaget and characterizes many of the so-called stage developmental theories in child psychology.

Adults, when faced with television advertising, have a variety of skills and abilities at their disposal to make sense of what is seen. There are three general classes of abilities that would structure any discussion of what skills the child possesses at different ages. Firstly, as a television commercial appears on television, the reader should be familiar with the forms and functions of television discourse. Television uses forms such as cuts and flashbacks to signal change and the past. Special signs are used to symbolize a dream state. Ellipsis is a common feature, with much of the intermediate activity in a sequence of events being omitted. Zooms and close-ups cause apparent change in the size of objects. Adults who are familiar with television understand these conventions and can 'read television', but children have to acquire this particular literacy as they grow up. The second general category of abilities would be concerned with the child's understanding of the nature and function of the ad itself. What is it there for? What does it do? The third class of skills would come under the comprehension of rhetoric. Advertising uses various rhetorical forms in the service of its different functions of persuading, entertaining and informing. Exaggeration, humour and various uses of metaphor can be detected. These three areas provide us with three topics under which various findings and theories can be classified. These are in order, the development of television literacy, the child's understanding of advertising, and the developmental psychology of rhetoric.

THE DEVELOPMENT OF TELEVISION LITERACY

The term 'television literacy' implies an analogy in that there are certain parallels between being able to read, write, use, and comprehend written language, and being able to understand and appreciate the forms and variety of content in television. The term is a popular one but there is a danger that the popularity of the expression may lead to a somewhat cavalier attitude towards its use.

The parallel between 'being literate' with language and 'being literate' with television should not be forced too far as there are extensive differences between descriptions and theories of language, and theories of the symbols and signs used in the mixture of spoken speech, sound, music, and moving pictures that constitute television's output. For example, the grammar of language has been formulated by linguists like Chomsky as having particular properties so that it can be described using a powerful system of rules characteristic of human language. These rule systems may apply to other systems as well but it is unlikely that they can be applied to a set of images that are continuous and analysable at one level, compared with language which consists of discrete units hierarchically organized into several levels.

In addition, literacy is a concept that is rooted in a social and historical milieu. 'Literacy to what purpose?' What skills should different groups in society possess and to what use will they be put? Should everyone be taught just the rudiments of reading texts or do all people have the right to be exposed to ideological or aesthetic analyses of great literary works? Who decides what's a 'great literary work'? These questions should be put and answered if the concept of 'television literacy' is to be developed to the same extent as the idea of literacy with print and the written word.

There are several books sources that describe how children become literate with television. Dorr (1986) discusses the general issue of television and children, and includes material on the child's growing understanding of the world of television whereas Bryant and Anderson (1983) review the more technical research on children's processing of the information in the television stimulus. Kelly and Gardner

(1981) edited a collection of papers, many of which have a bearing on aspects of television literacy. Consequently, the brief description below is only an outline of some of the more important features of television literacy.

Children begin to interact and respond to television at a very early age. There is evidence that infants orient to television's light and sound (Slaby and Hollenbeck, 1977). There is also evidence that from the age of 5 months infants are capable of recognizing pictorial representations, such as photographs of people and objects (Dirks and Gibson, 1977). By the time infants emerge into the world of language and friends from the world of infancy, they are interested in television and are able to react to television as a segment of their environment occupied with people and objects. The stage is set for the development of an understanding of this world.

There is evidence that the young child's understanding of television is exotically different from the older child's comprehension and an adult's awareness. Dorr (1980) draws on anecdotal evidence to claim that, for the young preschool child, the social reality displayed on television is much the same as the social reality in real life. Children of 2, 3, or even 4 years believe that the people they see on television can engage in social interaction with them; that they are as real as their own mums and dads, teachers, aunts and uncles, sisters and brothers. Lyle and Hoffman (1972) reported that young children, asked where people on television go when the set is turned off, seemed to believe that television people actually live in the box. Noble (1975) argued that young children engage in parasocial interaction with television characters and think they know the viewer just as the viewer knows them. These findings support the view that the early preschool child perceives television reality as similar to other real parts of social life. At least, young children communicate with television and reply to questions about television in a way that supports this view.

Young children's understanding of the content of television is very different from grown-up understanding. In an interesting study, Sparks and Cantor (1983) looked at the behaviour of *The Incredible Hulk* and how this influenced young children. In *The Incredible Hulk* the hero, David Banner, looks and acts like a normal person under most conditions. When he is very angry he is transformed into a frightening, green-faced muscular 'Hulk'. Although adults may find this amusing, children can be very frightened by this Jekyll-and-Hyde change. Three- to 5-year-olds were frightened more by the transformation itself and the Hulk after the transformation than by the situation David Banner found himself in before he changed into the Hulk. Older children aged from 9 to 11 years understood the theme of the series. Consequently they were more scared before the transformation, when Banner is in trouble, than by the transformation or the Hulk itself after the change. This is because older children expect everything to turn out right once the Hulk comes into being because this is the theme of the series. Younger children also tended to regard David Banner and the Hulk as distinct characters whereas older children would see the latter as a manifestation of the former. There is evidence from studies of children's recall of television episodes (Collins, 1979) that young preschool children are quite unable to integrate information from parts of television episodes into any resemblance of the story that is unfolding on the screen, and will confuse non-essential and essential information. This result is not unexpected as it is known that the preschool period is a time when the mental schemata available to structure stories is primitive and inadequate (Mandler and Johnson, 1977). There is some evidence, however, from natural language use, that pre-school children can produce an ordered narrative of a familiar situation like a birthday party (Nelson, 1978). Some system for organizing narrative, perhaps based on scripts for re-telling tales, is available but can only be utilized under restricted circumstances.

The first period in the development of television literacy, from infancy up to 3 or 4 years of age is typified by a child who attends to television especially when television itself uses attention-arousing effects. Wright and Huston (1983) showed that children in the late preschool period were susceptible to the attention-arousing effects of high-speed character movement, special effects not seen in the real world, loud music, sound effects, vocalizations, and non-human speech. These children have a very different understanding from adults of the content of television. People exist in the box and the child will often talk and shout to them and treat them no differently from real people. Information is assimilated, but not integrated within any schema or organization available for understanding stories. Children can be frightened of this social reality in a different way from older children because they do not organize dramatic information. The child at this stage has not developed a set of organized schemata that drives expectations of the expected content and structure of various television genres. The world of television is a world of change and novelty whose processing is driven by interest in and consequent attention to the stimulus itself.

It is from this very different and limited understanding of television in the early preschool period that the child gradually composes a more mature picture of what is going on. One important distinction that emerges is concerned with different degrees of television reality and everyday life. This presumes that a distinction between television reality and everyday life is already there, and it would appear that this is established in the majority of children between 3 and 4 years of age, although even some 5-year-olds will give unrealistic answers to Lyle and Hoffman's question (1972) about where the people go when the television is turned off (Hawkins, 1977, p. 305). Hawkins separated the perceived reality of television into two independent dimensions which he called 'magic window' and 'social expectations'. 'Magic window' refers to the degree to which children perceive television characters as real people or actors playing roles; that is, television characters are real people and television is like a magic window on the world. 'Social expectations' refers to the similarity of television characters and events to real life and how useful they are in guiding the child's own behaviour. For example, for an adult the British soap *Coronation Street* would have social expectations that are realistic in connection with what might happen whereas the American import, *The A Team*, will be regarded by most adults as an unrealistic portrayal of real life in the United States. In both programmes, the actors are acting and the cast of *Coronation Street* do not meet up in the Rover's Return of an evening or really live in the Street. Most adults will not perceive this soap as a 'magic window'. The developmental trend for 'magic window' is 'a gradual realization that most television programs present fiction and not pictures of actual events' (Hawkins, 1977, p. 315), the ages sampled ranging from 4 to 12 years. Over this age range, however, there was no obvious decline in 'social expectations'; the understanding that television programmes do not match up to real life because there is a dissimilarity between television theatre and the theatre of life comes much later in development.

Fernie (1981) discusses some of the problems children have in distinguishing between television characters of widely varying reality status. One particular problem is that television attempts to present all actions with equal visual realism, the difference between fantasy and reality not being so obviously marked. Furthermore, children who are already engaged in much fantasy play are likely to make fantastic interpretations of even ordinary events. Kelly (1981) looked at the reality–fantasy distinction in television and books, with children ranging from 7 to 11 years. The youngest children tended to consider first whether any parts of the television show existed in the real world. The argument would proceed on the lines that Kojak is real because Kojak is a policeman and there are policemen in real life. Another strategy is concerned with the child's judgement of the presentation's possibility or impossibility. High on the child's checklist of cues signalling fantasy is the presence of physical impossibility. *The Wizard of Oz* was not real, according to Kelly's 7-year-olds, because 'a lion can't talk'. Children of this age will use format rather than content to judge reality. There was unanimous agreement amongst Kelly's children that Superman is more real than Charlie Brown. The answer to the question 'Which is more real?' is, quite simply, whichever looks more real. By 10 years of age, the child has acquired an awareness of television's representational nature and this achievement radically alters the child's approach to the reality–fantasy distinction. Children will evaluate television programmes in terms of their inner content rather than their outward format. Consequently the child considers issues of possibility in his or her judgements and will relate them to social and behavioural phenomena. For example, Kelly quotes the 10-year-old who judged *The Odd Couple* to be real '. . . because Oscar and Felix are divorced and people can get divorced in life. It's possible.' By 12 years of age, reasoning about fantasy and reality has shifted to a different plane. Children are using plausibility as a criterion in their judgements and signalling their awareness that the question can be answered in a number of ways. They will ask, 'What do you mean, "real"? Real in what way?' and, if judging reality, will take into consideration violations of social and psychological reality rather than violations of physical reality. A soap is unreal because real people don't have all these problems coming at them in one half-hour episode. The resolution of problems in a 'happy ending' is considered unreal by 12-year-olds because this doesn't happen in real life. The 12-year-old's judgements of reality and fantasy now correspond more closely to those of an adult.

The ability to draw distinctions between reality and fantasy is a vitally important acquisition in the progress towards television literacy. As the evidence above has shown, the child applies different criteria of reality and fantasy at different stages of development. For the adult and the teenage child, the question of reality versus fantasy is more complex. An adult, if asked 'Is *Coronation Street* real?' might respond by asking you what you meant or in what way you meant it was 'real'. In addition, many adults will behave as if soaps were real. People write letters to actors and address them by their stage names, visit film locations and want to see where 'they (the characters) live', and mourn the death of favourite stars. This does not mean that the adult viewing population of Britain has regressed to the intellectual level of a preschool child and really believes that actors live on the set. In Coleridge's terms, it is the 'willing suspension of disbelief' that is occurring here and it is this willingness to enter into the role of audience member that keeps actors in business. At some stage in development, after children have acquired a working knowledge that actors are really acting and all the world is not a stage, they will begin to appreciate and enjoy this game of believing while really knowing it is only pretend.

Future research could examine the development of 'becoming an audience' with older children and explore some of the consequences of possessing multiple criteria for judging reality and fantasy. For example, the reality–fantasy distinction can operate on at least three levels. The level of representation deals with the medium involved. Cartoons are less real than films of people acting, and puppets lie somewhere in between. The level of behaviour is concerned with the reality of action by people. Events in the Lebanon and Northern Ireland are more real than *The A Team*. There is also reality of setting where the planet Krypton is less real than the streets of New York. All of these levels (and others) can operate simultaneously within one film, often to great dramatic effect. The fantasy of Superman's actions is made dramatic against the foil of the filmed reality of the streets of New York.

The judgement of reality or fantasy by children is also complicated by the fact that the frame of reference for such judgement can shift. This shift, however, is often predictable. In one programme of research, I interviewed children on their assessment of the reality of various television programmes. As expected, many children in middle childhood regarded fantasy programmes such as *He-Man* as not real. When asked about *Grange Hill*, however, which is a realistic school drama serial, children would often say that it was 'not real'. Further questioning revealed that it was 'not real' because it was not like their school. In other words, if the topic of judgement is personally close to the child, the frame of reference shifts and the reality–fantasy judgement is made relative to a different category than the category of 'all that's seen on television'.

During the preschool period there does not appear to be a system of mental organization to cope with the narrative nature of television. A more sophisticated system develops in the primary school years. This would appear to be related to a general trend connected with age in child development, also found in the child's changing criteria for distinguishing fantasy and reality, to detect information in stimuli that is deeper and more socially meaningful, and to use this information to draw distinctions. Collins, Wellman, Keniston, and Westby (1978) discovered that comprehension with children aged 11 years and older varied as a function of plot organization of the television narrative. With younger children, the organization of the plot did not appear to influence the child's comprehension of the programme, and younger viewers performed equally poorly regardless of plot organization.

The ability to predict future events in a narrative is also age-dependent although a difference emerges earlier than 11 years. At 7 years of age the average child is unable to predict what will happen in, say, a Western if the programme is stopped at an important point and the child is questioned. So, for example, Collins (1979) cites the scene where character A meets character B who resembled the man A had killed. A relevant prediction or reasonable dramatic inference from the context is that character A will think he hadn't killed the original person whom B resembles and consequently will go after B and try again to kill the unsuspecting B. Or so most adults would infer. Seven-year-olds rarely predicted this whereas the majority of 11-year-olds and 14-year-olds did. Another experiment, conducted by Collins and Westby (1975), found that presenting a random sequence of events from a crime drama programme had little detrimental effect, compared with the correct temporal sequence, on recall of the plot by 7-year-olds, whereas it did affect 10-year-olds, who recalled more effectively if the events were presented in correct sequence. The ability to construct dramatic inferences is a complex skill that develops into late childhood, adolescence, and adulthood. It is a research area that has not received the attention it deserves.

Television uses filmic conventions that instantaneously transfer the action from one space and one time to another space and another time; that focus attention on one part of a situation by zooming in on that part; that indicate mood by, for example, dissolving from one scene to another rather than cutting; that suggest dreams or fantasies by blurring parts of the screen, and so on. Do children understand how these conventions are used? There is some scattered research in this area. Dorr (1980) reports that the 5- to 7-year-olds she talked to could not understand how Steve Austin, the Six Million Dollar Man, could catch the bad guys when he ran so slowly. These children were misinterpreting the use of slow motion which, in this series, was an indicator of bionic strength. Tada (1969) examined the comprehension by Japanese children of film images. A film was shown which opened with scenes of quiet fishing villages and then cut to groups of factories being built along the shores. Fewer than half the group of 9-year-olds who saw this film were able to predict the effect of the factories on the fishing villages as intended by the producer. These children also had difficulty understanding any connection between the two scenes. Much work in this area, however, remains to be done.

Finally, there is a body of research concerned with children's attention to different aspects of the television message at different ages. A useful review can be found in the first four chapters of Bryant and Anderson (1983). The general principle of development that operates here is: as children grow older, their attention will be influenced more by what they expect to see. In other words, the mechanism of attention is initially stimulus-driven but, with age, becomes schema-driven too. The fact that attention could be activated by two different processes raises severe methodological problems. If attention is measured on a simple criterion of watching (*on*) and not-watching (*off*), there is no way of knowing whether the child shifts from one attentional state to another because of stimulus information or information from schemata. So, if a child looks away from the television screen, is this because the child is bored by what he or she sees (stimulus-driven), or expects and knows what's coming next and so thinks there's no need to watch any more (schema-driven)? It's difficult to answer this question on a simple *on-off* criterion of attention/no-attention. What can be established, however, is that attention to television is a composite process relying upon the salience of formal features and attention-arousing effects on the screen and the development of scripts or other mental representations of different television genres.

Salomon (1981) has discussed a form of attention to television that is concerned with the 'Amount of Invested Mental Effort' (AIME) the child puts into a television programme. The concept is akin to attention but is related more to engagement with what is going on. There are two main features of AIME. One is depth of processing. With some material, it is easy and tempting to skim the surface and simply extract the material there in the perceptual characteristics of the stimulus. That ad is colourful, loud, and fast. This one is soothing and sexy. With other material and in other moods, the processing of information can occur at deeper levels (to use the familiar metaphor) where inferences about what has happened, what something means and what is about to happen are made. Another concept is degree of automaticity. Deep processing can occur automatically if the skills involved have been learnt so that they operate independently of one's control. With other material and to other ends, processing information can be decidedly non-automatic and can involve much effort as one struggles to discover the logical flaws in a student's exam answer or to unpack the ideological assumptions in a political diatribe.

The AIME invested in a task will depend as much on the reader or viewer's expectations and history of success or failure as on the material to be read or viewed and the medium of presentation. For example, a student who has been relatively successful in achieving good results in the past and who is faced with reading material that is relatively familiar will tend to coast through the reading task with a small AIME. What is needed is a jolt. If a test is in the offing, the task is seen as more demanding and one would predict increased AIME. If the material is qualitatively different from what has gone before and appears more demanding then AIME should also increase. If the student has gone through a period of failure then the student should also increase AIME.

AIME also depends on the medium of learning and instruction. Television has certain characteristics that would discourage a large AIME. It is often fast-paced, leaving little time for mental elaboration. The visual nature of the medium means that, unlike radio and books, the viewer has little opportunity to use visual imagery and expend mental effort in constructing scenarios for the narrative. Television by its very nature needs less AIME in order to be assimilated and understood than other media. Salomon (1981) argues that adult co-viewers have a role to play to prevent low AIME when children watch television. The family should encourage a questioning attitude within the home towards television. Parents should take this medium seriously and discuss the content and form of television with children. In this way the AIME in television will be increased, leading to better understanding and recall of these messages. Salomon's approach is a valuable one and is an important theoretical contribution to issues in television literacy that are concerned with the assimilation of information from the television message to the child. For too many children television is moving wallpaper and for too many parents television is a silent babysitter. Television is worth more than that.

THE CHILD'S UNDERSTANDING OF ADVERTISING

This heading covers much of the research reviewed in Chapters 3 and 4. These dealt with the child's knowledge of the role advertising plays in the economic transactions involved in buying and selling goods and services, and of the persuasive function of advertising and the inferences that can be made and applied to advertising messages in general. These two aspects of advertising, which can be called the commercial and the persuasive functions, are frequently bracketed together in the literature as knowledge of the commercial and persuasive function of advertising although they are quite different and deserve separate theoretical accounts. The purpose of this section is to re-interpret the findings of the North American research of the 1970s into the question of the child's comprehension of advertising within, it is argued, a more adequate framework.

It is a well-established finding that a major advance in the understanding of advertising occurs round about 7 years of age. Children younger than that rarely refer to the persuasive and commercial function of advertising when interviewed. Children who are 7 years or older will refer to these functions, and the frequency of mention increases with age. Most explanations of this result have relied on accounts of cognitive development in children based on the theories and findings of Piaget (1926). There are a few exceptions such as Robertson and Rossiter's (1974) reference to attribution theory and Roedder's (1981) discussion of the information processing limitations of children, but in general the theories of Jean Piaget have been used to explain this change.

Piaget's theories have been very influential in contributing to our understanding of how the child's mind works from infancy to adolescence. Many developmental psychologists would regard his theories, as the popularity of his books both in European and North American developmental psychology of the 1960s and 1970s bears out, as one of the major contributions to child psychology. The word *theory* should be stressed because most of Piaget's investigations are designed to contribute to a developing body of theory that is ultimately concerned with the growth of knowledge in systems, both over time in society and over time in the individual child. Piaget has dignified this enterprise with the title of *genetic epistemology* which is the study of the growth of knowledge. Experiments and systematic observations are taken as evidence that support these theories or as findings that challenge their validity. Piaget was not only a theoretician, however, and his findings and popular versions of his theories have filtered down to the general public and have been incorporated into the training syllabuses of child health experts, teachers, social workers and many other child-care professionals. If Piaget's theories are to appear in the applied context of the child's understanding of advertising, other questions must be put. In particular the following should be considered.

1. Is it possible to take parts of Piagetian developmental psychology and use it to describe the child's cognitive development with particular reference to the child's comprehension of advertising?
2. Why choose a Piagetian model? In many other associated

areas of television's influence on the child, theories of
child development such as social learning theory in, for
example, the effects of televised violence on children's attitudes and behaviour are used and little reference is made to
Piaget.

3. Is a Piagetian model the most theoretically suitable
candidate to account for the child's comprehension or lack
of comprehension of advertising's intent?

One of the problems of setting up a theory in an applied
context is the distortion and simplification that occurs. The
original volumes or learned commentaries are reduced to
paperback textbooks, suitable for use by interested practitioners. The characteristics of Piaget's theories become
smoothed out, the rough edges are knocked off and, in
particular, the different perspectives are reoriented towards
one perspective dealing with one conception of childhood.
The main area in which Piaget has been applied is that
part of education dealing with the capacities of children at
different ages and with how the child assimilates and
accommodates to different classes of information at different
stages in development. Much emphasis, for example, is
given to the major shift in cognitive competence that occurs
at about 6 or 7 years of age when the younger child is
incapable of understanding that the amount of lemonade in
a glass changes only when you add some more or take some
away and that a change in the shape of the container does
not influence the amount of lemonade in it. In general, the
younger child in the preschool years is characterised as
inadequate, possessing exotic ideas about the world and
performing very differently from the older, primary-school
child. Such a picture of childhood is useful for teachers who
may become frustrated with the lack of comprehension of
5- to 6-year-olds in their classes. To be told that this is a
consequence of different mental structures and to present
material pitched at an appropriate level is reassuring and
useful. Teachers and other practitioners also welcome a
developmental psychology that offers cameos of childhood
at different ages and a stage-developmental theory can offer
just that by listing the characteristics of a preoperational

child and comparing them with those of a concrete operational child.

It has been argued in Chapter 1 that the image of the relationship of advertiser-as-seducer and child-as-innocent is a powerful one that can be found in much of the research into the effects of television advertising on children. There is some truth in the relationship as described. Advertisers are in the business of getting people to buy the brands they advertise and to consume products and persuasion is their technique. Children do display *naïveté*, and are over-trusting, and are in need of protection. If the relationship is presented in terms of advertiser-as-seducer and child-as-innocent then considerable emotional reactions can be unleashed because of the mythical overtones that such a relationship possesses. The Piagetian-based conceptions of childhood fit in very well just because they offer an image of childhood where children in one stage of development are naïve and older children are not.

Piagetian-based theories of cognitive development are not written in tablets of stone, and although the resurrection of Piaget's ideas in Britain and North America in the 1960s was a welcome antidote to some of the arid functionalism of postwar learning theory, a counter-reaction was established in the 1970s and many of his concepts and methods were subjected to criticism. Investigations into the acquisition of a child's language competence, inspired by the popularity of Chomsky's writings, revealed that the preschool child possessed a sophisticated syntactic competence that did not accord with her capabilities in cognitive tests based on Piaget's theories. Gelman (1978) reviewed the literature on cognitive development and concluded that the cognitive capabilities of preschool children had been seriously under-estimated. It would seem that researchers do not accept Piagetian norms completely and that findings are dependent on the methods of assessment used. The development of an understanding of advertising is a process that is complex and is built up over a period of time in the child. Nevertheless, the findings of Ward and others, that some change in understanding occurs at about 7 years of age, need to be accounted for. If the Piagetian explanation, that this change co-occurs with a cognitive change from preoperational to concrete operational thought, is limited at best then what alternative theoretical framework can be used to account for this shift in understanding?

Hakes (1980) reviewed evidence pertaining to children's abilities to make judgements on various types of sentences, for example to judge sentences as acceptable or non-acceptable, syntactically or semantically; to assess synonymy or ambiguity; to appreciate puns and riddles. The evidence points to a major change in language skill occurring during 'middle childhood', a period corresponding to an age of 7 or 8 years. This change is termed the attainment of 'metalinguistic' competence and, while the development of this competence may be spread over a period of several years, it can be characterized as constituting several attainments. There is a general ability to indulge in controlled, deliberate information processing. This is not peculiar to language or, indeed, communication, but can be found in cognition in middle childhood where children develop mnemonic strategies for rehearsal and become aware of the properties of their own memories and of what may need to be done in order to remember something (see, for example, Flavell and Wellman, 1977). They are able to stand back from the stream of language and to reflect on it, to regard language as 'transparent', something to be seen through, rather than 'opaque', something to be focused on in its own right. Hakes suggests that this metalinguistic ability may partly underpin the shift from preoperational to concrete-operational thinking that Piaget talks of although this is as yet a theoretically underdeveloped issue and is open to empirical evidence.

The development of metalinguistic abilities, if translated into the development of metacommunicative abilities with particular reference to media communication, is a much more likely candidate to account for that part of the child's understanding of advertising that develops in middle childhood. In order to answer questions like 'What do advertisements do?', 'What's the difference between advertisements and programmes?', or 'What is a television commercial?', one has to be able to stand back from the stream of television communication and evaluate it, think about it and judge it. Awareness and understanding of the general purpose of advertising, however, requires more than just an awareness of what the particular type of communication is for. An understanding of the function of the source of the communication is required as well as an appreciation of the message. Knowledge of the source of advertising, where ads come from, why they are delivered at regular intervals during programmes, is intimately related to the commercial function of advertising and an understanding of that is fixed in a knowledge system concerned with social and economic institutions. Much of the curriculum for schools relies, in a non-explicit way, on inculcating an awareness of process; of where things come from and where they're going to. This can embrace a perceptual learning of process such as the fact that this hedgerow or meadow has been there since the 'Domesday Book' and that it is under threat by developers, or that these ridges are remnants of strip cultivation. An awareness of process can involve a simple understanding of where things come from. The milk bottle is not just there on the doorstep but is the end product of a process of manufacture from commodity to product to brand. Children can be taught to see objects as the end result of a process with symbolic meaning. For example, that railway cutting did not just happen but was dug from the ground and cost the lives of hundreds of Irish navvies who died of typhoid. Some children are aware of this but many are not. Television is a case in point. Some children see the television as 'just there' as a utility that houses have whereas others see it as the end product of various processes such as those involving household expenditure, the physics of electromagnetic transmission, or even processes involving the social side of broadcasting.

The final part of this review of child development research that is relevant to an understanding of television advertising and children will deal with what has rather ambitiously been called:

THE DEVELOPMENTAL PSYCHOLOGY OF RHETORIC

I have used this rather grandiose title to cover a selection of quite recent research findings in developmental psychology. These are concerned with the child's comprehension of communication where there is a distinction between the propositional content of what is being said or communicated, and the way in which this content is conveyed. In addition, the manner frequently hides the propositional nature of the communication, and is often designed to persuade the receiver to act in accordance with the source's intention. This formulation approaches the conventional meaning of 'rhetoric' which is used in the context of 'dressing up' or 'hiding' the 'honest truth' with various devices. It is intended to cover non-language forms of rhetoric that are found in television advertising and magazine advertising, for example, as well as the more traditional rhetorical devices of language. The 'developmental psychology of rhetoric' will not be found in the index of books on child language or developmental psychology but, as the rest of this chapter will hopefully demonstrate, there is a small body of research that might constitute the basis for such a psychology.

Given the above definition of rhetoric one could possibly locate a developmental psychology of rhetoric within the growth of the child's pragmatic competence (see, for example, Ochs and Schieffelin, 1979; Haslett, 1987) but the latter has a wider brief than the former. Frequently in rhetorical communication a reading of the communication at its face value will be different from a reading once the propositional content is extracted from the rhetorical vehicle. It will be seen that children do not demonstrate a capacity to separate these two levels of interpretation until a certain age.

The various research papers that can be classified as belonging to a developmental psychology of rhetoric fall into several categories. The first group deals with the ability of the child to perceive and understand when someone is lying. This skill is relevant when examining how children respond to communication like advertising which, if not exactly lying, paints a rosy, unrealistic picture of life. It is also relevant as the stereotype of the 'trusting child' can be explored to see if there is any truth in that assertion.

What does it mean, formally, to say that a person lies? It means that the person intends to deceive the hearer (or else it could be a mistake). It means that there is a discrepancy between the facts of the matter and what is said about the facts. But people can be ironical. That is, they can deliberately make a statement where there is such a discrepancy but where the purpose is to make a particular point. The ironical use of language can be categorized as a figurative or non-literal use of language. Lying, therefore, must depend on working out a speaker's intent as the existence of a discrepancy between fact and utterance is inadequate to provide a unique account of lying. The skills that, when present and assembled, constitute an understanding of lying or deception, would appear to be as follows.

First, there should be an explicit representation, in the mind of the understander, of the deceiver's belief about the relevant state-of-affairs. Suppose the child watches his sister take some money from their mother's purse. The mother returns and asks the child's sister if she has taken the money. The girl says no. Before the child can judge whether his sister is telling a lie, or is being ironic, or is mistaken, or that the facts of the matter are ill-defined, he has mentally to represent (using images or words) his sister's belief about who took the money in relation to his own beliefs. This mental representation of the beliefs of another person must be there before any inference can be drawn.

Second, there are various information processing skills involved. Children need to possess an ability to code the information in the state-of-affairs, to code the information in the utterance, to retain both sets of information in some working memory, to compare information from the different sources and to detect inconsistency in the information. These could be called the necessary mental mechanics for detecting lying. If one link in this chain is down (the child forgets what his sister did; the comparison is too complex and overloads the child's information processing capacity) then the understanding of deception fails.

Finally, there should exist an ability to infer the speaker's conversational purpose in using the utterance. In order to establish that the deceiver was, or most likely was, deceiving, other alternatives have to be assessed and discounted. This is a developing social skill that progresses through life because the range of alternatives and preference from one or the other will depend on knowledge of other people and their social situations. The range of alternatives might include deliberate deceit, a poor joke, temporary insanity, hallucinations, irony, and so on. Some of these can be discounted immediately because of the person. The choice of the 'deceit' option will depend on further knowledge, for example, is the sister an inveterate, habitual, or occasional liar?

There is evidence that very young children have a basic understanding of the intent of others. Shultz, Wells, and Sarda (1980) showed that 3- to 5-year-olds were able to distinguish correctly between intended acts and unintended behaviour such as mistakes. This ability, however, does not yet constitute even the minimal specification of another person's knowledge that is necessary to understand deception. A further achievement on the way to understanding deception is for you to know that she does or doesn't know about something that you know. So, if a nursery school teacher tells children an important fact that is new ('There will be a parents' evening next Friday') and a late-comer enters the classroom at that moment, will the children know the late-comer doesn't have this information they have? Experimental results (Chandler and Greenspan, 1972; Flavell et al., 1968; Marvin, Greenberg, and Mossler, 1976; Mossler et al., 1976) demonstrate that, from four years onwards, children are able to differentiate between their own knowledge and the absence of this knowledge in the other person.

There is another situation where both observer A and observer B are familiar with a state-of-affairs. In B's absence and A's presence, the state-of-affairs changes. Will A know that B thinks that the old state-of-affairs exists? Wimmer and Perner (1983) created a story where a character called Maxi puts chocolate into cupboard X. In Maxi's absence his mother takes the chocolate from X and puts it into cupboard Y. Where will Maxi look for the chocolate when he returns? Most 4- to 5-year-olds point incorrectly to box Y whereas almost all 6- to 9-year-olds point correctly to box X. Wimmer and Perner argue that during the period from 4 to 6 years, a new cognitive skill is emerging. This skill consists of the ability mentally to represent wrong beliefs of others, an ability that is an important basis for knowing how to lie and for understanding others' deception. During this period from 4 to 6 years of age the child shows the capacity to construct a deceitful utterance as well as inferring a deceptive plan from an utterance under certain restricted conditions. Shultz and Cloghesy (1981) played a card game with children where the child or experimenter had to guess cards. Deceptive as well as truthful strategies were built into the game. It was found that evidence for a strategy by the child that took advantage of knowledge that the experimenter could be deceiving did not emerge until 5 years of age and older. This recursive awareness of intentions, that is that others are aware of intentions, is a necessary prerequisite for understanding deception.

It can be concluded that the ability to maintain an explicit representation, in the mind of the understander, of the deceiver's belief about the relevant state-of-affairs emerges between 4 and 6 years of age. Wimmer and Perner (1983) conclude that it is during this period that 'the ability to represent the relationship between two or more persons' epistemic states emerges and becomes firmly established' (p. 126). 'Epistemic states' means states of knowledge or belief. The relationship between my knowing a state-of-affairs and my knowing that you know or don't know, or have different knowledge about that state of affairs, would seem to be necessary before any inference (based on this knowledge) towards a conclusion of deceit can be made.

As for the other abilities mentioned above, Ackerman (1981a) demonstrated that children between 6 and 7 years are capable of detecting inconsistencies in stories where statements are made that are inconsistent with facts presented previously in the story. By this time, they are also capable of deciding upon the states of knowledge and belief of others. So the situation is one where the child perceives a lack of fit between utterance and reality and can utilize knowledge of speakers' belief states. Children of this age, however, possess literal interpretive strategies which mean that the possibility of the person's being sarcastic, ironic, or deliberately flouting the rules of conversation to some purpose does not occur to them.

The confounding of deceit with other forms of intent was noted by Piaget (1965) who described a brief scenario to the child, for example another child claiming to have seen a dog as big as a cow, and then asked if that child was lying. It was not until age 10 or 11 years that children become sensitive to the importance of intent and explicitly give the adult definition of a lie. At 6 years lies are thought of as utterances that are forbidden or punished. 'Naughty words', mistakes, and deliberately misleading utterances are all classified by the child at this age as lies. By 8 years of age the child regards lies as covering 'untrue' statements. There is no differentiation of intent, however, so mistakes are placed in the same category as deliberately misleading utterances.

There are many social situations where lying refers to states-of-affairs that are not available to both parties. 'I love you' can be a lie, designed to obtain compliance from the other partner. The statement refers to a hidden emotional state. The skill of distinguishing lies from truth in this context is a valuable and difficult social skill that not all adults possess and which cannot ever be completely achieved. De Paulo, Jordan, Irvine, and Laser (1982) found little evidence of this skill until late adolescence at 17 years.

There is some work in the child language literature that has examined the understanding and production of what are known in linguistics as speech acts. Speech acts usually refer to just one part of the act of saying something. They are concerned with the 'conventional force' associated with the act, whether it is a statement, promise, offer, and all the other conventional forces that are recognized by the language community. When the developmental literature on the acquisition of an understanding of speech acts is looked at, it is apparent that there is a wide divergence between the production side of the process and the comprehension aspect. In terms of production, there is evidence that the pre-linguistic child in late infancy is communicating with primitive communicative acts that have conventional force, such as conveying a request or directing adult attention to objects and events (Bates *et al.*, 1975). Certainly by the early preschool period it is possible to find a rich variety of forms that communicate different speech acts in the spontaneous speech of children.

Dore (1977) identified 32 types of illocutionary act in an analysis of 3,000 utterances of 3-year-old children. The most common type, comprising 10 per cent of all types, was coded as an action request and defined as 'soliciting H (hearer) to perform an act'. These illocutionary acts are found in various children's utterances and the child can select from a range to achieve the same effect on hearers. One strategy, described by Dore (1977), is where the child produces an utterance in circumstances which prevent it from being taken literally. The child points to a wooden box and says 'That's a train.' The intent of the child as speaker is to get the hearer to role-play as if the box were a train, and the non-literal way of doing this is to signal, using a strategy of non-literal usage to indicate that a non-literal interpretation of 'That's a train' is intended. If this strategy is used between children of the same age then the child cast in the role of hearer will have to understand non-literal usage and, assuming that the usage skill exists amongst preschool peers and has not disappeared because of the non-comprehension by peer hearers, it must be the case that children of this age comprehend such non-literal language use. This is one example of an apparent preschool understanding that disappears in the primary school years only to emerge in later childhood. Another example is the child's developing understanding of metaphor which is discussed below.

The child's comprehension of discourse and, in particular, the intent of a speaker, appear to depend largely on awareness of the separate elements in a communication situation. Much of the time, the different parts of communication are not made salient. The child will hear people say what they mean. Usually the context of reference (the things in the world that are being discussed) supports the ongoing communication in that people are not ironic or sarcastic, and do not lie or make mistakes. Much of what is said is accompanied by non-verbal behaviour that supports the message. In many situations the child comprehends and shows an understanding that is based on information where intent is reflected in content and where context reinforces content. There are situations, however, where a lack of agreement will occur. The child has to work out what is going on and establish a set of strategies to cope with, for example, a lack of agreement between information conveyed by language (a joke) and by non-verbal channels (a straight face). It is these disagreement situations that have been the subject of a lot of the research into the child's comprehension of communicator intent.

One problem young children have in detecting communicator intent where disagreement between channels of information occurs is concerned with the requirement that the information has to be compared and currently checked for inconsistency. Markman (1977, 1979) found that, even by 8 or 9 years, children were insensitive to logical inconsistencies in information in prose paragraphs. In terms of general principles of development, Piaget and his followers have argued that children before about 7 years of age tend to centrate or focus on one aspect of a situation and are incapable of simultaneously taking more than one aspect of a problem into account in solving it. Hakes (1980) has argued that the ability to indulge in controlled cognitive processing and detach oneself mentally from the ongoing stream of communication does not emerge until middle childhood.

One situation of disagreement, in the sense described above, is where the normal rules of conversation are disrupted. For example, if A asks B, 'Is this new dentist any good?' and B replies, 'He's got a nice waiting room', then adult A would have to re-interpret B's reply as reflecting an indirect way of saying something relevant about the new dentist. How do children cope with this? Ackerman (1981b) found that 5- to 6-year-olds did not discriminate consistently between these rule-violating utterances and conversationally consistent pairs. Older children were able to detect such a rule-violation but were not able to infer correctly a reasonable interpretation of B's intent in violating the normal conversation rule guiding replies to queries until 8 or 9 years of age.

Part of the metalinguistic (or metacommunicative) competence of older children will involve some awareness of the relation between intended meanings and their expressions in sentences. Sometimes communication fails because of an ambiguity or informational inadequacy in the message. 'Give me the white one' is not enough if there are five white ones on the table. Robinson and Robinson (1977*a*, 1977*b*) found that 5-year-olds blamed the listener on the grounds that it was he who chose wrongly, while by the age of 7, children tended to blame the speaker and the inadequate message. It can be said that the younger children, because they lack the metalinguistic skill of distinguishing between speaker's meaning and sentence meaning, will blame the hearer. A sentence means what it says and says what it means to these children. There is some evidence, however, from Robinson *et al.* (1983) that ambiguous and unambiguous messages are processed differently by preschool children. These authors found that children of this age understood and remembered better those messages which adequately express a clear intention although they were, in fact, more complex than the simpler ambiguous messages which were understood and remembered less well.

A large area of investigation in the field of children's understanding of communication situations where there is a lack of simple agreement between what is said and what is meant is concerned with the child's understanding of figurative language, including metaphor. Much of the literature on the child's comprehension, production and appreciation of metaphor is centred on a programme of research called Project Zero at Harvard University and the following conclusions can be extracted from this body of work.

There is some evidence that primitive precursors of metaphor are found in infancy. Wagner, Winner, Gardner, and Cicchetti (cited in Winner *et al.*, 1979) found that infants preferred to look at a long line accompanied with a continuous tone and a dotted line accompanied by a pulsing tone rather than other combinations of tone and line. The importance of this observation is that the presence of universal, basic preferences for the qualities of one sensory modality accompanied with certain qualities of another sensory modality can be related, theoretically, to the foundations of metaphor. One such argument would be that cross-modal functioning (for example, sight to sound) is neurologically and cognitively advanced in the infant and can act as a basis on which to build certain characteristics of language. Synesthesia, which is the experience of one sense in terms of the other, and synesthetic description (where the descriptive language appropriate to one sensory modality such as smell borrows extensively from that of another such as sound) conform to rules and these rules and principles form the foundation of much of our experience of meaning.

The classic measure of affective meaning called the semantic differential was based on synesthetic principles (Osgood et al., 1975). A 'bright sound' and a 'high tone' can be understood metaphorically. Winner et al. (1979) go so far as to claim 'that the capacity to perceive metaphorically . . . is one of our birthrights' (p. 75). Certainly the systematic preference for certain cross-modal relations continues through the preschool period and into later childhood and this preference is not limited to synesthetically-based connections. For example, preschool children could successfully map the spatial relationships in one concrete object onto another object, where these spatial relationships do not apply in 'standard' discourse (Gentner, 1977). They could respond in a principled way to the question 'If this tree had a knee, where would it be?'

Preschool children also produce constructions that are metaphorical in type. Gentner (1977) cites a 2-year-old saying when undressed 'I'm barefoot all over.' Gardner et al. (1978) quoted a 3-year-old who called a chimney 'a house-hat' and another preschooler who referred to shoes so tight that 'my toes are huddled together'. In addition, there is adequate evidence that these constructions are often produced with evident delight by the child in word-play situations. The alternative theory, which would be that these extensions are a consequence of inadequate semantic development in preschool children and are akin to mistakes, is less credible.

So it would seem that metaphor emerges early in development and is characteristic of child speech in the preschool period. However, these metaphors that are produced at 3 or 4 years of age are different from the ones we encounter in poetry, advertising or popular books on economics, and the difference lies in the acceptability of the metaphor. Many of the metaphors of the preschool period are 'wild'; they are idiosyncratic constructions that have no conventionally accepted interpretation. There is also no evidence that metaphors are products to any purpose apart from play whereas the adult metaphor has an important role to play in discourse, whether the purpose is persuasive, aesthetic or didactic.

By the early primary school years, children's metaphoric production has diminished and preoccupation with literal meaning emerges. The period of 'literalness' is a characteristic of the child's understanding of figurative usage in general, where the meaning read is the meaning said is the meaning intended. In situations where non-literal meaning is intended or a lack of correspondence between facts and words flags a change of intent by the speaker, the child seems unable or unwilling to grasp or acknowledge this shift, and provides a literal interpretation. An understanding of metaphor is constructed during the primary school period. Winner, Rosenstiel, and Gardner (1976) explored different types of apprehension of metaphor from 6 to 14 years of age and detected a limited and distorted metaphoric understanding before 10 years.

So, for example, the sentence 'Her perfume was bright sunshine' elicited a significant difference between children younger than 10 years and children older than 10 years in choosing and providing an appropriate paraphrase. Younger children frequently chose and gave responses that were coded magical ('Her perfume was made out of rays of the sun') or coded metonymic ('When she was standing outside in the bright sun she was wearing perfume'), whereas older children were able to choose and give primitive metaphoric responses ('Her perfume was a bright yellow colour like the colour of the sun'), or genuine metaphoric responses ('Her perfume had a wonderful smell'). The ability to judge, select and paraphrase metaphors correctly (relative to the adult norm which reflects the conventions of the literate community of which the child is becoming a member) does not emerge until about 10 years of age. This is later than the age when the child is capable of adopting a metalinguistic stance towards language.

There are other forms of non-literal usage, apart from metaphor, that have been investigated developmentally. Ackerman (1982*a*; 1983) and Demorest, Silberstein, Gardner, and Winner (1983) have used a methodology whereby children of different ages are presented with a story which has a punch-line designed to reflect various types of figurative use of language. Children are presented with the punchline and asked 'Why did she say that?' So, for example, Demorest *et al.* (1983) told a story about Jane cleaning up her bedroom and making a complete mess of the exercise. Her sister came in and said ... The ending was either literal ('Your room is very messy'), metaphorical ('You have been growing a garden full of weeds'), ironical ('Your room is a mess now after all that cleaning'), understated ('Your room still needs a few things straightened up'), or sarcastic ('Your room looks like it's totally clean now').

It was found that 6-year-olds usually recognized neither the discrepancy of the utterances nor the speaker's purpose. Eight-year-olds recognized the discrepancy from the truth but failed to attribute purpose successfully or at all. It wasn't until 11 years of age that discrepancy was recognized and communicative purpose identified. Even then, there was an order of difficulty in recognizing communicative purpose with irony least well understood, followed in order by metaphor, understatement, hyperbole, and sarcasm.

These norms should be interpreted with some caution, however. In real interpersonal communication situations sarcasm is not just signalled by a simple discrepancy between fact and statement but can be carried on other channels such as tone of voice, facial expression and communicative setting. Demorest *et al.* (1983) do not mention tone of voice as a variable whereas Ackerman (1982*a*) states that 'those utterances that could be interpreted as sarcastic received a heavy intonational emphasis appropriate to sarcasm' (p. 1078). The understanding of figurative forms may be a late achievement for children but the experiments described above are somewhat lacking in ecological validity to claim norms beyond 11 years of age.

There are other more 'frozen' forms of figurative usage where the non-literal meaning is encapsulated in a particular turn of phrase that has been preserved in the language of the culture for some time. Idioms, like 'to kick the bucket' or proverbs like 'a rolling stone gathers no moss' come to mind. Ackerman (1982b) found that 6- to 7-year-olds were sensitive to need for a non-literal explanation when the idiom was placed in an appropriate story context but were unable, in general, to give the appropriate explanation. By 10 years of age, correct explanations were provided most of the time.

The literature on proverb understanding is more long-standing and Piaget (1926) found that schoolchildren up to 11 or 12 years of age were unable either to interpret proverbs on their own or to match proverbs with candidate paraphrases. Proverb interpretation awaits the reasoning capacities that develop only in adolescence. Another ability that is detectable only in adolescence is the child's sensitivity to literary styles (Gardner and Lohman, 1975). Before this period, children will classify literary passages and works of art on the basis of content rather than style.

Humour is used frequently in advertising. Unfortunately, when the literature on the child's production and appreciation of humour is examined, it is difficult to establish firm age band boundaries. Humour comes in many different varieties. Some jokes are visual, others play on social conventions, whereas puns and word-play are basically linguistic. Each form requires different skills for comprehension. A state-of-the-art report at the end of the 1970s (McGhee and Chapman, 1980) concluded that 'in the final analysis, the comprehension and appreciation of humour must be a totally individual affair' (p. 296). Notwithstanding these differences across humour typology and individual children, the area of humour research is relevant and promising if only to establish whether the humour employed by advertisers is being understood by children or is beyond them.

That concludes this chapter on the different threads of

development that are relevant when considering the complex skills involved in advertising literacy. In the next chapter some empirical work that has been conducted in this country on the influence of television advertising on children will be described.

8

British Children's Understanding of Television Advertising: Experimental Research

MISCELLANEOUS STUDIES

British research into the influence of television advertising on children is limited compared with the programme of research conducted in the United States. In this chapter the findings of British researchers will be summarized with the author's own research (see Young, 1985, 1987a, 1987b, for a more detailed description). Going back to the earliest study on television and children we find only a brief passing reference to advertising. Younger children in Britain in 1956 liked advertisements better than the older children (Himmelweit et al., 1958, p. 106).

Durkin (1983) reports on an interesting finding in part of a programme of research into sex roles in children's television. A commercial for Impulse deodorant spray was shown to children. It depicted a young woman using the product with subsequent devastating effects upon a young man. On catching a scent of the spray as he alights from a train near the woman, the young man finds himself (impulsively) rushing to purchase flowers to present to her, despite the fact they appear to be previously unacquainted. The popularity of this story can be confirmed by the fact that the same dramatic structure with a different content was still being broadcast in Britain in 1989 and the theme has appeared internationally. After viewing, children were asked: 'Why did he give her flowers?' Although the sample sizes were small, consisting of six 5-year-olds, seven 7-year-olds and four 9-year-olds, the results were quite clear-cut. Children younger than 7 years replied 'Because he liked her', and the 9-year-olds replied 'Because she smelled nice'. A *post hoc* explanation of this finding could be that if the child understood the commercial intent behind the ad the whole point of the story is understood. The role of the product is central to the plot and the correct answer reflects this. For the younger children, who have established no such relationship between product, plot and intent of the communicator, the story is a simple romance with the product playing a secondary rather than a central role. This type of research is extremely valuable and provides a fresh insight into the problem of diagnosing an understanding of persuasive or commercial intent in the child but, unfortunately, it requires the choice or creation of appropriate ads like the Impulse Commercial.

Sweeney (1983) discusses the effects of television advertising on children in general terms based on the research conducted by the Children's Research Unit (CRU) in London. Much of the comment is unsubstantiated by reference to other work, not supported by empirical data, and based on vague generalizations. For example: 'CRU's research experience with UK children shows that they are aware of the purpose of advertising *at a very early age*' (p. 175, my italics).

Cullingford (1984) makes general points in his book based on responses from over 5,000 children to questions on television. Just what these questions were, or how results were analysed, or what the children's backgrounds were, is not revealed, and this lack of information devalues any conclusions he draws. We are told that 'nearly all children were consistent and positive in expressing their liking for advertisements' (p. 120). Humour is appreciated as a technique in commercials. Children aged 7 and 8 enjoy commercials for products that are not directed at them, such as carpets, telephones, savings banks, and so on. Many of these ads employ humour, or eye-catching visual devices, or memorable jingles. Sixty-nine per cent of children referring to their favourite advertisements cited those specifically aimed at adults.

Where it is possible to obtain facts from figures in Cullingford's book, results confirm the United States findings. For example 'By the age of twelve less than half the children believed even their favourite advertisement; only about ten per cent believed what their favourite advertisement said' (p. 126). This demonstrates the scepticism characteristic of late childhood and adolescence that was noted by Linn, Benedictis, and Delucchi (1982). Cullingford's message seems to be — don't worry, children remember ads, particularly the slogans reinforced by jingles, and are entertained, but not seduced, by them.

Sheehy and Chapman (1988) were interested in the representation of childhood and children found in television advertising and analysed the content of 88 advertisements recorded from British television that depicted children. The categories of child representation chosen (with the judged image as a percentage of all childhood representations in brackets) were naturalistic representation (34 per cent), angelic representation (34 per cent), 'impish' image (16 per cent), and 'mini-adult' (16 per cent).

STUDIES ON HEALTH-RELATED ISSUES

One of the major concerns of health education professionals is the extent to which advertising of certain products encourages their consumption by children, when that product cannot be sold to children legally, or when overconsumption poses threats to a child's health and well-being. Tobacco falls into this category. Cigarette advertising is restricted by law in Britain. It is banned on television and must be accompanied by a Government health warning on billboards, magazines, and newspapers. Cigarettes cannot be sold to children under 16. Is there any evidence, however, that cigarette advertising is influencing children to smoke? Many sporting events are sponsored by tobacco companies and it has been argued that the presence of brand names and brand colours, and logos on racing cars and around snooker tables is a method of advertising that evades regulations.

In research that received a lot of press publicity at the time, Ledwith (1984) found that many Manchester secondary schoolchildren were able to name cigarette brands that were associated with sponsored sports. In the first such study, he took a random sample of schools and classes in the Greater Manchester area and gave a questionnaire to 880 children aged from 11 to 16 years. They were asked to list the cigarette brands they knew and to describe their smoking habits, intentions and attitudes. In addition they estimated the time they had spent viewing a recent snooker championship sponsored by Benson and Hedges. Benson and Hedges was the predominant brand listed, and the one children claimed to smoke if they did admit to smoking. Children who watched more snooker were more likely to associate various cigarette brands with sport. In a second study, a similar survey was carried out in the week following the end of the Embassy World Snooker Championship. As was predicted, there was an increase in the recall of the brand Embassy.

Does this mean that cigarette advertising to children exists in Britain and does it influence children? The answer, on this evidence, must be a qualified 'yes'. Brand salience as measured by recall increases and, if advertisers claim that cigarette advertising influences brand choice only, salience must be a determinant of that choice. The question on the existence of cigarette advertising to children is one that could be discussed at length as the answer will depend on questions of definition. Symbols of the brand such as the name, logo, colours associated with the pack are all consistently present in the context of sports that are attractive and appealing to older children. This could be taken as one part of the complex process of promotion, marketing or advertising.

Is there any evidence that children use this information gained from advertising to smoke more or to start smoking? Research in Australia indicates that attitudes towards cigarette advertising can predict future changes in children's smoking behaviour (Alexander et al., 1983). This study of about 6,000 children ranging from 10 to 12 years looked at the change in their smoking behaviour over 12 months from 1979 to 1980. When children who did not smoke in either 1979 or 1980 (non-smokers) were compared with those who did not smoke in 1979 but smoked by 1980 (adopters), it was found that one of the factors distinguishing these two groups was approval of cigarette advertising. Children who approved of cigarette advertising were twice as likely to become smokers as children who disapproved. If children who smoked in 1979 and 1980 (smokers) were compared with those who smoked in 1979 but did not smoke in 1980 (quitters), then disapproval of cigarette advertising became a factor that separated the two groups. Children who disapproved of cigarette advertising were more likely to quit than those who approved of it. Of course there were many other factors that distinguished one group from the other, such as having friends or siblings who smoke, amount of pocket-money, and age of child. Nevertheless, children's attitude towards advertising would appear to influence their decision to continue or to quit smoking.

An earlier analysis of the 1979 cohort (O'Connell *et al.*, 1981) had established that children who smoked approved of cigarette advertising more than children who did not smoke. Results from a Scottish investigation where 726 children aged between 6 and 17 years of age were interviewed individually on a number of issues relating to smoking and cigarette advertising (Aitken *et al.*, 1986*a*) demonstrated that children who smoked and children who said they would smoke when they were older tended to be less in favour of a ban on cigarette advertising. This empirical evidence that liking and doing (or disliking and not doing) go together is predictable from theories of attitudes and their role in behaviour instigation, maintenance and change.

Smoking and not approving of, or not liking, advertisements for the product, would induce cognitive dissonance, a state of cognitive contradiction. Cognitive dissonance drives its own reduction because people find it mentally uncomfortable and seek ways to reduce it. One way of doing this is to increase approval of cigarette advertising, which would then be consonant with one's smoking behaviour. There is a tangled relationship here between feeling and doing, where attitudes towards advertising constitute the feeling aspect and smoking cigarettes the doing. There is no causal relationship, however, and it would be premature to claim causal models that describe the relationship for children or adolescents between thought and feeling about certain cultural representations of a brand of cigarette, and consumption of that brand or product. In recent comprehensive reviews of the literature on the role of tobacco advertising on the initiation (van Raiij, 1990) and maintenance (Poiesz, 1990) of smoking in young people, both authors conclude that there is no established set of findings that support the case that tobacco advertising contributes substantially to the initiation (van Raiij, 1990) or the maintenance (Poiesz, 1990) of such behaviour.

In the same paper, Aitken *et al.* (1986*a*) found that the percentage of children who wanted cigarette advertising banned decreased from 80 per cent at age 6 years to 44 per cent with 16- and 17-year-olds. When children were asked for reasons for banning cigarette advertisements, both younger and older children cited health issues such as cigarettes being harmful to health. The answers that reflect an understanding of the persuasive power of advertising, such as 'Adverts encourage people to smoke' or 'Adverts glamorize smoking and make you look tough', were age-related. Few children below the age of 10 mentioned these as arguments for banning but by 11 years and older they were cited frequently. This observation underlines the distinction between knowing that advertising has a persuasive function and applying that knowledge in an argument or assessment situation. This distinction is elaborated when the author's own research is discussed below.

In a further analysis of the same data base, Aitken, Leathar, and Squair (1986*b*) looked at the Scottish child's awareness of cigarette brand sponsorship of sports and games in Britain. By 10 years of age, about half the children claimed to know what 'sponsorship' meant but less than one in seven could give a full definition that embraced both the commercial and advertising aspects. Sponsorship is a transaction where the sponsor gives money (commercial side) and gets publicity (advertising side). It was the advertising component of sponsorship that most children failed to mention, even when prompted. Even by 16 years, fewer than half the adolescents were able to give a satisfactory definition that encompassed both parts. Given the lack of understanding of the term 'sponsorship', it is not surprising that over half the sample overall could not think of any brands of cigarettes that sponsor sports or games or any makes or brands that were connected with sports or games. When respondents did mention brands and sports being connected, the results replicated those of Ledwith (1984). The case that television sports sponsorship acts as cigarette advertising for children is therefore strengthened by these results.

Aitken *et al.* (1986*b*) acknowledge that their method of asking for answers to questions on definition of terms has weaknesses. For example, giving a satisfactory answer can tax the verbal and cognitive skills of the developing child, and any constraints on response may be imposed by limitations on cognitive or linguistic expression, or both, rather than being a consequence of a lack of understanding. There is a recurrent controversy in the literature on the assessment of the child's understanding of advertising between methods that rely on interview methodologies and those using nonverbal techniques.

Another method was used by Aitken *et al.* (1986*b*). Different cigarette advertisements were laid out on cards and the experimenter read out descriptions of different kinds of people. Each child had to point to the advertisement that showed the brand each person would like most. So, if someone was described as liking excitement and fast racing cars, we would expect children to point at the Marlboro ad if the ad has 'worked' by succeeding in having the cigarette associated with excitement and fast cars. With this method we do indeed find advertising 'working' with children. For example, although only 9 per cent of primary school children named Marlboro or John Player Special as being associated with or sponsoring racing cars, 47 per cent of these children pointed to advertisements as being liked by 'someone who likes excitement and fast racing cars'.

Aitken and his colleagues in the Advertising Research Unit at the University of Strathclyde have conducted qualitative research into children's understanding of advertising as well as the more quantitative survey research described above. The qualitative method employed in most of their studies used group discussion where children were led through a carefully selected schedule of topics and the tape-recorded comments were subsequently examined. This method is popular in advertising research and is one of a range of qualitative techniques designed to allow the free expression of opinion, unfettered by the strict procedures of experimental psychology.

It should be pointed out, however, that any analyses of children's comments on particular advertisements cannot provide normative data for that particular age, if these children are in a group. It can only give an indication of whether or not particular responses are available to that group of children at that particular age. Any measure of salience for an individual can only really be established during an individual interview by a trained interviewer who does not unconsciously promote or reinforce the 'correct' response. If one child in a group setting gives a subtle or sophisticated reply and the adult group facilitator unintentionally reinforces this by smiling, nodding or giving that reply more attention than other responses, then the other children will be more likely to perceive that reply as the one the grown-up expects, and will perform accordingly. Consequently, one would expect norms based on group discussion to be cited as earlier than the more valid norms established in individual assessments. Notwithstanding these criticisms, it is a popular and proven technique in advertising research.

The University of Strathclyde research on children's perceptions of cigarette advertising can be found in several sources (Aitken et al., 1985a, 1985b, 1986c; Aitken, 1988; Aitken et al., forthcoming). They worked with twenty-four groups of about ten children in each. The ages of the children ranged from 6 to 16 years and they were drawn from contrasting socio-economic areas of inner-city deprivation and leafy suburbia. All the groups discussed the imagery in magazine ads for various products including cigarettes.

The cigarette ads utilize special imagery techniques that have been cultivated as a distinctive feature of cigarette advertising in Britain. For example, Benson and Hedges cigarettes are advertised with surrealistic imagery and minimal brand name identification, with fragments of the pack identifiers such as a letter 'B' providing a cue to the brand name. 'Brand stretching' is practised with JPS Grand Prix Holidays where the brand identity is dissociated from the act of smoking and related to other activities and images such as high-status holidays and racing cars.

Under these conditions, a picture of the child's understanding of advertising imagery can be constructed and this picture suggests that there is a developmental progression from a superficial understanding of obvious, perceptually-based characteristics of the ad to a deeper understanding of ad imagery, driven by knowledge of what the ad is there for. The youngest children of 6 to 8 years, when faced with 'brand stretching', will focus on the visual content and argue that the ad advertises racing or racing cars. Older children aged from 8 to 10 years will still concentrate on the visual aspect, but this time more on the wording which concerns holidays, and will say it advertises holidays. By late childhood and early adolescence, however, most children will see that cigarette advertising is involved and will also question the credibility of placing the brand in such a remote context ('What's John Player holidays got to do with cigarettes?' from a 12-year-old inner-city boy), and even construct the advertiser's intent in producing such an irrelevant association ('using holiday pictures to say that cigarettes are relaxing', from a 14-year-old suburban boy).

The 'brandless' imagery of the Benson and Hedges ad worked with children in the sense that a majority at each age, except 6 years, said it advertised cigarettes. Several children mentioned during discussion that the Government Health Warning appeared on cigarette advertisements. Interestingly, about a quarter of the 6- to 10-year-olds misinterpreted this sign and said the ad represented anti-smoking publicity! Although norms are difficult to establish with this method of group discussion, Aitken and his colleagues do claim that the suburban groups were often capable of articulating the selling component in a definition of advertising, even at age 6 years.

Recognition of the symbolism in ads for cigarettes was detectable with 12-year-olds and older children who were capable of describing the sort of person who would 'like this ad'. So the ad used for Kim cigarettes, although quite muted by international standards, generated a woman, an office-worker in her twenties who wears colourful, up-to-date, trendy clothes, likes modern pop or disco music, and enjoys a lively night life and casual sports. This stereotype was quite different from the sort of person who would like the ad for More cigarettes. This finding partially confirms the research conclusions of Belk, Bahn, and Mayer (1982) in the United States on the recognition of consumption symbolism in school age children, the difference being that Belk *et al.* were concerned with the child's perception of the sort of person who might consume that brand of product.

It is apparent from the research of Aitken and his colleagues that there is more to the development of the child's understanding of advertising than recognition of persuasive or commercial intent. Going into adolescence the child is constructing an interpretation of the figurative forms found in advertising. Sometimes this understanding is not complete. The 12-year-old inner-city boy cited by Aitken *et al.* (forthcoming) who, when faced by the classic ad for Marlboro cigarettes, said, 'I don't see what horses have to do with cigarettes,' is misunderstanding the metaphorical nature of this representation or simply deciding not to search for a non-literal, intended meaning.

As well as investigating children's perceptions of cigarette advertising, Aitken and his colleagues were interested in the perceptions of advertisements for alcoholic drinks by groups of children from 10 to 16 years of age (Aitken *et al.*, 1987; Aitken, 1989). They also used a group discussion format. Results showed a developmental trend in that the group salience of alcoholic drink advertisements increased from 10 to 16 years. In other words, 10-year-old groups of children rarely mentioned alcohol advertising when listing advertisements seen recently and when describing favourite advertisements, but by 16 years of age advertisements for alcohol products like beers and lagers were among the first mentioned, and among the top favourites. One reason for this preference and salience could be the humour that characterized these ads. All children placed considerable emphasis on humour as a characteristic for liking an ad. The younger children also liked brightness and colour.

For older children from 14 to 16 years, preferred ads were often the stylish and innovative ones. Here can be seen the development of a critical evaluation of the world within the ad, not just the qualities the ad possesses, such as humour and brightness, but whether the world of style and glamour that the ad represents is a suitable one for their tastes. Even the youngest children were capable of identifying the target groups of different ads and saw some (such as Martini) aimed at 'posh ladies'. The symbolism became more sophisticated with the older groups. Adolescents aged from 14 years to 16 years saw beer and lager advertising campaigns as promoting masculinity, sociability, and working-class values, whereas the campaigns for Martini, for example, were seen as promoting a blend of sociability, style, sophistication, and attractiveness — for women.

Aitken, Eadie, Leathar, McNeill, and Scott (1988) explored the same problem using a more quantitative methodology where 433 Glasgow children aged between 10 and 17 years were interviewed about television advertisements for alcohol-related products. Findings were consistent with the results obtained with qualitative research. Older children tended to be more appreciative of such commercials and under-age drinkers were more adept at recognizing and identifying brand imagery, suggesting they paid more attention to alcohol commercials. Their evidence suggests that these commercials are reinforcing under-age drinking.

RESEARCH ON ADVERTISING LITERACY

In this section, results from the author's own programme of research stemming from an 18-month investigation funded by the Health Education Council in 1983 and subsequently supported by a grant from the University of Salford, will be described. It soon became apparent from an examination of the literature on the effects of television advertising on children, that the development of the child's understanding of the concept of a television advertisement was central to any research in this area. Consequently, any British investigation into how children understand television must tackle the central problem of what a television commercial means to a child in our culture.

An interview schedule was constructed that consisted of

questions that had already been tried and tested in the literature plus some innovative ones. For example, the child was asked what he or she thought the advertisement was really telling him/her, a question that had not been used in this research before. Subjects were taken from primary classes at two schools in an urban area in the north west of England. One school was deliberately chosen as representative of children drawn from a professional middle-class area, and the other was seen as taking in children from an inner-city catchment area, and in some cases the children came from socially disadvantaged and deprived homes. No claims were made that this sampling reflected the complex cultural and socio-economic divisions within this part of England, but given the sample size limitations it was considered necessary to sample children from two schools which are typically different. There were 39 5- to 6-year-olds, 36 7-year-olds, and 48 children older than 8 (within a range of 8 to 10 years), with approximately equal groups on sex and school.

When the results of the interviews were analysed it was decided to establish a category called 'commercial' which would normally include a reference to buying or selling. Within this category were two sub-categories of 'super-commercial' responses where in addition to reference to buying or selling, there was reference to additional functions. These were either 'informative' or 'persuasive'. It is important to note that the commercial/persuasive function of television commercials, which is often not distinguished in the literature, was clearly separated out in this analysis so it was possible for a child to refer to a commercial solely in terms of its persuasive function ('It gets you to do things'), or in terms of its commercial function ('It's to do with what to buy'), or in terms of its commercial and persuasive functions ('It's making you buy it').

Results from these interviews confirmed an age-related trend that had been discovered in the original American research reviewed in Chapter 3. That is, as children got older they tend to refer more to the commercial intent behind advertising when asked about television commercials. The age norms, however, for the frequency of these responses varied depending on the question asked. For example, if a specific television commercial was shown and the child was asked what this advertisement wanted him or her to do, over half the 7-year-olds made a response that could be classified as 'commercial'. On the other hand, a standard question from the literature such as 'What is a television advertisement?' presented without the benefit of a television commercial being shown as an example would only produce 'commercial' responses from one-third of the children aged 8 years and older.

Clearly, it was not possible to establish figures on number of children understanding commercial intent on the basis of one question. Some other method had to be found. This was done by categorizing responses across the whole battery of questions given during the interview. If the child never referred to the commercial function of television advertising during the whole interview, this child could be categorized as different from a child who made at least one reference to commercial intent when replying to at least one question during the interview. There is evidence that the commercial function response is not available to the former child whereas, in the latter child's case, just one reference is enough to establish the availability of this response in the child's repertoire. The child who replies frequently with a commercial function response to many questions during the interview has a salient commercial function response which is available.

The distinction between salience and availability of responses is a familiar one in psychology. Briefly, an available response is one that is there in the range of possible responses for a child of a particular age or stage of development. This particular available response may not be very likely to emerge or may require a particular set of contextual circumstances to promote its elicitation. That is, it may not be very salient compared with the other available responses. The importance of drawing this distinction between salience and availability in the literature on children and television advertising is discussed in more detail in Young (1986). Information on the availability of commercial function responses is given in Table 8.1.

The results in Table 8.1 can be taken as constituting a valid set of age norms for this British sample. Obviously,

TABLE 8.1.   *Number of children mentioning commercial function of advertising during interview*

Reference to commercial function	Age (in years)		
	5–6	7	8+
None	28	11	8
Some	11	25	40
TOTAL	39	36	48

both in the United States and in Britain, age norms are sensitive to the form of question used in interview and depend on methodology. What has been established is whether there is any evidence that the child considers 'buying the product' as a relevant function of television advertising or a relevant part of the definition of a television advertisement. In other words, Table 8.1 gives norms that are concerned with whether the minimal rudiments of a relationship between purchasing and television advertising are present in the child, or whether it never crosses the child's mind to consider purchasing the product as part of the concept of television advertising. They are norms concerned with the availability of a commercial reference response.

Although distinctions between commercial responses and 'super-commercial' responses were made in the analysis, the sample size was not large enough to reflect these differences in any significant way with different ages. Nevertheless, the difference between the commercial and persuasive function of advertising is an important theoretical distinction and one that should be made in any research in this field.

Understanding that advertising is there to persuade one to purchase is a skill that is intimately related to various important aspects of the child's development. It shows an ability to go beyond the face-value of a communication, to 'read between the lines', to be aware that all communications have a source and that often this source is intending to produce an effect on an audience or receiver of the communication.

Being able to understand that advertising persuades is a similar ability to knowing that some people will try to seduce you with words and other social actions, that there is a convention in courts and debating chambers that advocates present just one side of a case, and that in general people are not disinterested when communicating with others. Knowing these things and thus being able to interpret what is being said is a major part of growing up and surviving in an acquisitive and competitive society. On the other hand, reference to the commercial functioning of advertising need not reflect cognitive maturity, just as a lack of commercial reference does not reflect cognitive immaturity. The reply 'because it wants you to buy it' or 'to buy things', can reflect the extent to which 'buying and selling' as concepts are emphasized, culturally, in relation to television advertisements. Presumably, for most children who know what money is and what it means to purchase, the concept of buying will be most closely linked with contextual features of typical buying situations such as corner shop transactions, supermarket check-outs, and pocket money on Saturdays.

Given this relationship between 'buying' and what could be called the canonical or standard features of buying, what is interesting is the extent to which other aspects of the environment are then related to this core concept of purchase and economic transaction. To the adult, advertising in general is related via a common-sense understanding of economics and capitalism to economic exchange. So, for the adult, ads are there in order to 'make you want to buy the product'. For the child the relation between advertising and buying will be intimate or remote depending on whether the culture of the child establishes close or negligible links between the two. And this, in turn, is a function of educational programmes such as consumer education packages, or general features of the socialization process such as families, or peers, or TV commercials, or newspapers emphasizing the commercial role of advertising.

To pursue an analogy, for most people the concept

'politics' has some meaning. It is to be expected that there are some canonical features associated with 'politics' such as, in Britain, the symbolism of the House of Commons or political parties or famous MPs or ministers. The extent to which other aspects of life would be related to 'politics' would depend largely on the background of the respondent. For certain feminists, interpersonal relationships between men and women are intimately related to 'politics' and may even constitute the canonical features of the concept. The accretion of different features of meaning to social concepts will depend on socialization, culture and experience. Similarly, the extent to which the relationship between television commercials and buying/selling is seen as intimate or remote will depend on socialization as well as cognitive maturity.

There was one unexpected result from the interviews with this cohort of 123 children. One of the television commercials used was for a brand of biscuit called Star Wars. The ad consisted of 14 separate shots. The first and the last were shots of the pack in two different settings while the other 12 consisted of fast cut and closely edited excerpts from the film *Star Wars*. A voice-over provided a theme linking this visual information. When children were asked what they thought the advertisement was really telling them, the answers could be categorized as either referring to the brand or to other parts of the message. So children could say the ad was really telling them about the biscuit or they could claim the ad was really telling them all about *Star Wars* or Luke Skywalker (who featured prominently in the scenes).

It has been argued in Chapter 5 that the basic discourse structure of a television commercial is a topic, which is the brand, placed in a context, and that the context frequently has a metaphorical function of transposing the brand from the mundane world into the exotic and fantastical world-in-the-ad. Borrowing terms from theories of metaphor, we can categorize reference to the brand in answer to the question as 'topic' responses, and reference to other parts of the commercial as 'vehicle' responses. Table 8.2 gives this information by age. It should be noted that some responses

TABLE 8.2. *Responses categorized as 'topic' or 'vehicle' in reply to 'What do you think this advertisement is really telling you?' (%)*

Response	Age (in years)		
	5–6	7	8+
Vehicle	36	6	6
Topic	10	17	54
TOTAL	46	23	60

will not refer to either the topic or the vehicle but will be categorized differently. Consequently the total percentage is given as it may not always be 100 per cent.

The results are quite clear. There is a shift in response occurring about 7 years of age. Older children tend to reply with 'topic' responses but the majority of younger children give 'vehicle' replies. Why? For the adult (and older child) there is no problem in interpreting the question. Ads are telling you about brands and, as that is part of the generic information you possess about advertisements as a category, then the ad is really telling you about the biscuit. The presence of *Star Wars* simply serves the purpose of dressing up the topic (the brand).

There are two possible reasons for the 'vehicle' responses of the younger children. The question that was put to the children presumes there are two levels of discourse. One is an obvious, superficial, and perceptual level and the other is a deeper, hidden level. The younger child, because of cognitive limitations, is unable to operate at both of these levels and tends to choose the part of the commercial that is obvious and perceptually salient, that is, the *Star Wars* segment. An alternative explanation is that the child does not yet possess an adequate knowledge of the generic information carried by commercials. This information, common to the category of advertising, is that television commercials constitute a form of discourse where the topic is the brand

and all commercials are really about brands. The older child, by developing an ability to go beyond immediate perceptual data and by developing a literacy with advertising that incorporates this knowledge of advertising discourse, is able to pick the brand as the reply to the question.

CHILDREN'S CATEGORIZATION OF ADVERTISEMENTS

The results cited above confirmed a view of children's understanding of television advertising that had been developing as the results of these experiments emerged and as a critical examination of the literature on the topic was being done. It was becoming clear that the child's understanding of the nature and purpose of advertising was not a simple matter of 'acquiring' an ability to attribute persuasive and/or commercial intent to what was seen on television. There is no fixed age norm when this occurs and what occurs may best be described as consisting of several distinct developmental strands. The term 'advertising literacy' was coined (Young, 1986) to try to cover some of the characteristics of the child's understanding of advertising. This term presumes that there is more than a simple skill involved and suggests that several skills, serving the purpose of 'reading ads', will develop from infancy through to adulthood. The term also has the advantage of placing the child at the centre of the stage. Children and their growing and developing abilities are the object of study and the mould of the child being on the receiving end of some noxious stimulus called 'advertising' is (hopefully) broken.

The next step in the research by the author and Dr Alan Tuohy at the University of Salford tackled a fundamental problem, the basis on which children organize the concept of 'advertisement'. With adults, the procedure is quite clear. The adult is asked to think of the concept and, in particular, of different types that constitute the variety of instances of that concept. The adult then is required to provide as many characteristics as are needed to distinguish one type from another. If the concept to be explored is 'advertisement', one adult may conceive of ads as differentiated from each other because ads can be funny or serious, interesting or boring, animated or non-animated, and so on. The descriptions that distinguish ads from one another, the dimensions that provide internal structure to the concept 'advertisement' are kept as data.

The procedure had to be simplified for children, however, while still maintaining the purpose, which was to obtain dimensions of differentiation within the mental category of 'advertisement'. The eventual procedure used was as follows. Several 'warm-up' questions were given to each child, who was asked about most and least favourite television programmes and advertisements. The child was then asked to think of his or her favourite ad and write down what kind of ad it was. Some children may give only the brand mentioned in that particular ad but others could and would lay out various sub-categories such as 'boring' or 'funny', or categories based on product type such as food. The question was repeated for least favourite ad and any other kinds they could think of. Once a list of 'kinds of ads' had been obtained from the child, he or she was asked to write 'a short description of that kind of advertisement' for each entry.

The procedure was used on 65 children of 8 years and 66 aged 10 years drawn from three separate schools in the Manchester area, using one complete class at each (approximate) age level at each school. In addition, 60 adult university students were used. More than 1,000 descriptions (children) or ways of differentiating ads from each other (adults) were obtained, many of which were the same. These were reduced to 46 relatively separate attributes, by putting together synonyms and repetitions, which can be regarded as a list of ways children and adults possess for describing or differentiating 'kinds of ads'. A complete list of these 46 attributes is found in the Appendix at the end of this chapter. Of course, some of these may never or only rarely be mentioned by children. This provided the opportunity to create a data matrix that consisted of more than 1,000 rows comprising each obtained response and 46 columns which were the attributes. Each entry in the matrix marked either the presence (1) or absence (0) of that attribute for this response.

The data matrix was subjected to various forms of statistical manipulation in order to see what attributes 'go together' for different groups of respondents. Some attributes can be regarded as 'child-enhanced' in that they have a greater probability of elicitation from child than from adult groups. Other attributes are 'adult-enhanced' because they have a greater probability of elicitation from adult groups than from child groups. The child-enhanced attributes contain several that are product-oriented (such as *feature, variety*, and *brand*) and that are non-critically concerned with the ostensible purpose of advertisments (*sell, use*). Many of the adult-enhanced attributes are concerned with critically examining the advertisement in the larger context of the real world and do not accept its internal assumptions and intentions at face value. So, for example, adults are significantly more likely to recognize glamorization, ideological bias, the use of symbolism, and the exploitation of stereotypes although they may not use these very words.

By using various forms of factor analysis, it was possible to explore the organization of attributes with the two groups of children and the adult group. One particular method was to take certain attributes that did not differ in citation across groups. That is, the attribute emerged with approximately the same probability of occurrence in young children, older children and adults. This particular attribute need not be organized relative to other attributes in the same way for each group. It may 'go with' a certain set of attributes in the analysis for the young children and be related to a different constellation of attributes with the adult group. For example, *humour* emerged with all three groups and was not cited with different frequencies across the groups.

The following developmental sequence can be inferred from the data analysis. The young child construes *humour* in two ways. Firstly, it is part of the immediate texture of the advertisement itself, on a par with variables such as *animation* and *music*. However, a second construction is also present in which the variable *humour* is found with variables that begin to assess the relationship between viewer and advertisement (for example, *interest* and *annoyance*). By the age of 10 years separate functions appear to be integrated, in that *humour* occurs only in the context of both *interest* and *impact*. *Humour* is absent in the factorial structure of adults but this does not of course imply that adults have no sense of humour in advertisements. Since it is known that this variable was not elicited less often from adults, it may be concluded that it is not an important correlate of the structure of advertisement perception for this group, but remains as a background feature which is not relevant to classification. Tracing the changing structural role of these important attributes that are found throughout the sequence of development is a valuable technique for inferring the child's perception of 'an advertisement'.

A second group of correlated variables of extreme interest are those which can be described as having to do with the enhancement or transcendence of reality (*glamour, sex appeal*, and *stereotype*). For these variables, the probability of elicitation differs across groups with a strong advantage for adults as opposed to both groups of children. It was not surprising to find all these variables absent from the factorial structure of the youngest group. What was surprising and required an explanation was the strong presence of these variables in the factor structure of 10-year-olds. They 'went together' as a group in the statistical analysis. We thought this could be considered as evidence that children were beginning to disengage from the self-contained universe of the advertisement and that such detachment may herald the beginnings of appraisal. The child is not just commenting on the perceptual qualities of the ad or describing emotional feelings on viewing but is commenting on the ad as cultural object, detached from the immediate perceptual and affective context of viewing.

There are other, associated attributes, however, that also went with *glamour, sex appeal*, and *stereotype* as a factor in the factor analysis. These were *customer, creativity*, and *use*, and an examination of the gloss of these terms in the Appendix to this chapter led us to the conclusion that the origins of appraisal that can be detected in *glamour, sex appeal*, and *stereotype* are still firmly anchored as attributes of the advertisement *per se*. They are all descriptions of the content of advertisements. With adults, the structural arrangement is different. The cluster of three (*glamour, sex appeal*, and *stereotype*) are still there as a factor but are accompanied by *ego, information*, and *sponsor*. Examination of the gloss of these three in the Appendix would suggest that the cluster of three can be regarded as part of a process of detached appraisal by adults in contrast to children.

This approach seemed to us to be a good blend of the relative strengths of quantitative and qualitative methodologies. The analysis of a large data base, initially constructed from entries with simply two values corresponding to *presence* or *absence*, can be done with all the sophistication found in state–of–art statistical analysis packages. The inferences and construction of a general model of 'how the child understands advertising' constitutes interpretive activity and requires full discussion with peers and colleagues before the picture takes shape.

The picture that is beginning to take shape consists of a coherent developmental sequence with two main strands. The first of these defines a successive shift in perspective, in which the perceiver's viewpoint is disembedded from within the textural features of the advertisement itself, moves through the world shown in the advertisement, and finally steps outside the advertisement to regard it in a critical fashion in the real world. The second developmental strand suggested by the data refers to the ability to deal with indirectly expressed levels of meaning. 'Reading between the lines' (which is the original etymological meaning of the word 'intelligence') is a skill that presupposes a distinction held by the reader between content and intent, and which recognizes the likelihood that some maxims that characterize canonical forms of communication may not be complied with. Metaphor, for example, requires some form of recognition from the reader that ideas have been transposed into odd places before any new meaning is appreciated or any aesthetic pleasure caused by the created tension is enjoyed. Although these lines of development are theoretically distinguishable they will interact in practice, since the ability to analyse the advertisement in terms of, for instance, its rule-violation, in turn presupposes the ability to regard it as an object existing in the real world.

In the next and final chapter I shall attempt to provide a summary of the content of these eight chapters.

APPENDIX

The 46 advertisement attributes identified in subjects' typologies

Variable code	Definition of attribute
Aggression	Hectoring or aggressive 'hard-sell' tone
Animation	Uses animated characters or sequence
Annoyance	Likely to create annoyance or irritation
Attention	Impingement on the viewer's awareness
Audience	Designed to inform a wider audience about the product
Availability	Informs where and how the product can be obtained
Brand	Refers to a specific brand rather than to a generic product
Celebrity	Endorsement by celebrity or well-known cartoon character
Creativity	Uses clever or unusual ideas
Customer	Uses pseudo-biographical narrative sequences, shows satisfied customer
Cuteness	Uses 'cute' images, primarily animals or children
Deception	Attempts to deceive viewer or to misrepresent aspects of product
Ego	Appeals to the viewer's self-image, or exploits feelings of inferiority or uncertainty
Expert	Citation of research or survey findings, endorsement by scientist
Feature	Refers to specific features characteristic of the product advertised
Generic	Advertises a generic product rather than a specific brand
Glamour	Associates the product with a glamorous or enhanced life-style
Health	Emphasizes health or safety factors
Humour	Uses humour
Ideology	Gives an overt political message, or carries an ideological bias
Impact	Colour, movement, sound effects and vocalization, and so on, used for visual and auditory impact

Information	Refers to the amount of objective information given in an advertisement
In-group	Relies on previous or extraneous knowledge of the product or of earlier advertisements
Interest	Whether the advertisement is interesting or boring
Liking	Attempt to make the viewer well-disposed towards the product
Memorable	Easy to remember
Music	Uses jingles, mood-music, and so on
New product	Introduces a new product
Offer	Makes a free or special offer
Pace	Speed or changeability of visual images
Quality	Emphasizes the excellence of the product
Repetition	Uses repetition as a stylistic device
Rivals	Compares product with competitor's
Sell	Shows or refers to the sale of the product
Service	Claims to be performing a public service
Sex appeal	Uses sex appeal
Simplicity	Easy to understand, no unnecessary features
Slogan	Uses slogan, logo, catch-phrase, or distinctive trade-mark
Sponsor	Features sporting, artistic, or charitable sponsorship
Stereotype	Uses stereotypical roles
Symbolism	Part of the message expressed in an indirect or symbolic form
Sympathy	Engages the viewer's sympathy
Target	Specifies that the ad is aimed at a particular group of viewers, for instance, children, young couples
Threat	Emphasizes the consequences of not using the product
Use	Shows or refers to the consumption or use of the product
Variety	Shows the range of alternative forms of the product

Note: 'Definition of attribute' refers to the authors' glosses of the subjects' own definitions.

9

Summary

The purpose of this brief final chapter is to draw together the contents of the previous chapters and to summarize them. The reader should be able to assimilate what is stated here independently, since no knowledge of what has gone before is assumed.

Two pivotal concepts were introduced in Chapter 1. These were the notions of 'advertising', and 'the child'. Both concepts presume certain characteristics. So, a review of some of the criticisms that have been proposed concerning the nature of advertising established that many social theorists and critics see it as socially disruptive or dangerous in some way. Advertising is often viewed as a dry rot that pervades the building called society. Like dry rot, it gets in unnoticed and affects the solid values that are cherished in our society. The act of consuming goods and services is glorified and is often depicted, in advertisements, as the solution to our problems. The language of human relationships is applied to the world of objects so that brands are 'loved' and 'trusted'.

Advertising is a particular form of discourse where only the best side of a case is put forward so that the virtues of the topic are presented, to the relative neglect of the vices. This advocatory style of communication sits rather uneasily with other more 'balanced' modes of presentation that are found in education and certain areas of the mass media. Certainly in the history of British television broadcasting, advertising was kept at a distance and its introduction was fiercely opposed. Advertising, it was argued, should be kept apart from other varieties of media discourse and the lines of distinction had to be clearly drawn. The persuasive medium of advertising is by nature a pervasive creature which must be recognized and corralled, and not allowed to mix. Advertising that is broadcast on television is particularly pervasive as virtually all households have at least one television set, and many have two or more.

The content of advertising has frequently been criticized. Advertising is seen as accentuating existing human stereotypes and creating problems that can be solved by buying the brand promoted. Advertising borrows the symbols and forms of art and poetry to promote the consumption of goods and services. Advertising plays on existing fears and constructs irrational fears. Advertising raises the level of expectation of consumers and these aspirations can never be satisfied. Consequently, consumers feel powerless and this leads to frustration and possibly criminal behaviour. These and other criticisms contribute to a vision of advertising as a malignant rather than a benign influence, as having pervasive rather than limited influence, as being immoral rather than moral, and as devious as opposed to straight.

When the concept of child or childhood is examined there are various images that have been represented socially at different times in history, and in different cultures. The image of the child as a different person from the adult did not alway exist in all cultures. When children were regarded and treated as different, one of the images to emerge was of the child as 'sweet, simple and droll' (Aries, 1973). The inadequacies and immaturity of children were seen as sources of amusement. In contemporary Britain we find different images of childhood portrayed and reproduced in the media, in popular textbooks on child development and in handbooks aimed at the concerned parent. Among these can be found the image of the child as 'kid', frequently portrayed on television for children. The kid is streetwise, amusing, interested in excitement and fast action. Kids really know more than we give them credit for and should not be talked down to. Another prevalent image is of childhood as an age of innocence, of trusting naïveté without the critical, sceptical attitude and worldly-wise vision that characterizes being a grownup. This innocence can be embellished with a special vision, a purity of perception that is not yet tainted by adulthood.

When the idea of advertising is placed with the concept of the child then the quality of the relationship is determined both by advertising and by children. If the relationship strikes an emotional chord in members of the public then the way the relationship is characterized will frame any problems that are perceived as arising from children watching, or being exposed to advertising. The particular relationship that seems to emerge is of the advertiser seen as seducer and the child as an innocent. Advertising in this context is more than just an insidious threat, it is a positive evil. The model of childhood that blends with this vision of advertising is one where inadequacy is preferred to competence and where trust is assumed in contrast to cynicism. This special relationship between advertising and children will influence the way 'problems' are conceived of and coped with.

There is a short history of research into advertising and children and this was reviewed in Chapter 2. The vast bulk of the research has been done in the United States where the early days of television for children seemed to promise quality programmes. This was not to be. The basic interest of the television industry at this stage was to encourage viewers to buy television sets. As soon as a regular audience had been achieved the programmes were seen only as bait to catch audiences for advertisers and Saturday morning was a good time to catch children. In American commercial television the predominant driving force is advertising and there is no reason to suppose television for children was any different.

Public concern at television advertising on children's television in the United States was channelled in two directions. One was Action for Children's Television. One of the group's concerns was the separation of programme from commercial. The threat felt here is related to the pervasiveness of advertising and the need to keep it separate and distinguishable from programmes for children. The other was through the Council on Children, Media and Merchandising, and one of its concerns was the diet to which children are exposed through advertising. Junk food and products heavily loaded with sugar predominate in any analysis of the content of television advertising to children (Barcus and McLaughlin, 1978).

These two pressure groups lobbied the Federal Trade Commission in the 1970s with a view to changing the regulations that govern advertising to children. The Federal Trade Commission, no doubt aware of commercial interests that would not welcome any restrictions on competitive advertising, initially took the line that broadcasters should regulate themselves and establish guidelines on advertising to children. This was done. For example, commercials for breakfast-type products were to include at least one audio reference to and one video depiction of the role of a product within the framework of a balanced diet. This latter limitation meant that television commercials for heavily sugared breakfast cereals were inevitably presented with the ubiquitous glass of milk and the voice-over trailing '. . . part of a balanced breakfast'. The election of a Democratic president, Jimmy Carter, heralded a new toughness in the Federal Trade Commission's treatment of the children and television advertising issue. There was a fresh influx of petitions to the Commission and in 1978 a Federal Trade Commission Report on children and television advertising was published (Ratner et al., 1978). The report recommended that all television advertising for any product which is directed to, or seen by, audiences composed of a significant proportion of children who are too young to understand the selling purpose of, or otherwise comprehend or evaluate the advertising, should be banned. The report further recommended that televised advertising directed to, or seen by, audiences composed of a significant proportion of older children for sugared products, the consumption of which poses the most serious dental health risks, should either be banned or balanced by nutritional and/or health disclosures funded by advertisers (Ratner et al., pp. 345–6). By 1980, however, the Federal Trade Commission was under severe threat. At one stage its funding had been stopped and Government officials were considering terminating its activities.

The proceedings on television advertising to children were allowed to continue with the provision that any new regulation had to be based on the advertising being deceptive rather than being unfair. The distinction between

deceptive and unfair advertising is an important one. Deceptive advertising consists of communications from sellers to
buyers which are false or misleading and which induce
purchases. If the Federal Trade Commission found an
advertisement false or misleading it could either require the
seller to cease distribution of the ad, to disclose additional
information, or to correct the error affirmatively in future
ads. Unfair advertising deals with a particular class of advertisements. One cannot prove fairness empirically; one simply agrees or disagrees depending on one's ethical values.
Having to limit consideration to deceptive rather than unfair
advertising proved to be the final blow to the Federal Trade
Commission. In 1981 a *Final Staff Report* was published
(Elliott *et al.*, 1981) which recommended that the attempts
to put forward a regulation banning television advertising to
children be abandoned.

In Britain, television advertising is controlled by the Independent Broadcasting Authority. The Authority publishes a
Code of Advertising Standards and Practices (Independent
Broadcasting Authority, 1985) which is the latest in a line of
codes stemming from the *Principles for Television Advertising*
issued in 1955. The Annan Committee report of 1977 recommended, as did the Federal Trade Commission Report
of 1978 in the United States, the removal of television
advertising within children's programmes, a recommendation the Government in the following year did not pursue.
Both the Independent Broadcasting Authority and the Independent Television Companies' Association scrutinize new
ads to ensure that they fall within the guidelines for television advertising to children.

Given the political climate of the late 1980s going into the
1990s, it is unlikely that any further regulations or restrictions on general advertising to children will be introduced in
the United States or the United Kingdom.

The experimental literature on children and television
advertising is examined extensively in Chapters 3 and 4,
where the research is reviewed under various sub-headings.
Although these are organized in a sequential way covering
processes starting at viewing and finishing with doing, it
should be pointed out that a sequential model of the

influence of advertising on children or assumptions that
advertising has a direct effect on children's behaviour should
not be taken as the only way of conceptualizing its role in
the development of the child's thoughts, feelings, and behaviour. Advertising is only one factor amongst many that
influence the child. Family, friends, school, television,
magazines, and other media are constantly sending out messages on what to think and how to feel and act. The child is
at the centre, being buffeted by advice, coercion, demands,
and influences.

Advertising, and promotional activity in general, is advocatory and persuasive in intent. Advertising will present
only one side in order to persuade the child to consume a
good or service, or to influence other, more grown-up
financial decision makers in the family to buy this or try
that. Often, but not always, the interests of the source of
the advertising communication are not the same as the interests of the receiver, the child. It is always in the manufacturer's interests to see that the consumer buys and goes on
buying a particular brand. It need not always be in the
consumer's interest to consume that product and to be loyal
to the manufacturer's brand. Advertising is not unique in its
use of rhetorical and persuasive techniques, and those who
wish to see it banned or restricted would also, on the argument above, have to dismantle or severely modify the capitalist system and ban or restrict free enterprise and entre-
preneurial activity. The problems associated with advertising
are largely problems linked with free market economies.

If the experimental literature on television advertising and
children is examined we find that there are different sub-
headings under which research findings can be grouped.
One such area is concerned with the child's attention to
television commercials. There are three main developmental
threads. The first is concerned with the development of
schemata in children. Schemata are systems of mental
organization, often based on past experience, that are used
to predict future events. For example, as adults we know
that an interruption in a television programme is most likely
to signal the onset of a commercial, possibly the beginning
of a public service announcement, and maybe an apology

for a break in transmission. These expectations are based on our past experience with television. The first few seconds of a particular television commercial are possibly enough for us to anticipate the rest. Consequently, we need not watch continuously as a sampling attention strategy (occasionally looking) is adequate to process the information in the advertisement. Young children, however, have not yet developed a mature and complex organization of schemata. They will be more stimulus-driven than schema-driven when watching television. They are influenced by what's on right now and their attention to the commercial is dependent largely on the properties of the visual and auditory image on the box, rather than on any system of mental organization based on past experience with television advertising. There is a general drift, with increasing age, from stimulus-driven attention to schema-driven attention.

The second important aspect of attentional development in children that is relevant is the development of attentional control. The older child is able to use strategies of attention such as attending to relevant parts of the commercial or sampling sections of a commercial so that television viewing is integrated into other attractive or important tasks such as doing homework or talking to friends. The younger child is less able to exert such control and is more under the sway of the stimulus properties of the ad itself.

Finally, the phenomenon of attentional inertia should be outlined. Attentional inertia means that the longer a viewer looks continuously at television, the more likely it is that he or she will continue to do so. Conversely, the longer it has been since the viewer last looked at television, the less probable it is that he or she will look again. This attentional inertia is relatively independent of content and can be observed in children as young as 12 months through to adulthood. It would seem to build up as an influence over 15 seconds when it remains as a steady effect. It can be broken, of course, or else we would never start or stop watching, and it can be overridden by stimulus-driven and schema-driven information that is inherent in the content or features of what is seen or what is expected. As more complex and powerful schemata develop as the child grows older, attentional inertia becomes less important as a source of influence. Children can then expect, predict, and sample the parts of the television programme they want to rather than relying on the rather crude, content-free process of attentional inertia. For younger children, however, attentional inertia is a useful maintenance process that carries them over the parts of the programme that are uninteresting or incomprehensible when stimuli or schema do not drive attention to the screen.

The attention a child gives to any particular television commercial is not just a function of the stage of development of the child and consequently subject to the processes described above, but is also dependent on the content of the commercial itself and the context within which that commercial is found. The context encompasses the influence of neighbouring commercials and programmes as well as the context of viewing or so-called 'viewing ecology'. There is practically no published research that systematically explores these sources of influence on attention, although the available literature does produce general findings that can be described using the three developmental sequences discussed.

The child's ability to distinguish a television commercial from an adjacent programme is an area of research that has a small associated research literature. It is necessary for children to be able to distinguish between the two before they can begin to attribute functions to either. Consequently we would anticipate that any recognition that television commercials are different from other categories of television discourse is an early achievement and should be established before any of the norms on the child's knowledge of advertising intent, for example. The available literature was reviewed in Chapter 3 and one of the striking findings was that two cognitive categories which we can call 'television advertising' and 'the rest of television' emerge very early in development, at about 3 years of age. There is no theoretical difficulty in claiming an early emergence for this distinction as the difference between ads and the rest is carried on very salient perceptual features. Ads are short and programmes are long. Other research that uses verbal or behavioural indicators requires children to communicate to the experi-

menter when they think they have seen a programme or a
commercial. Evidence from this kind of research places the
beginning of awareness of a distinction at some age between
4 and 7 years depending on the methodology used.

The research done on the ability of the child to understand the intent behind television advertising is of central
importance within the portfolio of work produced on television advertising and children. Why? Knowing that advertising exists in order to persuade people, knowing that it
presents only one side of a case, and knowing that it is
designed to get one to buy goods and services, are all acquisition that enable the child to comprehend and process
advertising as a different genre from other forms of media
communication. As adults, our knowledge of advertising
intent means that we approach it with a degree of scepticism. We 'read' advertising as a type of communication full
of rhetorical forms that are not meant to be taken literally
but are designed to attract attention and convey characteristics of the good or service being promoted. The child's
literacy with advertising grows and develops towards the
adult norm and one of the major milestones on this road to
literacy is an understanding of the intent behind the ad.

The complete range of this research was reviewed, critically and in detail, in Chapter 3. Early work had established
that there was an important cognitive change in middle
childhood. If children were asked about the difference between television commercials and programmes, most children in the 5- to 8-year age group would refer to salient
perceptual characteristics of difference such as a programme
being long and a commercial short. The majority of older
children, aged 9 to 12 years, would use a functional distinction that exists between commercials and programmes, such
as commercials being about selling things and programmes
being about telling stories. A complete understanding of
advertising intent takes some time to emerge, however, and
one study (Ward, Reale, and Levinson, 1972) gave evidence
that only a quarter of 11- to 12-year-olds were able to
provide an explanation of why commercials were shown on
television that demonstrated an understanding of selling and
profit motives. It would appear that knowledge of the

economic and commercial function of television advertising is
built upon a basic ability to infer functional characteristics of
advertising as opposed to just being able to perceive and
conceive of advertising in terms of perceptually salient features. This developmental change from a set of inference
procedures based on perceptually available features to deeper inferences founded on conceptually based characteristics
of the world is a well-known structural change in the child's
mental world.

Advertising has several functions and commentators have
said that it informs, entertains, and persuades. It is the last
of these that defines advertising as different from other
forms of communication and places it alongside similar
forms such as advocacy and seduction. Persuasion is a
powerful and essential part of the definition of advertising
whereas the informative and entertainment functions of
advertising are not intrinsic to the definition but simply
define the form. The ability to attribute persuasive intent to
advertising emerges in practically all children by 10 or 11
years of age (Robertson and Rossiter, 1974). This same
study demonstrated that children who attribute persuasive
intent are also capable of understanding that television commercials are symbolic in nature, that they only represent
situations and emotions in the outside world.

By the end of the 1970s a consensus had developed in the
literature that the child's understanding of the purpose and
intent of advertising emerged at some stage in middle childhood, although the norms of emergence differed greatly
depending on the nature of the questions asked. Non-verbal
techniques that bypass verbal expression were being used
more frequently in the research published in the early 1980s
and, not surprisingly, the norms of emergence were placed
somewhat earlier than middle childhood. Some children as
young as 4 or 5 years seemed to understand the intent of
television advertising by choosing correct pictures or performing appropriate actions.

Is it possible to integrate the findings that come from
experiments with different methodologies into a coherent
theory of the child's comprehension of advertising intent?
Advertising persuades but it also sells. These two functions

would appear to be distinct in the development of the child as there is evidence (Blosser and Roberts, 1985) that understanding that television commercials are 'to do with' buying and selling things precedes any understanding that persuasion is intrinsic to advertising. The former should be kept theoretically distinct from the latter in any account of the development of advertising literacy. Knowing that advertising is to do with buying and selling, that it is a genre firmly located in the context of the exchange of goods and services, and that it is the communicative arm of commerce and industry is connected with learning about the arrangements and organization of the economic and social world. This knowledge and understanding should be viewed as a part of economic psychology that is concerned with economic socialization.

Understanding that ads persuade and present the best face of a case to people constitutes a different skill. This skill is better placed with a range of other abilities that emerge in middle childhood and develop through to early adolescence. They cover being able to 'read between the lines', being able to recognize that a literal interpretation of a communication is not the only possibility, and that classes of communication differ in their ground rules for production and comprehension depending on assumptions shared by the individual participants or their culture. In other words, there should be a developmental psychology of rhetoric within which the child's comprehension of the persuasive and advocatory function of advertising is found.

Although the literature on the child's understanding of advertising's intent is basic to an understanding of the development of advertising literacy, there are several other areas that contain valuable research. One such area is the influence of the content of television advertising on children. The content of ads does not just include the basic episodic features of 'who did what to whom and when', but as a cultural product that is attractive and used for rhetorical purposes, much of the content is full of symbolic meaning. Wearing designer jeans means more than just owning trousers with a name on them. Ads for designer jeans communicate a social identity to the viewer that he or she may share or aspire to and, hopefully, will recognize. The research evidence indicates that children younger than 7 or 8 years of age have not yet developed an understanding of such symbolic meaning and are limited in their awareness. For example, they do not possess a systematic and consistent picture of the sort of person who owns a particular brand. This awareness of 'consumption symbolism' emerges in middle childhood and develops into a notoriously complex system in adolescence. Research evidence (Belk et al., 1984) indicates that girls are more skilled than boys, and higher social class children have stronger consumption symbolism than children from lower social classes.

The child's ability to recognize and recall commercials is an area where results are in accord with general principles of memory development in children, although there are wide variations in results depending on what kind of commercial is used as a stimulus. Between 5 and 8 years of age the child develops schemata for television commercials that can be utilized to organize recall and aid recognition. Consequently, younger children will remember perceptually salient and odd features of the commercial that 'stood out'. Older children will recall more product and commercial line information since those are integrated into the schema of the commercial as a coherent piece of discourse. There is some evidence that, for certain commercials such as those for foods, recall and recognition is high, even for primary school children. It is difficult, however, to generalize and say that certain product categories are more easily remembered than others as the variability across commercial styles is so great. It is likely that this differentiating feature, together with involvement or engagement with the product and brand advertised, will influence remembering after exposure.

Knowledge of the function of television commercials can assist in reading advertising and can control decisions whether to purchase or not. Knowing that an advertisement persuades and that it should be read rhetorically is one line of defence against the onslaught of advertising (to use a metaphor that is popular in the literature). But there are more defences. Eight-year-old children may be aware of the intent of a television commercial and might demonstrate scepticism about the claims of advertisers in general, but will still be influenced by the immediate presence of an ad to change their liking or preference or intention to buy. Of course, adults do this too, or advertising would not work. Knowledge of advertising and its techniques constitute only the cognitive component of an attitude towards advertising. It would help in developing a healthy scepticism toward the claims and rhetoric of advertising. The ability to control and manage information-processing strategies is necessary to avoid inconsistency between product preference going into the situation of watching the ad, and the subsequent preference after watching the ad. Finally, and perhaps most importantly, the feelings and emotions generated while watching as well as the emotional 'after-taste' when the ad is retrieved from memory are important factors in influencing the child's preference and choice.

Television advertising, over a period of time, will influence the attitudes, values, and knowledge the child holds and expresses. The general principle that is derived from studies based on United States experience with television is that children evolve a more cynical, negative attitude towards television advertising than younger children. Why? One would expect that a growing awareness of the rhetorical nature of advertising will breed a cynicism with advertising in general. Nevertheless, the cultural basis of United States advertising should be taken into account. It is not necessarily the case that all children will become more cynical about advertising as they grow older. If advertisers wish to appeal to a particular segment of the youth market it is not inevitable that the older end of this market will be less susceptible to television commercials than the younger end. It is up to the craft and skills of the advertiser to appeal to just that group. If market research establishes that adolescents do not regard conventional advertising of product X or sub-genre Y as credible or trustworthy and in general devalue the source of such communications, then the agency should use rhetorical devices such as mild parody to re-establish credibility by creating a new genre of 'anti-ads' for example.

Television advertising, by its continual presence, cultivates a picture in the child's mind of the world out there. Most of the analyses of the content of commercials (see Chapter 6) show that so-called junk food is advertised frequently whereas other foods like vegetables and fruit are rarely represented. This is not unexpected given the economics of food, the nature of promotional activity, and the competitive state of certain markets in food products. Does the child possess a distorted view of food as a consequence of watching the biased portrayals in television advertising? The experimental evidence on this issue is equivocal. There is some evidence that children think that heavily sugared products, such as sweets and ice cream, are good for you and healthy and that this view is expressed more frequently by heavy television viewers than by those who watch little television. Other results appear to demonstrate that television advertising does not influence nutritional knowledge and that other influences based on parental socialization and parental socio-economic status are more important. This latter result is in line with other evidence in the general area of unintended media effects on audiences. For example, the portrayal of violent acts on television may influence the vision of the world held by viewers to the extent that they use more violence and conclude that there is more violence in the streets than statistics reveal. Although there may be 'special audiences' for whom this effect is dominant and powerful, such media influence is generally best conceived of as a 'weak force' when compared with other sources of influence such as family and friends.

There is also limited evidence that exposure to television advertising influences the values children possess about the world. In particular, there is a 'sharpening' of social categories where the definition is heightened and the differences are clarified. The classic roles of gender with their associated stereotypes become well defined and clearly distinguished in the child who watches television advertising. This result is not unusual and would characterize exposure to television and media in general where characterization tends toward caricature and the brush strokes used to paint the performers are bold.

Television advertising influences the thoughts, feelings,

and values of the child as summarized above and children go through various social-cognitive and communicative development stages that affect the way they assimilate and understand the advertising. The development of advertising literacy and the specific effects advertising has on the cognitive, affective, and conative components of the child's mental life are not the only aspects of the television advertising and children literature. Television advertising affects other people apart from the child. The young child is not an independent consumer but is part of a family where much of the decision-making on products of interest to children is conducted by parents who are subject to influence by their sons and daughters. In summary, there is research evidence that children ask for food products advertised on television and that parents will often comply with these requests. In addition, there is some evidence that purchase requests by children cause conflict between parent and child, although this will depend on the accustomed strategies of the child and ways parents have of handling these strategies. The methodology employed obtains opinions and reported facts from parents and children and uses methods of assessment of child-rearing style that are based on questionnaire responses and structured interviews. Much research still needs to be done in this area and would benefit from a more intensive, clinically-based approach that explored family dynamics and basic values concerning consumerism and materialism.

Finally, television advertising to children should affect the child's behaviour in some way. Most people in the street as well as advertisers and policy makers would view that as the central question to be answered. Does watching affect doing? Perhaps some psychologists would consider the development of advertising literacy as the core question rather than the issue of how watching influences behaviour. Other psychologists would take the behaviourist line that the stimulus of an advertisement should result in some observable response at the level of purchase or other consumer behaviour. One well-defined area within this field of behavioural effects of advertising is concerned with the behavioural consequences of watching food advertising for the child. The methodology often involves 'watching', then 'doing'. Children are assigned to different groups for different treatment conditions where they watch particular commercials. Afterwards they are given a choice from a range of available snacks, including the advertised brand. Under these somewhat artificial conditions researchers often, but not always, find that advertising brand X makes subsequent choice of this brand by the child more likely.

There are various reasons why this would occur, however, and with this research we are really no further towards finding an answer to the question of whether advertising snacks on television causes children to eat more snacks. This methodology has high internal validity but low external or ecological validity. That is, the results are true within the artificial universe of this kind of experimental, laboratory investigation but may not hold in the real world out there. Research using this format can, however, tell us something about the relative effectiveness of different kinds of stimulus arrangements using brand choice as an indicator. For example, using repetitive presentation of the same commercial with 8- to 10-year-old children, Gorn and Goldberg (1980) showed that exposure to more than one commercial for a brand of ice cream increased the probability that the brand would be chosen but did not influence the amount consumed.

No discussion of the role of advertising in the development of children is complete without at least a passing reference to the analysis of advertising. This issue was aired in Chapter 5. Much of the literature on the meaning of ads relies on basic assumptions, either ideological or metaphysical, concerning what parts of the ad are important and relevant to consider or the nature of the relationships between different elements within the advertisement. In addition there is a metaphor employed in the analysis of advertising that implies a particular model of meaning in ads. The meaning is hidden, deep down, and the ad needs to be 'decoded' or 'unpacked' in order to establish the truth. The analyst is, of course, equipped with the correct instruments of exploration, carefully tuned to the right ideological or metaphysical wavelength. For example, one may make certain ideological assumptions concerning power relationships between men and women and the culturally expressed forms of these. Consequently, a woman looking up into the eyes of a man, or a man with his hand on a woman's shoulder are both interpreted as reflecting these implicit relationships and will be interpreted accordingly when encountered on a billboard or in a magazine. In a similar vein, the relationship between a chocolate bar and a woman's mouth is selectively perceived as symbolic of sexual activity with the brand portrayed as a penis. The viewer occupies the role of voyeur or else enters the ad and becomes a receptive consumer. In any case, the ad will work if the psychoanalytic explanation is only partially valid because people will stare, or desire, or both.

There are certain structural analyses of advertisements that make metaphysical assumptions about the way of the world. The cultural world is seen as being structured on dimensions of binary opposition of the form *A/not-A*. An example would be the contrast *sacred/profane*. A structuralist analyst would attempt to make sense of the television commercial, or sample of commercials, by establishing the set of oppositions that make sense of all the elements in the ad. Functional analyses exist (for example, Andren *et al.*, 1978) where the rhetorical function of the ad is taken into account and categorized. What is needed, however, in the context of advertising to children, is an analysis that makes psychological sense. The model that drives such an analysis need not have been used in conjunction with models of child development or, indeed, of different audiences in the general field of advertising and its influence on people. It should be possible to implement it, if the need should arise, by setting it in a psychologically real framework and using psychologically valid concepts.

A suitable candidate for such a model of advertising is framed in the theory of communication and is derived from a branch of linguistic theory known as pragmatics. Pragmatics considers the context of a communication and the intent behind the communicator as well as the text of what is being communicated. Any interpretation of the text of an ad, whether the text is considered in visual or auditory terms or both, must be influenced by the context within which the ad is located and the presumed intent of the source of the ad. Now the presumed intent (by adult audiences) of advertising is persuasion. It is possible to place this function in a category along with other communicative roles such as pleading, exhorting, and advocating. They all share a certain similarity which has been formalized by May (1981), under the so-called maxim of Best Face. This maxim requires the reader to treat the case that is being put as the strongest case that can be made and applies to certain communicative arrangements where one party wishes to produce a preferred response in the other.

We expect ads to display the best apples in the stall and we read the rhetoric accordingly. This approach to the study of communication specifies certain ground rules for communication overall, and a set of ground rules that are peculiar to particular categories of communication is laid out, and even more specific rules for categories within categories could be listed. I am assuming that these rules are psychologically real in the sense that a fully knowledgeable communicator in a particular culture would behave and communicate as if he knew these rules, although he or she may not be able to articulate them. It is then appropriate to ask whether special audiences, like children, possess these rules for interpretation. Knowledge of ground rules will affect the 'reading' given to the ad. We expect families to be idealized. We would predict that the images surrounding the brand-in-the-ad are there to enhance the brand and not as neutral accompaniments, nor as devices to devalue the brand image. When we perceive families as more real than ideal, we assume that this slight breach of the standard or canonical rules of advertising communication exists to some rhetorical purpose. Perhaps this depiction of the family as less than perfect is done to establish audience credibility, or to increase identification with the characters, or to make this ad stand out from the rest.

The model of advertising communication that is being suggested consists of two parts. There are the genre-specific rules that guide interpretation of advertising. In addition, the internal discourse structure of the advertisement has to be considered. The minimal specification of this structure (which would be common to all ads) is *'brand* in *context'*, where *brand* occupies the topic role of the discourse and *context* occupies the comment role. Given the maxim of Best Face, we would expect the context to enhance the brand. If the brand is not apparently visible in the ad (as in some UK cigarette advertising), then we search for it. The 'brandless' ad breaches the basic rule of advertising discourse. We assume that this breach is to some purpose, that it is relevant in some way, and we attempt to make deeper inferences.

The brand exists in three kinds of context. There is the immediate context of the 'brand-in-the-ad'. Each brand found in an ad may be associated with people holding it, eating it, using it, music and sounds accompanying it, a voice-over extolling its virtues, related images, and so on. This context of the brand-in-ad is found nested in the next setting, the communicative context. For television advertising, the communicative context would be the surrounding ads in the block of advertising spots which would be embedded in a programme or between programmes. Finally, there is the non-communicative context of the physical setting itself which would include the people in the room co-viewing and characteristics of the television set. These three contexts will influence any reading of the ad, although one would expect the rhetorical and well-crafted immediate context surrounding the brand-in-ad to be the most forceful. Brands do not always live in ads, however. Their everyday existence is in the context of the real world. Brands do not exist in ideal settings only, but in the real world of supermarket shelves, schoolboys' satchels, or the back of the freezer. In the change from the brand-in-world to brand-in-ad the context of the everyday, mundane world is replaced with the context of the ideal, occasionally fantastical, and eventful world of the ad. This transition can be characterized as metaphorical, in the general sense of taking ideas from their accustomed context and transplanting them into a different context. Usually, in such metaphorical shifts, the new context is semantically inappropriate to a certain extent so that a non-literal, figurative interpretation is sought. For example, in the linguistic metaphor 'The tree wept in the wind', the standard concept of trees blowing in the wind is placed in a fresh context of the act of weeping. This combination breaches the conventional selection restrictions on verbs that take animate and human subjects. The metaphorical shift from brand-in-world to brand-in-ad can be described using various labels such as *real* to *ideal*, or *profane* to *sacred*. There are other metaphorical occurrences within the world of brands in ads that distinguish some ads from other ads and these are described in Chapter 5, but the major operation occurs when entering the world of brands in ads.

This summary description of a theory of meaning in advertising can act as a model for achievements in advertising literacy. For example, an understanding that advertising is a genre of communication that possesses its own rhetoric will emerge at some stage in the development of the child. When does the child know that the discourse structure of ads should include a brand, either visible or implied? When do children grasp the principles of metaphor or hyperbole or other non-figurative forms? Answers to these and other questions can be found in Chapters 7 and 8.

There was a brief excursion into the content analysis of ads in Chapter 6. The American evidence is fairly clear on the issue of what is shown to children. The diet of television commercials in the USA in the 1970s on Saturday mornings was composed predominantly of sugared food products directed at children. The content of this 'kid-vid ghetto', as it has been called, has certain characteristics. Food is fun, fantasy, and sensuality. The qualities advertised are taste, texture, and shape. A content analysis of British television advertising to children (Young, 1985; 1987a; 1987b) did not find this clear picture of a well-defined child market in the UK in the 1980s. In Britain, Saturday morning television advertising, which was taken as the classic child market place in the United States, contained much advertising that was adult-oriented rather than directed to children. The period leading up to Christmas (October and November) and, to a lesser extent, a pre-Easter season, was demographically purer in that there was intensive toy advertising to children. Outside these seasonal periods Saturday morning television advertising in the UK was directed both to children and to adults. A similar lack of definition was found in after-school television advertising.

An analysis of a set of 58 different commercials directed at children established the presence of several rhetorical devices. Some of these are conventional tropes found in language such as metaphor and hyperbole. Others are characteristic of advertising such as 'romdom', a highly romanticized presentation of the family and household, and 'rompast', a presentation of scenes from the past in a romanticised and nostalgic way.

There are some relevant findings in developmental psychology that should inform theories of advertising's influence on children. These were discussed in Chapter 7. Three classes of abilities were identified as relevant. They were the development of television literacy, the child's understanding of advertising, and a developmental psychology of rhetoric.

The concept of television literacy assumes a parallel between literacy with the printed word and literacy with the moving image. It is a useful analogy but does not necessarily hold up at all points of comparison. For example, the grammar of a language can be conceived of as consisting of various discrete units at different levels of representation, organized hierarchically. Speech sounds are combined into word units which are integrated into sentences. There is no evidence that the structure of television images is similarly organized. The expression 'grammar of television' should be used carefully, rather than in the somewhat cavalier way it has appeared in writings recently.

There is evidence that the young child's understanding of television is exotically different from adult's or an older child's. For example, 3-year-olds seem to believe that the people on television are as real as their own parents and friends and that television reality is very similar to other parts of real social life. There is a lack of understanding of the narrative or dramatic structure of television episodes.

In summary, these young children have a very different understanding of the content of television from adults. People exist in the box and the child will often talk and shout to them and treat them no differently from real people. Information is assimilated, but not integrated within any schema or organization available for understanding stories. Children can be frightened of this social reality in a different way from older children because they do not organize dramatic information. The child at this stage has not developed a set of organized schemata that drives expectations of the expected content and structure of various television genres. The world of television is a world of change and novelty, and the processing of this world is driven by interest in and consequent attention to the stimulus itself. As the child grows older, the distinction between television reality and the reality of the world outside the box is established. By the end of the preschool period, the majority of children will understand that there is a fundamental difference between the reality of the world of television and the world of real people and that people do not live in the television set.

The child will, however, develop distinctions between different kinds of television reality over a long period until adolescence. Before 10 years of age most children will judge television reality by referring to physical impossibility. So, *The Wizard of Oz* for 7-year-olds is not real because lions can't talk. Cartoon characters are less real than actors on film or video. By 10 years of age a new dimension of judgement has emerged and issues of possibility are raised. A 10-year-old judged *The Odd Couple* as real '. . . because Oscar and Felix are divorced and people can get divorced in life. It's possible.' By 12 years of age, most children can make reality judgements by considering plausibility so that 'happy endings' are unreal because life is not like that. Older children are also capable of predicting what will happen next, based on an understanding of the plot. Older children possess an understanding of filmic conventions that younger children lack. For example, Dorr (1980) reports that the 5- to 7-year-olds she talked with could not understand how Steve Austin, the 'Six Million Dollar Man' could catch the bad guys when he ran so slowly.

The literature on the child's understanding of advertising

was reviewed in Chapters 3 and 4, a core concept being the child's awareness of the purpose or intent of advertising. One such purpose is to persuade. Theoretical accounts of the development of children's understanding of advertising's intent have relied on Piagetian theory and it has been argued that the emergence of such an understanding in childhood is part of a general transition from a preoperational mode of thinking to a concrete-operational mode. One of the characteristics of preoperational thought is a reliance on the appearance of things when making inferences about the way of the world whereas the concrete-operational child can produce deeper inferences based on conceptual rather than perceptual reality. Although such an account will provide a general theoretical backdrop against which the specific achievement of understanding advertising intent can be placed, a more appropriate theory can be found in the literature on the development of metacommunicative abilities in children.

A major change in the child's understanding of communication occurs in middle childhood (see Hakes, 1980). About this time (7 to 8 years of age), the child is capable of standing back from the stream of communication and reflecting on it, of regarding language as 'transparent', as something to be seen through, rather than 'opaque', or something to be focused on in its own right. Being able to detach oneself from the ongoing stream of advertising communication and evaluate, judge, and consider that brand of communication is an ability that must exist in order for the child to be aware of the rhetorical and persuasive function of advertising.

There is not as yet a full developmental psychology of rhetoric that would consolidate and underwrite the collection of findings in the television advertising and children literature. There are, however, several research strands that are relevant in this context. For example, the ability of the child to perceive and understand when someone is lying. This ability can be analysed into various other skills that emerge at different ages. The ability to represent mentally the wrong beliefs of others emerges in the period 4 to 6 years. The relationship between my knowing a state-of-affairs and my knowing that you know, or don't know, or have different knowledge about that state of affairs would seem to be necessary before any inference (based on this knowledge) towards a conclusion of deceit can be made.

At 6 years lies are thought of as utterances that are forbidden or punished. 'Naughty words', mistakes, and deliberately misleading utterances are all classified by the child at this age as lies. By 8 years of age the child regards lies as covering 'untrue' statements. There is no differentiation of intent, however, so mistakes are placed in the same category as deliberately misleading utterances. It is not until age 10 or 11 years that children become sensitive to the importance of intent and explicitly give the adult definition of a lie. A lack of agreement between what is said and what is intended can signal the presence of non-literal, figurative language use as well as deception.

There is evidence that an understanding of irony or sarcasm does not emerge until late childhood or early adolescence. The development of metaphor in children shows an interesting although bewildering sequence. There is good evidence that the preschool child is able to produce linguistic metaphors intentionally and with pleasure. Metaphoric production diminishes in the early school years when the young school child enters a period of 'literalness' on production and comprehension. The meaning read is the meaning said is the meaning intended. Gradually, metaphoric comprehension improves from late childhood into adolescence.

The British research into children and television advertising, including the author's own work, was reviewed in Chapter 8. There are several studies on health-related issues concerning the promotion of cigarettes and alcohol, and their effects on children and adolescents. The results from this work demonstrate that cigarette promotion does enhance brand awareness in children. In particular, 'brand stretching', where cigarettes are associated with sporting activities such as snooker or motor racing, work to such an extent that children will recall the heavily-promoted brands more than other brands, and will remember the associated imagery. These results should be interpreted with caution, however, as there is no direct evidence that such tobacco promotion influences the consumer behaviour of the child. The results are not exactly unexpected given simple principles of psychology, such as more frequent exposure to a stimulus improving recall of that stimulus relative to other stimuli. Research with ads for alcohol with adolescent subjects show that they are able to identify the kinds of groups of consumers at whom the ads are aimed.

The author's own research on the comprehension of advertising intent with British children was discussed in Chapter 8. A distinction between salient and available responses was made. That is, if a child is asked about the purpose and function of advertising using a battery of different questions, he or she may never reply with a reference to the persuasive or commercial function of advertising at any point during the interview. Under these circumstances, this type of response is unavailable. The salience of a commercial or persuasive response is the probability that the response will be produced in answer to any relevant question during the interview, as measured by the frequency of those responses. Zero salience means that the response is unavailable. Available 'commercial' responses in the child's repertoire emerged from 7 years of age but the salience of these responses was low for older children, compared with North American norms. This cross-cultural difference can be explained by the relative lack of hard-sell, frequent television advertising in the UK where the style is more indirect and the selling points are swathed in layers of rhetoric.

Another change occurring about 7 years of age was detected by asking children what a particular ad was really telling them. The ad in question was predominantly composed of extracts from *Star Wars*, with the brand in question mentioned at the end. The majority of children younger than 7 years said the ad was telling you about *Star Wars*. The *Star Wars* part of the commercial was perceptually dominant. Younger children tend to judge situations on the basis of their appearance. Older children can infer deeper, more conceptual aspects of a situation, and the one of the characteristics of ads that can be inferred is that all ads have a brand as topic of the advertising discourse. The majority of children older than 7 years said that the ad was telling you about the biscuit (the brand being promoted) even in the face of the perceptual dominance of *Star Wars*.

It is perhaps appropriate to conclude this chapter, and the book, with a summary of as yet unpublished research (Tuohy and Young, in preparation). The methodological starting point is to elicit, from a particular audience, a set of descriptions of ads or distinguishing characteristics that separate one kind of ad from another kind. So, for example, the gloss given to one characteristic called 'humour' might emerge (with different turns of phrase) with adults, younger children, and older children. Another characteristic, which could be called 'glamour', does not emerge with younger children but can be found, expressed in different ways, in adults and older children.

The labels and constructs that carve up the world of television commercials and the different dimensions that provide content and contrast within this world are interesting in their own right. Powerful statistical analyses, however, can add more structure to this picture and an account of the development of an understanding of advertising is emerging. Two main themes of development seem to be important. The first of these is concerned with the perspective of the perceiver and consists of a gradual detachment from the immediate world of the textual features of the ad, through the world depicted in the advertisement, to an eventual critical evaluation of the ad as a member of the world of culture. The second of these refers to the ability to read between the lines, to deal with levels of meaning not directly expressed in the text. Certainly, one of the major research lines in the future should be an exploration of the diversity of different kinds of television commercials and how different audiences, including children, classify and categorize them.

It is with the benefit of hindsight that we are able to see the significant results and shortcomings of the work done in the 1970s and 1980s. Perhaps we can hope that the 1990s sees a revival of interest in the research issue of the role of television advertising in the development of the child, with the questions framed in terms of advertising literacy and the developmental psychology of rhetoric.

REFERENCES

Ackerman, B. P. (1981a). 'Young children's understanding of a speaker's intentional use of a false utterance'. *Developmental Psychology*, 4: 472–80.

—— (1981b). 'When is a question not answered? The understanding of young children of utterances violating or conforming to the rules of conversational sequences'. *Journal of Experimental Child Psychology*, 31: 487–507.

—— (1982a). 'Contextual integration and utterance interpretation: The ability of children and adults to interpret sarcastic utterances'. *Child Development*, 53: 1075–83.

—— (1982b). 'On comprehending idioms: Do children get the picture?' *Journal of Experimental Child Psychology*, 33: 439–54.

—— (1983). 'Form and function in children's understanding of ironic utterances'. *Journal of Experimental Child Psychology*, 35: 487–508.

Adler, R. P. (1980). 'Children's television advertising: History of the issue'. In E. L. Palmer and A. Dorr (eds.), *Children and the Faces of Television: Teaching, Violence, Selling*: 237–49. New York: Academic Press.

—— Lesser, G. S., Meringoff, L. K., Robertson, T. S., Rossiter, J. R., and Ward, S. (1980). *The Effects of Television Advertising on Children: Review and Recommendations*. Lexington, Mass.: D. C. Heath.

—— Friedlander, B. Z., Lesser, G. S., Meringoff, L., Robertson, T. S., Rossiter, J. R., and Ward, S. (1977). *Research on the Effects of Television Advertising on Children: A Review of the Literature and Recommendations for Future Research*. Washington, DC: US Government Printing Office.

Aitken, P. P. (1988). 'Children and cigarette advertising'. In P. White (ed.), *Pushing Smoke: Tobacco Advertising and Promotion*. Copenhagen: World Health Organization Regional Office for Europe and the Commission of the European Communities.

—— (1989). 'Television alcohol commercials and under-age drinking'. *International Journal of Advertising*, 8: 133–50.

—— Leathar, D. S., and O'Hagan, F. J. (1985a). 'Children's perceptions of advertisements for cigarettes'. *Social Science and Medicine*, 21/7: 785–97.

—— —— —— (1985b). 'Monitoring children's perceptions of

advertisements for cigarettes'. In D. S. Leathar, G. B. Hastings, K. M. O'Reilly, and J. K. Davies (eds.), *Health Education and the Media: Proceedings of the 2nd International Conference:* 155–61. Oxford: Pergamon Press.

—— —— and Scott, A.C. (1987). 'Ten- to sixteen-year-olds' perceptions of advertisements for alcoholic drinks'. Unpublished paper. Glasgow: Department of Marketing, University of Strathclyde.

—— —— and Squair, S. I. (1986a). 'Children's awareness of cigarette brand sponsorship of sports and games in the UK'. *Health Education Research,* 1/3: 203–11.

—— —— —— (1986b). 'Children's opinions on whether or not cigarette advertisements should be banned'. *Health Education Journal,* 45/4: 204–7.

—— —— —— (1986c). 'Young people's perceptions of advertisements for cigarettes'. Unpublished paper. Glasgow: Department of Marketing, University of Strathclyde.

—— —— O'Hagan, F. J., and Squair, S. I. (1987). 'Imagery, advertising, smoking and youth'. In A. Burr (ed.), *The Symbolism of Addictive Behaviours.* London: Tavistock (forthcoming).

—— Eadie, D. R., Leathar, D. S., McNeil, R. E. J., and Scott, A. C. (1988). 'Television advertisements for alcoholic drinks do reinforce under-age drinking'. Submitted to *British Journal of Addiction.*

Alexander, H. M., Callcott, R., Dobson, A. J., Hardes, G. R., Lloyd, D. M., O'Connell, D. L., and Leeder, S. R. (1983). 'Cigarette smoking and drug use in schoolchildren: IV—Factors associated with changes in smoking behaviour'. *International Journal of Epidemiology,* 12: 59–66.

Anderson, D. R., and Lorch, E. P. (1983). 'Looking at television: Action or reaction'. In Bryant and Anderson (1983): 1–33.

—— Alwitt, L. F., Lorch, E. P., and Levin, S. R. (1979). 'Preschool children's visual attention to attributes of television'. *Human Communication Research,* 7: 52–67.

—— Field, D. E., Collins, P., Lorch, E. P., and Nathan, J. G. (1985). 'Estimates of young children's time with television: A methodological comparison of parent reports with time-lapse video home observation'. *Child Development,* 56: 1345–57.

Andren, G., Ericsson, L. O., Ohlsson, R., and Tannsjo, T. (1978). *Rhetoric and Ideology in Advertising.* Stockholm: Liber-Forlag.

Aries, P. (1973). *Centuries of Childhood.* Harmondsworth: Penguin.

Arlen, M. J. (1981). *Thirty Seconds*. New York: Farrar, Strauss and Giroux.

Atkin, C. K. (1975*a*). 'Effects of television advertising on children — Second year experimental evidence'. Report 2. Ann Arbor, Mich.: Michigan State University, June.

—— (1975*b*). 'Effects of television advertising on children — Parent–child communication in supermarket breakfast selection'. Report 7. Ann Arbor, Mich.: Michigan State University, October.

—— (1978). 'Observation of parent–child interaction in supermarket decision making'. *Journal of Marketing*, 42: 41–5.

—— (1979). 'Children's advertising rulemaking comment: A study of children and TV advertising'. Presented at the Federal Trade Commission Hearings on Children's Television Advertising. San Francisco. January.

—— and Gibson, W. (1978). 'Children's responses to cereal commercials'. Report to Public Advocates, Inc.

—— and Heald, G. (1977). 'The content of children's toy and food commercials'. *Journal of Communication*, 27/1: 107–14.

—— Reeves, B., and Gibson, W. (1979). 'Effects of televised food advertising on children'. Paper presented to the Association for Education in Journalism. Houston, Texas.

Austin, J. L. (1962). *How to Do Things with Words*. Oxford: Clarendon Press.

Barcus, F. E. (1971*a*). 'Description of children's television advertising'. Statement to Federal Trade Commission Hearing on Modern Advertising.

—— (1971*b*). *Saturday Children's Television: A Report on TV Programming and Advertising on Boston Commercial Television*. Newtonville, Mass.: Action for Children's Television.

—— (1972). *Network Programming and Advertising in the Saturday Children's Hours: A June and November Comparison*. Newtonville, Mass.: Action for Children's Television.

—— (1975*a*). *Television in the After-School Hours*. Newtonville, Mass.: Action for Children's Television.

—— (1975*b*). *Weekend Children's Television*. Newtonville, Mass.: Action for Children's Television.

—— (1976). *Pre-Christmas Advertising to Children: A Comparison of the Advertising Content of Children's Programmes Broadcast in April and November of 1975*. Newtonville, Mass.: Action for Children's Television.

—— (1980). 'The nature of television advertising to children'. In E. L. Palmer and A. Dorr (eds.), *Children and the Faces of Television: Teaching, Violence, Selling*: 273–85. New York: Academic Press.

—— and McLaughlin, L. (1978). *Food Advertising on Children's Television: An Analysis of Appeals and Nutritional Content*. Newtonville, Mass.: Action on Children's Television.

—— and Wolkin, R. (1977). *Children's Television: An Analysis of Programming and Advertising*. New York: Praeger.

Barenblatt, L. (1981). 'A critical review of recent research on the effects of television advertising on children'. In Esserman (1981c): ch. 1.

Barling, J., and Fullager, C. (1983). 'Children's attitudes to television advertisements: A factorial perspective'. *Journal of Psychology*, 113: 25–30.

Barry, T. E. (1977). *Children's Television Advertising*. American Marketing Association Monograph Series, 8. Chicago: American Marketing Association.

—— and Gunst, R. F. (1982). 'Children's advertising: The differential impact of appeal strategy'. In J. H. Leigh and C. R. Martin, Jr. (eds.), *Current Issues and Research in Advertising*: 113–25. Ann Arbor, Mich.: Graduate School of Business Administration, University of Michigan.

Barthes, R. (1964). 'Rhétorique de l'image'. In S. Heath (ed. and trans.), *Image, Music, Text*: 32–51. London: Fontana, 1977.

Bates, E., Camaioni, L., and Volterra, V. (1975). 'The acquisition of performatives prior to speech'. *Merrill-Palmer Quarterly*, 21/3: 205–26.

Baumrind, D. (1971). 'Current patterns of parental authority'. *Developmental Psychology Monograph*, 4: 1–103.

Bearden, W. O., Teel, J. E., and Wright, R. R. (1979). 'Family income effects on measurement of children's attitudes toward television commercials'. *Journal of Consumer Research*, 6: 308–11.

Bechtel, R. B., Achelpol, C., and Akers, R. (1971). 'Correlates between observed behaviour and questionnaire responses on television viewing'. In E. A. Rubinstein, G. A. Comstock, and J. P. Murray (eds.), *Television and Social Behaviour*, iv. *Television in Day-to-Day Life: Patterns of Use*. Washington, DC: US Government Printing Office.

Bednall, D., and Hannaford, M. (1980). *Television and children: Recall of television advertising and programmes by children*. Melbourne: Australian Broadcasting Tribunal Research Report.

Belk, R. W., Bahn, K. D., and Mayer, R. (1982). 'Developmental recognition of consumption symbolism'. *Journal of Consumer Research*, 9: 4–17.

—— Mayer, R., and Driscoll, A. (1984). 'Children's recognition of consumption symbolism in children's products'. *Journal of Consumer Research*, 10: 386–97.

Berger, A. A. (1974). 'Drug advertising and the pain–pill–pleasure model'. *Journal of Drug Issues*, 4: 208–12.

Blatt, J., Spencer, L., and Ward, S. (1971). 'A cognitive developmental study of children's reactions to television advertising'. In E. A. Rubinstein, G. A. Comstock, and J. P. Murray (eds.), *Television and Social Behavior*, iv. *Television in Day-to-Day Life: Patterns of Use*. Washington, DC: US Government Printing Office.

Blosser, B. J., and Roberts, D. F. (1985). 'Age differences in children's perceptions of message intent: Responses to TV news, commercials, educational spots, and public service announcements'. *Communication Research*, 12/4: 455–84.

Böcker, F. (1986). 'Children's influence on their mothers' preferences: A new approach'. *International Journal of Research in Marketing*, 3: 39–52.

Bohuslav, B., Egan, M. F., and Morgan, J. (1985). Content analysis of children's Saturday morning television advertising. Working paper. College Station, Tex.: Department of Marketing, Texas A and M University.

Bolton, R. N. (1983). 'Modeling the impact of television food advertising on children's diets'. In J. H. Leigh and C. R. Martin, Jr. (eds.), *Current Issues and Research in Advertising*. Ann Arbor, Mich.: Graduate School of Business Administration.

Brehm, J. W., and Cohen, A. R. (1962). *Explorations in Cognitive Dissonance*. New York: Wiley.

Brewer, W. F. (1980). 'Literary theory, rhetoric and stylistics: Implications for psychology'. In R. J. Spiro, B. C. Bruce, and W. F. Brewer (eds.), *Theoretical Issues in Reading Comprehension*. Hillsdale, NJ: Erlbaum.

Brown, G., and Yule, G. (1983). *Discourse Analysis*. Cambridge: Cambridge University Press.

Brucks, M., Armstrong, G. M., and Goldberg, M. E. (1988). 'Children's use of cognitive defenses against television advertising: A cognitive response approach'. *Journal of Consumer Research*, 14/4: 471–82.

—— Goldberg, M. E., and Armstrong, G. M. (1986). 'Children's cognitive responses to advertising'. In R. J. Lutz (ed.), *Advances in Consumer Research*, 13.

Brumbaugh, F. N. (1954). 'What effect does television advertising have on children?' *Educational Digest*, 1: 32–3.

Bryant, J., and Anderson, D. R. (1983) (eds.). *Children's*

Understanding of Television: Research on Attention and Comprehension. London: Academic Press.

Butter, E. J., Popovich, P. M., Stackhouse, R. H., and Garner, R. K. (1981). 'Discrimination of television programs and commercials by preschool children'. *Journal of Advertising Research*, 21/2: 53–8.

Calder, B. J., Robertson, T., and Rossiter, J. (1975). 'Children's consumer information processing'. *Communications Research*, 2: 307–16.

Cantor, J. (1981). 'Modifying children's eating habits through television ads: Effects of humorous appeals in a field setting'. *Journal of Broadcasting*, 25: 37–47.

Chandler, M. J., and Greenspan, S. (1972). 'Ersatz egocentrism: A reply to H. Borke'. *Developmental Psychology*, 7: 104–6.

Choate, R. B. (1972). 'The sugar coated children's hour'. *The Nation*, January 31: 146–8.

—— (1981). 'The politics of change'. In E. L. Palmer and A. Dorr (eds.), *Children and the Faces of Television: Teaching, Violence, Selling*: 323–37. New York: Academic Press.

Chomsky, N. (1965). *Aspects of the Theory of Syntax.* Cambridge, Mass.: MIT Press.

Christenson, P. G. (1980). 'The effects of consumer information processing announcements on children's perceptions of commercials and products'. Unpublished doctoral dissertation. Stanford, Calif.

—— (1982). 'Children's perceptions of TV commercials and products: The effects of PSAs.' *Communication Research*, 9/4: 491–524.

Clancy-Hepburn, K., Hickey, A., and Nevill, G. (1974). 'Children's behavior responses to TV food advertisements'. *Journal of Nutrition Education*, 6/3: 93–6.

Collins, W. A. (1979). 'Children's comprehension of television content'. In E. Wartella (ed.), *Children Communicating: Media and Development of Thought, Speech, Understanding*. Beverly Hills, Calif.: Sage.

—— and Westby, S. D. (1975). 'Children's processing of social information from televised dramatic programs'. Paper presented at the biennal meeting of the Society for Research in Child Development. Denver, Colo. April.

—— Wellman, H., Keniston, A., and Westby, S. (1978). 'Age-related aspects of comprehension and inference from a televised dramatic narrative'. *Child Development*, 49/2: 389–99.

Comstock, G., and Paik, H.-J. (1987). 'Television and children:

New knowledge on persistent questions'. Paper for Educational Resources Information Clearinghouse. Syracuse, NY: School of Education, Syracuse University.

Cooper, D. E. (1986). *Metaphor*. Oxford: Basil Blackwell.

Cosmas, S. C., and Yannopoulos, N. (1981). 'Advertising directed to children: A look at the mother's point of view'. *Journal of the Academy of Marketing Science*, 9/3: 174–90.

Crosby, L. A., and Grossbart, S. L. (1984). 'Parental style segments and concern about children's food advertising'. In J. H. Leigh and C. R. Martin (eds.), *Current Issues and Research in Advertising*, i. *Original Research and Theoretical Contributions*. Ann Arbor, Mich.: Graduate School of Business Administration.

Culley, J. D., Lazer, W., and Atkin, C. K. (1976). 'The experts look at children's television'. *Journal of Broadcasting*, 20: 3–21.

Cullingford, C. (1984). *Children and Television*. Aldershot: Gower.

Cuozzo, P. F. (1971). 'An inquiry into the image of food and food habits as presented by television food commercials'. Unpublished Master's thesis. Annenberg School of Communications, University of Pennsylvania.

Dahl, A. G. (1984). 'Children's confrontation with commercial TV: A Norwegian perspective on future investigation'. Paper presented to conference on International Perspectives on Television Advertising and Children. Mallemort en Provence, France.

Dawson, B., Jeffrey, D. B., Peterson, P. E., Sommers, J., and Wilson, G. (1985). 'Television commercials as a symbolic representation of reward in the delay of gratification paradigm'. *Cognitive Therapy and Research*, 9/2: 217–24.

Demorest, A., Silberstein, L., Gardner, H., and Winner, E. (1983). 'Telling it as it isn't: Children's understanding of figurative language'. *British Journal of Developmental Psychology*, 1: 121–34.

—— Meyer, C., and Phelps, E. (1984). 'Words speak louder than actions: Understanding deliberately false remarks'. *Child Development*, in press.

De Paulo, B. M., Jordan, A., Irvine, A., and Laser, P. S. (1982). 'Age changes in the detection of deception'. *Child Development*, 53: 701–9.

Dirks, J., and Gibson, E. (1977). 'Infants' perception of similarity between live people and their photographs'. *Child Development*, 48: 124–30.

Donohue, T. R., Henke, L. L., and Donohue, W. A. (1980). 'Do kids know what TV commercials intend?' *Journal of Advertising Research*, 20/5: 51–7.

Doolittle, J., and Pepper, R. (1975). 'Children's TV ad content: 1974'. *Journal of Broadcasting*, 19: 131–42.

Dore, J. (1977). 'Children's illocutionary acts'. In R. O. Freedle (ed.), *Discourse Processing and Comprehension*: 227–44. Norwood: Ablex.

Dorr, A. (1978). 'Children's advertising rulemaking comment'. In Barcus (1975*b*).

—— (1980) 'When I was a child I thought as a child'. In S. B. Withey and R. P. Abeles (eds.), *Television and Social Behavior: Beyond Violence and Children*: 91–230. Hillsdale, NJ: Erlbaum.

—— (1986). *Television and Children: A Special Medium for a Special Audience*. Beverly Hills: Sage.

Durand, J. (1970). 'Rhétorique et image publicitaire'. *Communications*, 15. Paris: Éditions du Seuil.

Durkin, K. (1983). *Sex Roles and Children's Television*. Report to the Independent Broadcasting Authority. Canterbury: Social Psychology Research Unit, University of Kent.

Dyer, G. (1982). *Advertising as Communication*. London: Methuen.

Elliott, S., Wilkenfeld, J. P., Cuarino, E. T., Kolish, E. D., Jennings, C. J., and Siegal, D. (1981). *Federal Trade Commission Final Staff Report and Recommendations in the Matter of Children's Advertising. 43 Fed. Reg. 17967*. Washington, DC.

Esserman, J. (1981*a*). 'A study of children's defenses against television commercial appeals'. In Esserman (1981*c*): 48–54.

—— (1981*b*). 'Viewing of commercials and children's understanding of the rules of nutrition'. In Esserman (1981*c*): 173–94.

—— (1981*c*) (ed.). *Television Advertising and Children: Issues, Research and Findings*. New York: Child Research Service.

Faber, R. J., Meyer, T. P., and Miller, M. M. (1984). 'The effectiveness of health disclosures within children's television commercials'. *Journal of Broadcasting*, 28/4: 463–76.

—— Perloff, R. M., and Hawkins, R. (1982). 'Antecedents of children's comprehension of television advertising'. *Journal of Broadcasting*, 26/2: 575–84.

Fernie, D. E. (1981). 'Ordinary and extraordinary people: Children's understanding of television and real-life models'. In Kelly and Gardner (1981): 47–58.

Feshbach, N. D., Dillman, A. S., and Jordan, T. S. (1979). 'Children and television advertising: some research and some perspectives'. *Journal of Clinical Child Psychology*, 8/1: 26–30.

Feshbach, S., Feshbach, N. D., and Cohen, S. E. (1982). 'Enhancing children's discrimination in response to television advertising: The effects of psychoeducational training in two elementary school groups'. *Developmental Review*, 2/4: 385–403.

Fischer, M. A. (1985). 'A developmental study of preference for advertised toys'. *Psychology and Marketing*, 2/1: 3–12.

Flavell, J. H. (1963). *The Developmental Psychology of Jean Piaget*. Princeton, NJ: Van Nostrand.

—— and Wellman, H. W. (1977). 'Metamemory'. In R. V. Kail, Jr., and J. W. Hagen (eds.), *Perspectives on the Development of Memory and Cognition*: 3–33. Hillsdale, NJ: Erlbaum.

—— Botkin, P. T., Fry, C. L., Wright, J. W., and Jarvis, P. E. (1968). *The Development of Role-taking and Communication Skills in Children*. New York: Wiley.

Fox, D. T., Jeffrey, D. B., McLellarn, R. W., Hickey, J. S., and Dahlkoetter, J. (1980). 'Television commercials and children's eating habits'. Paper presented at meeting of the American Psychological Association. Montreal.

Frazer, C. F., and Reid, L. N. (1979). 'Children's interaction with commercials'. *Symbolic Interaction*, 2/2: 79–96.

Gaines, L., and Esserman, J. F. (1981). 'A quantitative study of young children's comprehension of television programs and commercials'. In Esserman (1981*c*): 95–105.

Galst, J. P. (1980). 'Television food commercials and pro-nutritional public service announcements as determinants of young children's snack choices'. *Child Development*, 51/3: 935–8.

—— and White, M. A. (1976). 'The unhealthy persuader: The reinforcing value of television and children's purchase-influencing attempts at the supermarket'. *Child Development*, 47: 1089–96.

Gardner, H., and Lohman, W. (1975). 'Children's sensitivity to literary styles'. *Merrill-Palmer Quarterly*, 21/2: 113–26.

—— Kirchner, M., Winner, E., and Perkins, D. (1975). 'Children's metaphoric productions and preferences'. *Journal of Child Language*, 2: 125–41.

—— Winner, E., Bechhofer, R., and Wolf, D. (1978). 'The development of figurative language'. In K. E. Nelson (ed.), *Children's Language*, i. 1–38. New York: Gardner.

Garfinkel, A. (1983). 'A pragmatic approach to truth in advertising'. In Harris (1983): 175–94.

Garvey, C. (1984). *Children's Talk*. London: Fontana.

Geis, M. (1982). *The Language of Television Advertising*. London: Academic Press

Gelman, R. (1978). 'Cognitive development'. *Annual Review of Psychology*, 29: 297–332.

Genter, D. (1977). 'If a tree had a knee where would it be? Children's responses on simple spatial metaphors'. *Papers and Reports on Child Language Development*, 13: 157–64.

Gianinno, L. J., and Zuckerman, P. A. (1977). 'Measuring children's reponses to television advertising'. In C. Leavitt (ed.), *Proceedings: American Psychological Association Division 23*. 85th Annual Convention. San Francisco. August.

Ginsburg, H., and Opper, S. (1969). *Piaget's Theory of Intellectual Development. An Introduction*. Englewood Cliffs, NJ: Prentice Hall.

Giudicatti, V., and Stening, B. W. (1980a). 'An empirical evaluation of a test measuring children's attitudes towards TV advertisements'. *Psychological Reports*, 46/3: 1222.

—— (1980b). Socioeconomic background and children's cognitive abilities in relation to television advertisements. *Journal of Psychology*. 106/2: 153–5.

Goffman, E. (1979). *Gender Advertisements*. London: Macmillan.

Goldberg, M. E., and Gorn, G. J. (1977). 'Material versus social preferences, parent–child relations, and the child's emotional responses: Three dimensions of response to children's TV advertising'. Unpublished paper presented at the Telecommunications Policy Research Conference. Airlie, Va.

—— —— (1979). 'Experimental assessment of the effects of TV food messages on children'. Paper presented to the annual meeting of the American Psychological Association. New York.

—— —— (1983). 'Researching the effects of TV advertising on children: A methodological critique'. In M. Howe (ed.), *Learning from Television: Psychological and Educational Research*. London: Academic Press.

—— —— and Gibson, W. (1978). 'TV messages for snacks and breakfast foods: Do they influence children's preferences?' *Journal of Consumer Research*, 5: 73–81.

Gorn, G. J., and Goldberg, M. E. (1978). 'Possible moderating influences of TV advertising's effects on children: Repetitive exposure and a hierarchy of effects'. Unpublished paper. Montreal: Faculty of Management, McGill University.

—— —— (1980). 'Children's responses to repetitive television commercials'. *Journal of Consumer Research*, 6: 421–4.

—— —— (1982). 'Behavioral evidence of the effects of televised food messages on children'. *Journal of Consumer Research*, 9: 200–5.

Greenberg, B. S., Fazal, S., and Wober, M. (1986). *Children's Views on Advertising*. London: Research Department, The Independent Broadcasting Authority.

Greer, D., Potts, R., Wright, J. C., and Huston, A. C. (1982).

'The effect of television commercial form and commercial placement on children's social behavior and attention'. *Child Development*, 53: 611–19.

Grice, H. P. (1975). 'Logic and conversation'. In P. Cole and J. L. Morgan (eds.), *Syntax and Semantics 3: Speech Acts*: 41–58. New York: Academic Press.

—— (1978). 'Further notes on logic and conversation'. In P. Cole (ed.), *Syntax and Semantics 9: Pragmatics*: 113–28. New York: Academic Press.

Griffin, E. (1980). 'The future is inevitable: but can it be shaped in the interest of children?' In E. L. Palmer and A. Dorr (eds.), *Children and the Faces of Television: Teaching, Violence, Selling*: 339–52. New York: Academic Press.

Gunter, B. (1981). 'Measuring children's comprehension of television commercials'. *Current Psychological Reviews*, 1: 159–70.

Gussow, J. (1972). 'Counternutritional messages of TV ads aimed at children'. *Journal of Nutrition Education*, 4: 48–52.

—— (1973). 'It makes even milk a dessert—a report on the counternutritional messages of children's television advertising'. *Clinical Pediatrics*, 12: 68–71.

Haefner, J. E., Leckenby, J. B., and Goldman, S. L. (1975). 'The measurement of advertising impact on children'. Paper presented at the American Psychological Association. Chicago. August.

Hagen, J. W. (1967). 'The effect of distraction on selective attention'. *Child Development*, 38: 685–94.

Hakes, D. T. (1980). *The Development of Metalinguistic Abilities in Children*. Berlin: Springer-Verlag.

Hamilton, R., Haworth, B, and Sardar, N. (1982). *Adman and Eve*. Manchester: Equal Opportunities Commission.

Hancher, M. (1979). 'The classification of co-operative illocutionary acts'. *Language in Society*, 8/1: 1–14.

Hardes, G. R., Alexander, H. M., Dobson, A. J., Lloyd, D. M., O'Connell, D., Purcell, I., and Leeder, S. R. (1979). 'Cigarette smoking and drug use in school children in the Hunter region (NSW)—tobacco, alcohol and analgesic use in 10–12 year-old primary school children'. *Medical Journal of Australia*, 1: 579–81.

Harris, R. J. (ed.) (1983). *Information Processing Research in Advertising*. Hillsdale, NJ, and London: Erlbaum.

Haslett, B. J. (1987). *Communication: Strategic Action in Context*. Hillsdale, NJ, and London: Erlbaum.

Hawkins, R. P. (1977). 'The dimensional structure of children's perceptions of television reality'. *Communication Research*, 3: 299–320.

Hayes, D. S., and Birnbaum, D. W. (1980). 'Preschoolers' retention of televised events: Is a picture worth a thousand words?' *Developmental Psychology*, 16: 410–16.

Henry, B. (ed.) (1986). *British Television Advertising: The First 30 years*. London: Century Benham.

Heslop, L. A., and Ryans, A. B. (1980). 'A second look at children and the advertising of premiums'. *Journal of Consumer Research*, 6: 414–20.

Himmelweit, H. T., Oppenheim, A. N., and Vince, P. (1958). *Television and the Child*. London: Oxford University Press.

Home Office (1977). *Report of the Committee on the Future of Broadcasting*. London: HMSO.

Horowitz, H. (1979). 'Update on Federal Trade Commission's Hearings on Children's Television Advertising and Testimony of Dr Richard F. Murphy Representing the American Association of Public Health Dentists'. *Journal of Public Health Dentistry*, 39/4: 298–305.

Hughes, C. (1983). 'Children's understanding of television: Implications for policy'. Paper presented to the Canadian Communication Association. Vancouver.

Husson, W. (1982). 'Theoretical issues in the study of children's attention to television'. *Communication Research*, 9/3: 323–51.

Huston, A. C., and Wright, J. C. (1983). 'Children's processing of television'. In J. Bryant and D. R. Anderson (eds.), *Children's Understanding of Television: Research on Attention and Comprehension*. New York: Academic Press.

Independent Broadcasting Authority (1985). *The IBA Code of Advertising Standards and Practice*. London.

Independent Television Companies' Association (1987). *An Introduction to Independent Television*. London: Independent Television Companies' Association.

Jaglom, L. M., and Gardner, H. (eds.) (1981). 'The preschool television viewer as anthropologist'. In Kelly and Gardner (1981): 9–30.

James, W. (1891). *The Principles of Psychology*, i. London: Macmillan.

Jeffrey, D. B., McLellarn, R. W., and Fox, D. T. (1982). 'The development of children's eating habits: The role of television commercials'. *Health Education Quarterly*, 9/2–3: 174–89.

—— —— Hickey, J. S., Lemnitzer, N. B., Hess, M. J., and Stroud, J. M. (1980). 'Television food commercials and children's eating behaviour: Some empirical evidence'. *Journal of the University Film Association*, 32/1, 2.

Johnson, M. (1987). *The Body in the Mind*. Chicago: University of Chicago Press.

Kaplan, E. A. (1987). *Rocking around the Clock*. New York: Methuen.

Kaufman, L. (1980). 'Prime-time nutrition'. *Journal of Communication*, 30/3: 37–46.

Keenan, E. O. (1976). 'The universality of conversational implicature'. *Language in Society*, 5: 67–80.

Kelly, H. (1981). 'Reasoning about realities: Children's evaluation of television and books'. In Kelly and Gardner (1981): 59–72.

—— and Gardner, H. (1981) (eds.). *Viewing Children Through Television*. San Francisco: Jossey-Bass.

Klapper, H. L. (1981). 'Children's perception of the realism of televised fiction: New wine in old bottles'. In Esserman (1981c): 55–82.

Krull, R., and Husson, W. G. (1980). 'Children's anticipatory attention to the TV screen'. *Journal of Broadcasting*, 24: 36–47.

Kumatoridani, T. (1982). *The Structure of Persuasive Discourse: A Cross-Cultural Analysis of the Language in American and Japanese Television Commercials*. Ph.D. thesis. Washington, DC: Georgetown University.

Lakoff, G. (1987). *Women, Fire and Dangerous Things*. Chicago: University of Chicago Press.

—— and Johnson, M. (1980). *Metaphors We Live By*. Chicago: University of Chicago Press.

Lambo, A. M. (1981). 'Children's ability to evaluate television commercial messages for sugared products'. *American Journal of Public Health*, 71/9: 1060–2.

Lavidge, R., and Steiner, G. A. (1961). 'A model for predictive measurements of advertising effectiveness'. *Journal of Marketing*, 25: 59–62.

Ledwith, F. (1984). 'Does tobacco sports sponsorship on television act as advertising to children?' *Health Education Journal*, 43: 85–8.

Leech, G. (1974). *Semantics*. Harmondsworth: Penguin.

—— (1983). *Principles of Pragmatics*. London: Longmans.

Leiss, W. (1983). 'The icons of the marketplace'. *Theory, Culture and Society*, 1/3: 10–21.

—— Kline, S., and Jhally, S. (1986). *Social Communication in Advertising*. Toronto: Methuen.

Lévi-Strauss, C. (1968). *Structural Anthropology*. London: Allen Lane.

Levin, S. R., Petros, T. V., and Petrella, F. W. (1982).

'Preschoolers' awareness of television advertising'. *Child Development*, 53/4: 933–7.

Levinson, S. C. (1983). *Pragmatics*. Cambridge: Cambridge University Press.

Leymore, V. L. (1975). *Hidden Myth: Structure and Symbolism in Advertising*. London: Heinemann.

Liebert, D. E., Sprafkin, J. N., Liebert, R. M., and Rubinstein, E. A. (1977) 'Effects of television commercial disclaimers on the product expectations of children'. *Journal of Communication*, 27: 118–24.

Linn, M. C., Benedictis, T., and Delucchi, K. (1982). 'Adolescent reasoning about advertisements: Preliminary investigations'. *Child Development*, 53: 1599–1613.

Loughlin, M., and Desmond, R. J. (1981). 'Social interaction in advertising directed to children'. *Journal of Broadcasting*, 25: 303–7.

Lyle, J., and Hoffman, H. (1972). 'Children's use of television and other media'. In E. A. Rubinstein, G. A. Comstock, and J. P. Murray (eds.), *Television and Social Behavior,* iv. *Television in Day-to-Day Life: Patterns of Use*. Washington, DC: US Government Printing Office.

Mac Cormac, E. R. (1985). *A Cognitive Theory of Metaphor*. Cambridge, Mass.: MIT Press.

McGhee, P. E., and Chapman, A. J. (1980). *Children's Humour*. Chichester: Wiley.

Macklin, M. C. (1982). 'The influence of task demands on outcomes: Preliminary findings and theoretical implications to advertising research involving children'. In R. Bagozzi and A. Tybout (eds.), *Advances in Consumer Research*, x. Ann Arbor Mich.: Association for Consumer Research.

—— (1983). 'Do children understand TV ads?' *Journal of Advertising Research*, 23/1: 63–70.

—— (1985). 'Do young children understand the selling intent of commercials?' *Journal of Consumer Affairs*, 19/2: 293–304.

—— (1987). 'Preschoolers' understanding of the informational function of television advertising'. *Journal of Consumer Research*, 14: 229–39.

—— (forthcoming). 'The relationship between music in advertising and children's responses: An experimental investigation'. In D. W. Stewart and S. Hecker (eds.), *Nonverbal Communication in Advertising*. Lexington, Mass.: Lexington Books.

 —— and Kolbe, R. H. (1984). 'Sex role stereotyping in children's advertising: Current and past trends'. *Journal of Advertising*, 13/2: 34–42.

Mackworth, N. H., and Bruner, J. S. (1970). 'How adults and children search and recognise pictures'. *Human Development*, 13: 149–77.

McNeal, J. U. (1987). *Children as Consumers: Insights and Implications*. Lexington: Lexington Books.

Malone, J. (1984). 'Self-regulation of children's television advertising: Current practices and future proposals'. *Media Information Australia*, 31: 57–61.

Mandler, J., and Johnson, N. (1977). 'Remembrance of things parsed: Story structure and recall'. *Cognitive Psychology*, 9: 111–51.

Markman, E. M. (1977). 'Realizing that you don't understand: A preliminary investigation'. *Child Development*, 48: 986–92.

—— (1979). 'Realizing that you don't understand: Elementary school children's awareness of inconsistencies'. *Child Development*, 50: 643–55.

Marschark, M., and Nall, L. (1985). 'Metaphoric competence in cognitive and language development'. *Advances in Child Development and Behavior*, 19: 49–81.

Marvin, R. S., Greenberg, M. T., and Mossler, D. G. (1976). 'The early development of conceptual perspective taking: Distinguishing among multiple perspectives'. *Child Development*, 47: 511–14.

May, J. D. (1981). 'Practical reasoning: Extracting useful information from partial informants'. *Journal of Pragmatics*, 5: 45–59.

Melody, W. H. (1973). *Children's Television: The Economics of Exploitation*. New Haven: Yale University Press.

—— and Ehrlich, W. (1974). 'Children's TV commercials: The vanishing policy options'. *Journal of Communication*, 24: 113–25.

Meringoff, L. (1980). *Children and Advertising: An Annotated Bibliography*. New York: Children's Advertising Review Unit.

Michaels, S., and Collins, J. (1984). 'Oral discourse styles: Classroom interaction and the acquisition of literacy'. In D. Tannen (ed.), *Coherence in Spoken and Written Discourse*.: 219–44. Norwood: Ablex.

Moschis, G. P., and Moore, R. L. (1982). 'A longitudinal study of television advertising effects'. *Journal of Consumer Research*, 9/3: 279–86.

Mossler, D. G., Marvin, R. S., and Greenberg, M. T. (1976). 'Conceptual perspective taking in 2- to 6-year-old children'. *Developmental Psychology*, 12: 85–6.

National Science Foundation (1977). *Research on the Effects of Television Advertising on Children*. Washington, DC: US Government Printing Office.

Nelson, K. (1978). 'How young children represent knowledge of their world in and out of language'. In R. S. Siegler (ed.), *Children's Thinking: What Develops*. Hillsdale, NJ: Erlbaum.

Noble, G. (1975). *Children in Front of the Small Screen*. London: Constable.

Observer (1988). 'Sweden's war on toys'. London. 10 January.

Ochs, E., and Schieffelin, B. B. (1979). *Developmental Pragmatics*. London: Academic Press.

O'Connell, D. L., Alexander, H. M., Dobson, A. J., Lloyd, D. M., Hardes, G. R., Springthorpe, H. J., and Leeder, S. R. (1981). 'Cigarette smoking and drug use in children: 2.–Factors associated with smoking'. *International Journal of Epidemiology*, 10: 223–31.

O'Meara, V. A. (1982). 'FTC deceptive advertising regulation: A proposal for the use of consumer behaviour research'. *North Western University Law Review*, 76/6: 946–79.

Ortony, A. (ed.) (1979). *Metaphor and Thought*. Cambridge: Cambridge University Press.

Osgood, C. E., May, W. H., and Miron, M. S. (1975). *Cross-Cultural Universals of Affective Meaning*. Urbana, Ill.: University of Illinois Press.

Packard, V. (1957). *The Hidden Persuaders*. London: Longmans.

Palmer, E. L., and McDowell, C. N. (1979). 'Program/commercial separators in children's television programming'. *Journal of Communication*, 29: 197–201.

Parsons, M., Johnston, M., and Durham, R. (1978). 'Developmental stages in children's aesthetic responses'. *Journal of Aesthetic Education*, 12/1: 83–104.

Pateman, T. (1980). 'How to do things with images: An essay on the pragmatics of advertising'. *Theory and Society*, 9: 603–22.

—— (1983). 'How is understanding an advertisement possible?' In H. Davis and P. Walton (eds.), *Language, Image, Media*, 187–204. Oxford: Blackwell.

Paul, A. A., and Southgate, D. A. T. (1978). *McCance and Widdowson's The Composition of Foods*. 4th edn. London: HMSO.

Pearce, A. (1972). *The Economics of Network Children's Television Programming*. Staff report submitted to Federal Communications Commission.

Piaget, J. (1926). *The Language and Thought of the Child*. New York: Harcourt Brace.

—— (1965). *The Moral Judgement of the Child*. New York: Free Press. Originally published 1932.

Poiesz, T. B. C. (1990). 'Advertising and smoking maintenance'.

Paper presented at Advertising and Tobacco seminar. Windsor, England. To appear in the *International Journal of Advertising*.

Pollay, R. W. (1986). 'The distorted mirror: Reflections on the unintended consequences of advertising'. *Journal of Marketing*, 50: 18–36.

Pollock, L. A. (1983). *Forgotten Children: Parent–child Relations from 1500 to 1900*. Cambridge: Cambridge University Press.

Prasad, V. K., Rao, T. R., and Sheikh, A. A. (1978). 'Mother vs. commercial'. *Journal of Communication*, 28: 91–6.

Quarfoth, J. M. (1979). 'Children's understanding of the nature of television characters'. *Journal of Communication*, 29/3: 210–18.

Raiij, F. van (1990). 'The effect of marketing communication on the initiation of juvenile smoking'. Paper presented at Advertising and Tobacco seminar. Windsor, England. To appear in the *International Journal of Advertising*.

Ratner, E. M., Hellegers, J. F., Stern, G. P., *et al.* (1978). *Federal Trade Commission Staff Report on Television Advertising to Children*. Washington, DC: Federal Trade Commission.

Reardon, K. K. (1981). *Persuasion: Theory and Context*. London: Sage.

Reddy, M. (1979). 'The conduit metaphor'. In Ortony (1979): 284–324.

Reid, L. N. (1979a). 'Viewing rules and mediating factors of children's responses to commercials'. *Journal of Broadcasting*, 23: 15–26.

—— (1979b). 'The impact of family group interaction on children's understanding of television advertising'. *Journal of Advertising*, 9: 13–19.

—— and Frazer, C. F. (1980). 'Studying the child–television advertising relationship'. *Journal of Advertising*, 9: 13–19.

Reilly Group Inc. (1973a). *Assumptions by the Child of the Role of the Consumer*. Darien, Conn.

—— (1973b). *The Child*, ii. *Meals and Snacking: The Child and what he eats*. Darien, Conn.

Resnick, A. J., Stern, B. L., and Alberty, B. (1979). 'Integrating results from children's television advertising research'. *Journal of Advertising*, 8: 3–12.

Riecken, G., and Samli, A. C. (1981). 'Measuring children's attitudes toward television commercials: Extension and replication'. *Journal of Consumer Research*, 8: 57–61.

Roberts, D. F. (1982). 'Children and commercials: Issues, evidence, interventions'. *Prevention in Human Services*, 2/1–2: 19–35.

Roberts, D. F., Christenson, P. C., Gibson, W. A., Mooser, L., and Goldberg, M. E. (1980). 'Developing discriminating consumers'. *Journal of Communication*, 30: 229–31.

Robertson, T. S., and Feldman, S. (1976). 'Children as consumers: The need for multitheoretical perspectives'. In B. B. Anderson (ed.), *Advances in Consumer Research*, 3. Cincinatti: Association for Consumer Research.

—— and Rossiter, J. (1974). 'Children and commercial persuasion: An attributional theory analysis'. *Journal of Consumer Research*, 1: 13–20.

—— —— (1976). 'Children and commercial persuasion: A reply to Ryans and Deutscher. *Journal of Consumer Research*, 3: 58–61.

Robinson, E. J., and Robinson, W. P. (1977a). 'Children's explanations of failure and the inadequacy of the misunderstood message'. *Developmental Psychology*, 13: 151–61.

—— —— (1977b). 'The young child's explanation of communication failure: A reinterpretation of results'. *Perceptual and Motor Skills*, 44: 363–66.

—— Goelman, H., and Olson, D. R. (1983). 'Children's understanding of the relation between expressions (what was said) and intentions (what was meant)'. *British Journal of Developmental Psychology*, 1: 75–86.

Roedder, D. L. (1981). 'Age differences in children's responses to television advertising: An information-processing approach'. *Journal of Consumer Research*, 8: 144–53.

—— Didow, N. M., and Calder, B. J. (1978). 'A review of formal theories of consumer socialization'. In H. K. Hunt (ed.), *Advances in Consumer Research*, 5. Ann Arbor, Mich.: Association for Consumer Research.

—— Sternthal, B., and Calder, B. J. (1983). 'Attitude-behavior consistency in children's responses to television advertising'. *Journal of Marketing Research*, 20: 337–49.

Root J. (1986) *Open the Box*. London: Comedia.

Rosch, E. (1978). 'Principles of categorization'. In E. Rosch and B. B. Lloyd (eds.), *Cognition and Categorization*. Hillsdale: Erlbaum.

—— Mervis, C. G., Gray, W. D., Johnson, D. M., and Boyes-Braem, P. (1976). Basic objects in natural categories. *Cognitive Psychology*, 8: 382–439.

Ross, R. P., Campbell, T., Huston-Stein, A., and Wright, J. C. (1981). Nutritional misinformation of children: A developmental and experimental analysis of the effects of televised food commercials. *Journal of Applied Developmental Psychology*, 1: 329–47.

—— —— Wright, J. C., Huston, A. C., Rice, M. L., and Turk, P. (1981). 'When celebrities talk, children listen: An experimental analysis of children's responses to TV ads with celebrity endorsement'. Working paper. Lawrence, Kan.: Center for Research on the Influence of Television on Children, University of Kansas.

Rossano, M. J., and Butter, E. J. (1987). 'Television advertising and children's attitudes toward proprietary medicine'. *Psychology and Marketing*, 4/3: 213–24.

Rossiter, J. R. (1977). 'Reliability of a short test measuring children's attitudes toward television commercials'. *Journal of Consumer Research*, 3: 179–84.

—— (1979). 'Does TV advertising affect children?' *Journal of Advertising Research*, 19: 49–53.

—— (1980). 'Children and television advertising: Policy issues, perspectives and the status of research'. In E. L. Palmer and A. Dorr (eds.), *Children and the Faces of Television: Teaching, Violence, Selling*: 251–72. New York: Academic Press.

—— (1981). 'Children and television advertising: policy issues, perspectives and the status of research'. In Esserman (1981*c*): 107–32.

—— and Robertson, T. S. (1974). 'Children's TV commercials: Testing the defenses'. *Journal of Communication*, 24: 137–44.

Rothschild, M. L. (1987). *Advertising: From Fundamentals to Strategy*. Lexington, Mass.: D. C. Heath.

Ryans, A. B., and Deutscher, T. (1975). 'Children and commercial persuasion: Some comments'. *Journal of Consumer Research*, 2: 237–9.

Rychtarik, R. G., Jeffrey, D. B., and Kniivila, C. (1978). 'Methodological considerations in research on television advertising and children's behavior: A critical review'. Paper presented to the American Psychological Association. Toronto.

Saatchi and Saatchi Compton (1985). 'What children watch and when'. *Marketing*: 76. 11 April.

Salomon, G. (1981). 'Introducing AIME: The assessment of children's mental involvement with television'. In Kelly and Gardner (1981): 89–102.

Sarson, E. (ed.) (1971). *The First National Symposium on the Effects of Television Programming and Advertising on Children*. New York: Avon Books.

Saussure, F. de (1915). *Cours de linguistique générale*. Paris: Payot. Trans. W. Baskin. *Course in General Linguistics*. New York: The Philosophical Library, 1959. London: Fontana, 1974.

Scammon, D. L., and Christopher, C. L. (1981). 'Nutrition

education with children via television: A review'. *Journal of Advertising*, 10/2: 26–36.

Schlinger, M. J. (1979). 'A profile of responses to commercials'. *Journal of Advertising Research*, 19: 37–46.

Schramm, W., Lyle, J., and Parker, E. B. (1961). *Television in the Lives of our Children*. Stanford, Calif.: Stanford University Press.

Searle, J. R. (1969). *Speech Acts*. Cambridge: Cambridge University Press.

—— (1976). 'The classification of illocutionary acts'. *Language in Society*, 5: 1–24.

Sharaga, S. J. (1974). 'The effects of television advertising on children's nutrition attitude, nutrition knowledge and eating habits'. *Dissertation Abstracts International*, 75: 145.

Shaw, J. H. (1983). 'Political and commercial influences on dental health: The Federal Trade Commission looks at television advertising to children'. *Journal of Dentistry*, 11/2: 168–74.

Sheehy, N. P., and Chapman, A. J. (1988). 'The representation of children in British television advertising'. Unpublished paper. Leeds: Department of Psychology, Leeds University.

Sheikh, A. A., and Moleski, M. L. (1977). 'Conflict in the family over commercials'. *Journal of Communication*, 27: 152–7.

—— Prasad, V. K., and Rao, T. R. (1974). 'Children's TV commercials: A review of research'. *Journal of Communication*, 24: 126–36.

Shultz, T. R., and Cloghesy, K. (1981). 'Development of recursive awareness of intention'. *Developmental Psychology*, 17: 465–71.

—— Wells, D., and Sarda, M. (1980). 'The development of the ability to distinguish intended actions from mistakes, reflexes and passive movements'. *British Journal of Social and Clinical Psychology*, 19: 301–10.

Singer, J. L., and Singer, D. G. (1984). 'Parents as mediators of the child's television environment'. *Educational Media International*, 4: 7–11.

Slaby, R. G., and Hollenbeck, A. R. (1977). 'Television influences on visual and vocal behaviour of infants'. Paper presented at the biennal meeting of the Society for Research in Child Development. New Orleans. March.

Smith, G., Gullen, P., and Wood, M. (1983). *Children's Hour*. London: J. Walter Thompson.

Soldow, G. F. (1983). 'The processing of information in the young consumer: The impact of cognitive developmental stage on television, radio and print advertising'. *Journal of Advertising*, 12/3: 4–14.

—— (1985). 'The ability of children to understand the product package: A study of limitations imposed by cognitive developmental stage'. *Journal of Public Policy and Marketing*, 4: 55–68.

Sparks, G. G., and Cantor, J. (1983). 'Developmental differences in fright responses to a television program depicting a transformation of a character'. Unpublished paper. University of Wisconsin.

Sperber, D., and Wilson, D. (1986). *Relevance: Communication And Cognition*. Oxford: Blackwell.

Stephens, N., and Stutts, M. A. (1982). 'Preschoolers' ability to distinguish between television programming and commercials'. *Journal of Advertising*, 11/2: 16–26.

Stern, B. L., and Harmon, R. R. (1984). 'The incidence and characteristics of disclaimers in children's television advertising'. *Journal of Advertising*, 13/2: 12–16.

Stiles, W. B. (1986). Levels of intended meaning of utterances. *British Journal of Clinical Psychology*, 25: 213–22.

Stoneman, Z., and Brody, G. H. (1981). 'Peers as mediators of television food advertisements aimed at children'. *Developmental Psychology*, 17/6: 853–8.

—— —— (1982). 'The indirect impact of child-oriented advertisements on mother-child interactions'. *Journal of Applied Developmental Psychology*, 2: 369–76.

—— —— (1983). 'Immediate and long-term recognition and generalization of advertised products as a function of age and presentation mode'. *Developmental Psychology*, 19/1: 56–61.

Stutts, M. A., Vance, D., and Hudleson, S. (1981). 'Program-commercial separators in children's television: Do they help a child tell the difference between Bugs Bunny and the Quik Rabbit?' *Journal of Advertising*, 10: 16–25.

Swartz, J. E. (1985). 'Comic book advertising: Directions and implications for research'. *Southwestern Mass Communication Journal*, 1/2: 35–42.

Sweeny, E. (1983). 'Commercial and political influences on dental health: The effects of television advertising on children'. *Journal of Dentistry*, 11/2: 175–81.

Tada, T. (1969). Image-cognition: A developmental approach. In *Studies of Broadcasting*. Tokyo: Nippon Hoso Kyokai.

Tuohy, A. P., and Young, B. M. (in preparation). 'The factorial structure of advertisement perception in children and adults'.

US National Archives (1974). 'Proposed rules'. *Federal Register*, 39, 11 November. 39844.

US Senate Select Committee on Nutrition and Human Needs (1977). *Dietary Goals for the United States*. Washington, DC: US Government Printing Office.

Van Auken, S., and Lonial, S. C. (1985). 'Children's perceptions of characters: Human versus animate assessing implications for children's advertising'. *Journal of Advertising*, 14/2: 13–22, 61.

Van Peer, W. (1986). *Stylistics and Psychology: Investigations of Foregrounding*. London: Croom Helm.

Wackman, D., Wartella, E., and Ward, S. (1979). 'Children's information processing of television advertising'. Unpublished paper. Minnesota, Minn.: University of Minnesota.

Ward, S. (1972). 'Children's reactions to commercials'. *Journal of Advertising Research*, 12/2: 37–45.

—— and Wackman, D. B. (1973). 'Children's information processing of television advertising'. In P. Clarke (ed.), *New Models for Communication Research*: 119–46. Beverly Hills, Calif.: Sage.

—— Levinson, D., and Wackman, D. (1972). 'Children's attention to television advertising'. In P. Clark (ed.), *New Models for Communication Research*. US Government Printing Office. Beverly Hills, Calif.: Sage. (Also in E. A. Rubinstein, G. A. Comstock, and J. P. Murray (eds.), *Television and Social Behavior*, iv. *Television in Day-to-Day Life: Patterns of Use*. Washington, DC: US Government Printing Office.)

—— Popper, E., and Wackman, D. (1977). *Parent Under Pressure: Influences on Mothers' Responses to Children's Purchase Requests*. Report No. 77–107. Cambridge, Mass.: Marketing Science Institute.

—— Reale, G., and Levinson, D. (1972). 'Children's perceptions, explanations and judgements of television advertising: A further exploration'. In E. A. Rubinstein, G. A. Comstock, and J. P. Murray (eds.), *Television and Social Behavior*, iv. *Television in Day-to-Day Life: Patterns of Use*: 468–90. Washington, DC: US Government Printing Office.

—— —— Robertson, T. S., and Brown, R. (1986). *Commercial Television and European Children: An International Research Digest*. Aldershot: Gower.

—— Wackman, D., and Wartella, E. (1975). *Children Learning to Buy: The Development of Consumer Information Processing Skills*. Cambridge Ma.: Marketing Science Institute.

—— —— —— (1977). *How Children Learn to Buy*. Beverly Hills: Sage.

—— Robertson, T. S., Klees, D., Takarada, K., and Young, B. M. (1984). 'A cross-cultural analysis of children's commercial television viewing and product requesting behavior'. Paper presented at American Psychological Association Conference. Hawaii. December.

Ward, T. B. (1984). 'Opinions on television advertising to children: A content analysis of letters to the Federal Trade Commission'. *Merrill-Palmer Quarterly*, 30/3: 247–59.

Wartella, E. (1980). 'Individual differences in children's responses to television advertising'. In E. L. Palmer and A. Dorr (eds.), *Children and the Faces of Television: Teaching, Violence, Selling*: 307–22. New York: Academic Press.

—— (1984). 'Cognitive and affective factors of TV advertising's influence on children'. *The Western Journal of Speech Communication*, 48: 171–83.

—— and Ettema, J. (1974). 'A cognitive developmental study of children's attention to television commercials'. *Communication Research*, 1: 46–69.

—— and Hunter, L. S. (1983). *Children and the formats of television advertising*. Advertising Working Paper No. 14. Urbana-Champaign: Department of Advertising, University of Illinois.

—— Wackman, D. B., Ward. S., Shamir, J., and Alexander, A. (1981). 'The young child as consumer.' In Esserman (1981*c*): 196–221.

Wells, W. D., and LoScuito, L. A. (1966). 'Direct observation of purchasing behaviour'. *Journal of Marketing Research*, 3: 227–33.

Williams T. M. (ed.) (1986). *The Impact of Television: A Natural Experiment in Three Communities*. London: Academic Press.

Williamson, J. (1978). *Decoding Advertisements: Ideology and Meaning in Advertising*. London: Marion Boyars.

Wiman, A. R. (1980). 'Attitudes of parents and children toward children's television advertising'. Paper presented at annual conference of the Academy of Marketing Science.

—— (1983). 'Parental influence and children's responses to television advertising'. *Journal of Advertising*, 12/1: 11–18.

—— and Newman, L. M. (1987). 'Television advertising exposure and children's nutritional awareness'. To appear in *Journal of the Academy of Marketing Science*.

Wimmer, H., and Perner, J. (1983). 'Beliefs about beliefs: Representation and constraining function of wrong beliefs in young children's understanding of deception. *Cognition*, 13: 103–28.

Winick, C., Williamson, L. G., Chuzimir, S. F., and Winick, M. P.

(1973). *Children's Television Commercials: A Content Analysis*. New York: Praeger.

Winick, M. P., and Winick, C. (1979). *The Television Experience: What Children See*. Beverly Hills, Calif.: Sage.

Winner, E., Rosenstiel, A. K., and Gardner, H. (1976). 'The development of metaphoric understanding'. *Developmental Psychology*, 12/4: 289–97.

—— Wapner, W., Cicone, M., and Gardner, H. (1979). 'Measures of metaphor'. *New Directions for Child Development*, 6: 67–75.

Wober, J. M. (1986). *Children and How Much they View*. London: The Independent Broadcasting Authority.

Wohlwill, J. F. (1962). 'From perception to inference: A dimension of cognitive development'. In W. Kessen and C. Kuhlman (eds.), *Cognitive Development in Children*. Monographs of the Society for Research in Child Development. Chicago: University of Chicago Press.

Wright, J. C., and Huston A. C. (1983). 'A matter of form: Potentials of television for young viewers'. *American Psychologist*, July: 835–43.

Wright, P. L. (1973). 'The cognitive processes mediating acceptance of advertising'. *Journal of Advertising Research*, 10: 53–62.

Young, B. M. (1985). *The Incidence and Content of Television Advertising of Sugared Products to Children: A British Study*. London: The Health Education Council.

—— (1986). 'New approaches to old problems: The growth of advertising literacy'. In S. Ward and R. Brown (eds.), *Commercial Television and European Children: An International Research Digest*. 67–77, 82–3. Aldershot: Gower.

—— (1987a). Television advertising of sugared products to children: A UK study. In L. Schou (ed.), *Health Policy Aspects of Dental Caries Prevention*. 28–37. Edinburgh: The Scottish Health Education Group.

—— (1987b). *Sugar, Children and Television Advertising*. London: Health Education Authority Research Report No. 15.

Zuckerman, P., and Gianinno, L. (1981). Measuring children's response to television advertising. In Esserman (1981c): 83–93.

—— Ziegler, M. E., and Stevenson, H. W. (1978). 'Children's viewing of television and recognition memory of commercials'. *Child Development*, 49: 96–104.

AUTHOR INDEX

SUBJECT INDEX